Philosophy For, With, and Of Children

Philosophy For, With, and Of Children

Edited by

Monica B. Glina

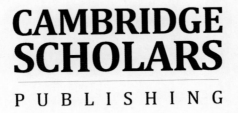

Philosophy For, With, and Of Children,
Edited by Monica B. Glina

This book first published 2013

Cambridge Scholars Publishing

12 Back Chapman Street, Newcastle upon Tyne, NE6 2XX, UK

British Library Cataloguing in Publication Data
A catalogue record for this book is available from the British Library

ISBN (10): 1-4438-4480-2, ISBN (13): 978-1-4438-4480-2

TABLE OF CONTENTS

FOREWORD

BEATE BØRRESEN
OSLO AND AKERSHUS UNIVERSITY COLLEGE

We know that knowledge and understanding are the result of dialogue and argumentation—with ourselves, with our experiences, with texts, and with others. However, we also know that there is little dialogue and little argumentation in schools across the world. What is often referred to as *dialogue* is dominated by the teacher and consists of exchanges of information, fact checking, or just an exchange of opinions. In philosophy, one participates in a dialogue in which the goal is to reach something true and good or truer and better, and the way to do this is to listen to different ideas and pieces of information, argue for and against, evaluate what is said, and make a choice. We do not exchange opinions but try to find out how things are, might be, or should be. A philosophical dialogue is structured and focused, and in it, everyone must participate, at least through listening, understanding, and connecting to what is said.

After many years of having philosophy in the schools, we know that doing philosophy with children is possible and valuable. Several research projects, for example, in Clackmannanshire, Scotland, and in Stockholm, Sweden, have shown that students who engage regularly in structured philosophical dialogue over a longer period of time develop cognitive and oral skills. Their schoolwork improves, especially in languages and mathematics, and they get better at listening, asking questions, and giving reasons. These projects also reveal that a number of elements need to be in place if we are to begin achieving a favorable outcome. Specifically, the success of these projects relies on teacher determination, a faithful adherence to doing philosophy at least once a week, quality stimulus material, training, and administrative commitment. We have also seen that it is difficult to continue with philosophy once the project that brought it to the classroom ends. Both teachers and students soon fall into old routines. Most teachers either will not or cannot do the work that is required for practicing good philosophy in the classroom.

What shall we do then? I am sorry to say that I do not think it is possible to get teachers to do philosophy regularly in their classrooms.

They lack training, time, and support. However, what they can do is to take the general attitudes and implement ways of working that are associated with the practice of doing philosophy into the classroom, and they can better challenge the students *and* use their questions and problems as starting points for work in the classroom. What does this mean in practice?

Attitude

Philosophical activity is based on the recognition of ignorance. The philosopher's thirst for knowledge is shown through attempts to find better answers to questions even if those answers are never found. At the same time, a philosopher also knows that being too sure can hinder the discovery of other and better possibilities. In a philosophical dialogue, the participants are aware that there are things they do not know or understand. The goal of the dialogue is to arrive at a conception that one did not know or understand beforehand. In traditional schools, where philosophy is not present, students often work with factual questions, they learn specific content listed in the curriculum, and they are not required to solve philosophical problems. However, we know that an attitude of ignorance or awareness of what one does not know can be a good way to acquire knowledge. Knowledge and understanding are developed through thinking and talking. Putting things into words makes things clearer. Therefore, students must not be afraid of saying something wrong or talking without first being sure that they are right. They must get experience with how mistakes and misunderstanding can lead to knowledge. In turn, teachers must value mistakes and use them for better understanding. The students must be given time and space to express their ideas and thoughts even if they are themselves unsure of those ideas and thoughts. Then, the class together shall find out if and in what ways these ideas may or may not be good. In this way, students can use their knowledge, experience, and reason to try find a good answer instead of guessing or just repeating what is in their textbooks.

Structure

Philosophers work in a systematic way. They formulate a problem, collect different suggestions, and compare, evaluate, and decide what the best possible answer is, and they do not go to the next step until everything is as clear as possible. Furthermore, we can use these methods in day-to-day work in the classroom, for example, by not answering or explaining something before we are sure that everybody has heard and understood the question or the problem and by letting students instead of the teacher offer answers and explanations. It is also important to let students have time to think and make notes before they answer questions and to explain their answer before the teacher evaluates it. In addition, when students are engaged in dialogues or discussions, it is helpful to keep a discussion map on the board to keep track of what has been done. This might help students focus on one thing at a time and delve into matters more deeply instead of just exchanging opinions.

Students can be helped to be more aware on a meta-level by having to say what they are about to do, for example, "I am going to ask a question," "I will explain in what way John disagrees with Ann," or "I will show how Sara's reason is not sufficient." In this way, it is easier for those who listen to grasp what is said and for the dialogue to be more accurate. In the same way, a concluding final round of meta-talk, during which students explain what was difficult, what they have learned, and so on, can help the class to be more aware of what they have understood, what skills they have mastered, and what they still have to practice.

In philosophy, we find answers and understand more by entertaining other peoples' ideas and different possible answers. We become suspicious when everyone agrees with a general belief and no one argues against it. Rather than simply accept that belief, it is exactly at this point that we should try to explore the belief in a deeper way by listening to more ideas or by looking at the matter from a different angle. It is, therefore, important for a teacher or facilitator not only to let those who raise their hands speak but to involve all students by distributing opportunities for students to talk in class by using dice, pulling names out of a box, or letting the students listen to each other in rounds. For this to work well, students must be encouraged to speak even if they are not sure what to say and to help each other develop their ideas and not simply repeat what has already been said.

Challenge

Understanding often occurs when we are confronted with a perspective that is different from or goes against the views that we initially had, and we are forced to think about how things are or might be. In philosophy, there is an ideal that one shall seek other views and other ways before one decides on a problem or question. For students to learn, they have to be put in situations where they must think, give reasons, and evaluate their words and actions and those of others by listening to themselves and each other and by having to present their ideas. In such situations, students are confronted with a wealth of information and opinions to which they have to actively relate. So, even if it might be faster for the teacher to tell students what to think, the students will learn by arriving at these notions themselves with help from the teacher.

The process of giving reasons and evaluating words and actions is central to education in Norwegian schools and educational politics. Each student has to formulate and evaluate goals for his or her work. Pedagogically, they learn by having to be aware of what they need to do, why they need to do it, and in what ways they have been doing it well. Philosophy is helpful in this process because it is open, it seeks different views, and it helps individuals decide on what and why something is good. Philosophy with children, in particular, emphasizes that understanding and learning are processes in which we engage in together, with others, and with help from others' knowledge, experiences, and ideas.

One can increase room for thinking by presenting students with problems that cannot be solved immediately instead of concrete tasks with easily found, short, and clear answers. When the students, instead of the teacher, are allowed to describe a problem, present and discuss different solutions, try them out, and evaluate the results, they are forced to build strategies for school work and to reflect on and explain what they are doing. To enable students to find good answers, it is necessary that their discussions be more than general conversations during which everyone "has a right to their own opinion" and in which they are never challenged. Instead, they have to go deeper by relating to what is said, require clarification and explanation, take a stand, and evaluate their words and their actions.They need to involve themselves in an inquiry, as people who do philosophy with children would argue.

Apart from these attitudes and ways of working, one can also introduce philosophy to students by letting them work with philosophical questions connected to different subjects, for example:

- "Where are the numbers when we don't use them?" (math)
- "Are languages invented?" (language)
- "Is someone in a prison free?" (social studies)
- "Do laws take away our freedom?" (social studies/civics)
- "Who decides what is just?" (law)
- "What makes something beautiful?" (art)

Although this volume offers a number of suggestions for ways in which this can be done, this breadth of options also reminds us to be aware that there are many ways of working in a classroom. When there is more variety in the kinds of teaching methods, the hope is that students will learn more. In the end, we must not forget that both philosophy and school are about being better persons and creating better communities. As Gregory underlines in his chapter, work in school must focus not only on how philosophy can help children to be better students or get ahead but also on the fact that philosophy is also about living well.

INTRODUCTION

MONICA B. GLINA
UNIVERSITY OF OSLO

Philosophy for Children (P4C) is more than simply a way to engage in shared, substantive inquiry into narrative or informational text; it offers ways to open discourse channels for interacting with and contemplating the perspectives of others. This volume illustrates the considerable diversity of perspectives that can be brought to P4C, and the ways in which these agendas sometimes complement and sometimes undermine one another. Although approaches and conceptions vary, there is an undercurrent of pervasive themes that flows throughout P4C practice, which is represented in these chapters. First, there is an emphasis on the active, reasoned role of the participants in the community of inquiry (CI). Many of the authors in this volume directly or indirectly reference the transformation that can occur for the individual thinker and the community, as well as the symbiotic impact that they can have on one another. Second, there is an epistemological requirement and practical commitment from the teacher to divest himself or herself from the trappings typically associated with being the classroom expert and the authority to allow for the recalibration and redistribution of power. Third, P4C can be viewed as a systematic, process-driven pedagogy that promotes powerful cognitive and social dispositions whose outcomes follow from the rigor associated with reasoned inquiry. Engaging in sustained, collaborative thinking helps students learn how to think and how to think about thinking. Lastly, the content of philosophical inquiry can range from the exploration of contestable concepts within and across school subjects to social and ethical quandaries to the biggest theoretical concepts and existential questions about the meaning of personhood and how to live a worthwhile life.

Our authors take the common position that humility and a certain kind of scholarly ignorance can be seen as keys to philosophical inquiry. In this collection, we offer multiple and divergent perspectives on philosophy for, with, and of children and hope that it will arouse reactions, critical examination and discussion.

Gregory opens the volume by reviewing the variety of purposes that have been articulated for pre-college philosophy historically, and by arguing for a more ambitious purpose: to relate thinking well with living well. He draws on the tradition of ancient schools that undertook philosophy as the pursuit of wisdom and proposes that P4C practice be broadened to combine discursive with ethical and contemplative practices. In a similarly ameliorative vein, Kennedy and Kennedy suggest the need to continually deconstruct and reconstruct our ideas of how things are and how they should be, not only in individual classrooms but within the school as a whole. They argue for exploration of the potential connections among content areas by extending and relating contestable concepts across disciplines, and they begin to explore the potential for these relationships in the mathematics classroom.

Parker moves the discussion from the school setting to cultural venues, where kids are inspired to develop poetry within the CI and to use their poetry as stimuli to inspire further and future inquiry. Parker argues that poetic thinking cultivates pertinent behaviors, such as addressing individuals in the community, responding to one another respectfully, and being empathetic.

Splitter makes a case for the unique moral value of each person as one among others and applies a Davidsonian model of triangulation in which the person, those with whom he or she is in a dialogical relationship, and the world as a whole are conceptually and epistemologically intertwined. In the classroom, this model is the CI. The theme of language and, specifically, the role of dialogue in understanding moral and ethical issues are picked up by other contributors, including Rogers, who revisits the importance of empathy, emotion, and thinking, and argues that ethics not only should not be but cannot be taught as a prescribed formula. Room must be made for deliberation and choice about ethical concepts, and this room is absent when a didactic approach to teaching morality is present. These themes manifest themselves practically in my own investigation of structured philosophical dialogue as a means by which to explore issues of aggression. In this study, I analyzed indicators of dialogic interaction to assess whether complex notions of caring, empathy, fairness, and respect were operationalized and, ultimately, internalized by participants in a CI.

Lin makes the case that the CI can help us meet the theoretical demands of conceiving dialogic pedagogy as a means for delivering democracy, and Sequeira explains the impact that such a democratic practice can have on the cultivation of a compassionate citizenry in which the individual differences and perspectives of the marginalized are valued and celebrated. The discussion comes full circle to Gregory's suggestion that philosophy can help us to live well. Should individuals be able to explore content domains, their surroundings, and those around them in a thoughtful and respectful manner, this may indeed be the outcome.

In traditional P4C practice, the philosophical story is the traditional stimulus from which students derive contestable questions and launch their own inquiries and explorations. Because there is a broadly personal and psychological domain of background knowledge that is shared among people, the narrative form of the philosophical novel is a highly egalitarian tool. For example, we all know from a young age what it means to feel sad or hurt, so people reading narratives about sadness or hurt can readily relate to these emotions. On the other hand, specific ways of thinking are required for accessing domains, such as history, mathematics, and science. These domains, however content-specific, offer manifold opportunities for inquiry around contestable concepts and questions. Many of the words and phrases that we see emerge during philosophical inquiry, including *practical application, proficient, theory, test, hypothesize, reinforce, factor, elaborate, confirm,* and *negotiate,* are core terms in other domains as well, streaming fluidly from one content area to another.

Analogous to Kennedy and Kennedy's recommendation that content should be considered across different domains because of the inherent and pervasive connections that exist among them, so, too, is the case with the chapters in this volume. What has preceded is a summative, if intentionally cursory, introduction. We hope that this volume serves as a stimulus from which to mine and explore contestable concepts and questions; readers are invited to engage its material, weigh it against their existing dialogues, and respond to those elements that they find inspiring, as well as those with which they disagree or deem problematic.

This volume is by no means the beginning of the dialogue but represents our own modest contribution to an already robust discourse.

PART I:

PHILOSOPHY FOR CHILDREN IN THE SERVICE OF EDUCATIONAL OBJECTIVES

CHAPTER ONE

WISDOM AND OTHER AIMS FOR PRECOLLEGE PHILOSOPHY EDUCATION

MAUGHN ROLLINS GREGORY
MONTCLAIR STATE UNIVERSITY

The diversity of materials and methods developed for precollege philosophy programs signifies different conceptions of what it means to engage children in philosophical practices. The development of program-specific objectives and standards would make it possible to judge the relative merits of various programs and to prevent the unfair comparison of programs with very different objectives. Precollege philosophy programs commonly work toward four objectives: the development of cognitive skills and dispositions, the understanding of inquiry and the development of inquiry strategies, the development of dialogical skills, and the development of familiarity with philosophical content. These objectives might lead to a wider appreciation of the educational merits of studying philosophy but might also reinforce education aimed at students getting ahead rather than living well. The Stoics distinguished three components of living well that can provide categories of wisdom-oriented objectives for precollege philosophy education: a moral component of living ethically and virtuously, a psychological component of maintaining tranquility in the midst of chaos, and an intellectual component of disciplined thinking and the construction of a value-oriented vision of the world. Reinstating these objectives in the context of precollege philosophy education could help to return philosophy to its original identity as the disciplined study and practice of living well.

The Need to Develop Objectives for Precollege Philosophy Education

The year 2009 marked the 40th anniversary of Matthew Lipman's first philosophical novel for children, *Harry Stottlemeier's Discovery,*[1] which was piloted in schools in Montclair and Newark, New Jersey. Today *Harry* has been translated into scores of languages and dialects, and

Philosophy for Children has become a worldwide movement. However, the diversity of curriculum materials and pedagogical protocols that this movement has spawned signifies not merely different approaches to teaching philosophy to children but also different conceptions of what it means to teach philosophy to children or to engage children in philosophical practices. Other disciplines that have become a regular part of children's education, such as mathematics, science, and history, have initiated educational objectives and standards that describe the knowledge and skills that children should be able to demonstrate at various stages in their education. These objectives make it possible to judge the merits of various educational approaches, to make formative and summative program assessments, and to regulate the consistency and equity of educational experiences across diverse populations. Also, the formulation of educational objectives and standards occasions professional dialogue about what it means to practice a discipline well and about likely means for initiating newcomers into the discipline, and this dialogue benefits the discipline itself.

All of this is instructive for precollege philosophy and, in particular, Philosophy for Children, which aspires to make philosophy a standard school subject for all age groups (see Cam, 2006; Splitter & Sharp, 1995). Although philosophy is a relative newcomer to precollege and especially presecondary education, the proliferation of materials and methods in the last few decades has resulted in four important problems for this field that we can solve only by giving attention to the issue of objectives and standards for meeting them. First, approaches to teaching philosophy to children and youth are so diverse that it is difficult to compare their relative merits. There has been confusion and unfairness in comparing and criticizing programs with widely different objectives. This confusion is increased when philosophers argue (correctly) that school programs in critical thinking, ethics, art, democratic citizenship, and character education have, or ought to have, philosophical components.

Second, precollege philosophy programs are rarely evaluated even about their own objectives, or they are evaluated for external objectives, such as raising grades or test scores. Most of the empirical evaluation of Philosophy for Children has been done with regard to its effect on children's thinking skills (Garcia-Moriyón, Rebollo, & Colom, 2004), which is only one of the program's objectives. As a result, the program is often misconstrued (e.g., Willingham, 2007) as a nondisciplinary thinking curriculum rather than an introduction to the discipline of philosophy. The lack of authentic program evaluation is a problem for precollege philosophy because, without it, neither program developers nor their clients have evidence of the program's effectiveness for either internal or external objectives (see Reznitskaya, 2005).

Two obstacles to the authentic evaluation of precollege philosophy education are that (a) philosophers are not trained in methods of empirical research and so must cross-disciplinary boundaries to collaborate with colleagues in the social sciences, who themselves may not be interested in philosophy, and (b) authentic objectives for philosophy education, such as dialogical competence and acumen with philosophical concepts, have been difficult to observe and measure empirically until relatively recently. Most evaluative studies of precollege philosophy education (e.g., Dolz, 1996; Morehouse & Williams, 1998; Shipman, 1983) have relied on measurement tools, such as standardized vocabulary, reading comprehension, and logic tests, which capture only a small range of the outcomes that are important to philosophy education. However, recent advances in qualitative and quantitative research methods in education, influenced primarily by sociocultural learning theories (see Reznitskaya, 2005), make this work increasingly suitable for the evaluation of philosophy education and particularly classroom dialogue (e.g., Alexander, 2003; Kuhn, Shaw, & Felton, 1997; Mercer, Wegerif, & Dawes, 1999; Nystrand, Wu, Garmon, Zeiser, & Long, 2003; Soter et al., 2008).

The lack of institutional and professional rapprochement between philosophers and educational researchers also contributes to a third problem facing the field of precollege philosophy: many programs are uninformed by research literature in the educational sciences, including pedagogy, educational psychology, and even cognitive science, in the way that programs in other subjects are. As a result, philosophy programs may not be developmentally appropriate or pedagogically sound. Philosophy has an important role to play in the critique of educational aims, concepts, and methods, but philosophy educators also have much to learn from educational research, particularly when it comes to the development of a curriculum for philosophy education.

A fourth problem is the lack of collaboration or even communication among precollege philosophy program developers, with the result that new programs often do not build on the successes or deliberately avoid the mistakes of past programs. Over the past 4 decades, a body of philosophical and empirical research on philosophy for, of, and with children and adolescents has been built up; this amounts to thousands of academic books, articles, and doctoral dissertations from scores of countries. Precollege philosophy is the topic of dozens of academic conferences and special conference sessions every year in every part of the world and is the primary thematic focus of four academic journals[2] and a frequent focus of numerous other journals in philosophy and education. The problem is not merely that many programs touted as new or unique are actually neither but, more importantly, that they are uninformed by the past 40 years of scholarship on precollege philosophy. Today, it is simply uncreditable for developers of precollege philosophy programs to claim ignorance of this field of scholarship, and the creation of new materials or methods for use in schools, let alone their sale, without consultation of this scholarship is not merely unprofessional but unethical.

The articulation of objectives and standards for precollege philosophy education would help to solve or alleviate these problems. Of course, professional and educational standards can be misused and can have unintended negative consequences, one of which, for precollege philosophy education, could be the insulation of a majority opinion on aims and methods from minority criticism and innovation. More serious negative consequences could be the fragmentation of teaching and learning in precollege philosophy into discreet, measurable outcomes and the valuing (i.e., assessment) of predetermined, narrowly defined performance objectives over the experience and process of philosophical inquiry itself (see Hyland, 1994, p. 54) and the unexpected but educationally significant outcomes that might emerge from that process (Osberg & Biesta, 2008). As Kotnik (2008, p. 8) argued, this consequence would be particularly damning to Philosophy for Children, for whom the educational benefit of philosophical inquiry depends on its being a holistically meaningful experience for children.

The setting of standards also raises the perennial danger of the determination of program objectives on the basis of what can be readily assessed instead of the determination of what and how to assess on the basis of authentic program objectives.[3] Moreover, despite the tremendous amount of work done in the past 40 years, precollege philosophy is still an experimental field, in that there is no meaningful consensus about the proper aims of precollege philosophy education, and few of the aims that have been advanced have been studied empirically with regard to the kinds of materials and methods likely to achieve them. For these reasons, rather than attempt to promulgate standards with any official status, the work that needs to be accomplished by practitioners and theorists working in precollege philosophy includes the following:

- The articulation of authentic purposes, objectives, and standards for their programs.
- The defense of these with value-oriented arguments and with arguments and evidence from relevant philosophical and

educational research.

- The formulation of research-based guidelines for educational materials, methods, and professional development likely to achieve their stated objectives.
- The determination of ways to gather evidence for whether or not those objectives are being achieved.

This kind of work has been occurring over the past 4 decades (e.g., Lipman, Sharp, & Oscanyan, 1980, section II) but not systematically enough or to the extent that the problems will be alleviated or bring the benefits described previously.

Some Common Objectives for Precollege Philosophy

A review of Philosophy for Children and other precollege and undergraduate philosophy programs and the academic literature examining them reveals four kinds of objectives commonly stated or implied for these programs:

1. To help students acquire cognitive skills and dispositions, enabling them to make sound inferences and other reasoning moves (Cannon & Weinstein, 1985; Gratton, 2000; Weinstein, 1988), construct and critique logical arguments (Imbrosciano, 1993; Slade, 1989; Splitter, 1988), and learn broader inquiry strategies, such as identifying problems, formulating inquiry questions, constructing original hypotheses, and finding and analyzing relevant data (Dalin, 1983; Haynes & Haynes, 2000; Matsuoka, 2004).
2. To help students learn the concept of philosophical inquiry as the disciplined, open-ended, self-corrective search for reasonable beliefs and values (Dewey, 1933/1997; Fisher, 2008b; Lipman, 1991; Splitter & Sharp, 1995; Walton, 1998).
3. To help students learn the concept of dialogue as a method of collaborative inquiry and peer accountability (Fisher, 2008a; Gregory, 2008; Kennedy, 2004; Sternberg, 1999) and learn to dialogue with cognitive and social competence (Splitter & Sharp, 1995).
4. To help students learn canonical philosophical content, including questions, problems, concepts, arguments, and some of the key figures within the subdisciplines of ethics, aesthetics, metaphysics, political philosophy, and logic (Lim, 2003; van

der Leeuw & Mostert, 1987), and learn to discern philosophical concepts and issues wherever they arise. This is sometimes referred to as the development of "a philosophical ear" (Gregory, 2008, p. 1).

In addition to alleviating the problems mentioned previously, the establishment of objectives, such as these for precollege philosophy, could bring the additional benefit of a wider appreciation among educators and parents of the educational merits of studying philosophy and especially the cultivation of cross-disciplinary habits of rigorous intellectual engagement and a nuanced understanding of philosophical concepts, such as justice, person, mind, beauty, cause, number, truth, citizen, good, and right, which are foundational to the arts and sciences. The recognition that these merits come not merely from the study of philosophy as a high school elective but from "growing up with philosophy" (Lipman & Sharp, 1978) would also, no doubt, benefit the profession with more college philosophy majors.

However, to work for the wider inclusion of philosophy in precollege education on the basis of its intellectual and academic merits alone is to risk allowing precollege philosophy to be co-opted in the enterprise of education for socioeconomic advancement, an enterprise severely criticized by philosophers since ancient times:

> Sophists had claimed to train young people for political life, but Plato wanted to accomplish this by providing them with a knowledge …inseparable from the love of the good and from the inner transformation of the person. Plato wanted to train not only skillful statesmen, but also human beings. (Hadot, 2002, p. 59)

The timeless distinction that Plato drew was between education aimed at getting ahead and education aimed at living well, or wisdom. "Getting ahead" means acquiring the disciplinary knowledge and the intellectual, social, and technological skills necessary for academic and professional advancement. "Living well" means learning to cultivate personal and collective well-being, which involves the regulation of one's desire and action in ways that bring meaning and purpose to one's life. Of course, making a living is part of living well, and being wise does not preclude being successful, but education that focuses exclusively on getting ahead prepares students ultimately to be successful at pursuing unexamined desires in a free-market economy. Indeed, as Sternberg (1999) observed, this is the intended aim for many parents and educators:

Education is seen more as an access route…toward obtaining…the best possible credentials for individual socioeconomic advancement. Education is seen not so much as a means of helping society but of helping one obtain the best that society has to offer socially, economically, and culturally. (p. 62)

It is ironic that this distinction between getting ahead and living well applies to teaching philosophy, which originated as the disciplined pursuit of wisdom. However, precollege philosophy has often been used for getting ahead, especially in its instrumental role of teaching excellent thinking, which has been justified in the following terms:

- To help children do better in school by helping them to make more sense of subject content, to develop cross-curricular skills (Haynes, 2002, pp. 127–129), to think in ways characteristic of particular disciplines (Lipman, 1991, p. 18), and to offer them more intellectually stimulating experiences that will increase their motivation (Fisher, 2008b, pp. xi and 2–3).
- To prepare students to do well in college and to perform better on college entrance exams (Willingham, 2007, p. 8).
- To prepare students to be successful in business (Willingham, 2007, p. 8) and other sectors of employment, particularly given the rapid "rate of change within society" (Fisher, 2008b, p. 3).
- To prepare students to participate in democratic decision making (Lipman, 1998) and thereby strengthen democratic society, which is characterized as a thinking society (Fisher, 2008b, p. 3).

These largely instrumentalist aims contrast dramatically with the following, which are also offered as aims for teaching thinking but are focused on improving the quality of children's lives more immediately:

- To allow students to experience the enjoyment of intellectual challenge (Fisher, 2008b, pp. 1 and 3).
- To give students cognitive tools and dispositions to solve current life problems and to achieve personal autonomy by avoiding manipulation (Murris, 2008; Splitter, 1986).
- To help students learn to make better moral, aesthetic, and other kinds of judgments that will enhance their life experiences (Lipman, 1991, p. 19).

The former set of aims for teaching thinking are largely compatible with the latter, but the latter cannot be realized by education that focuses exclusively on the former, nor will educational aims for living well be realized if they are merely added onto to the standard curriculum for getting ahead, even if some kind of balance is attempted between the two sets of aims. Rather, as a growing number of educational philosophers and psychologists are proposing (Gregory & Laverty, 2009; Noddings, 2005; Sternberg, 2003), living well must become the primary educational aim to which other aims should be expected to contribute.

Wisdom Objectives for Precollege Philosophy

In contradiction to philosophers for whom "to apply philosophy is not thereby to do it" (Pollack, 2007, p. 246), a number of philosophers have argued the reverse: that philosophy is most authentic as a way of life:

Philosophy is love of wisdom; wisdom being not knowledge but knowledge-plus; knowledge turned to account in the instruction and guidance it may convey in piloting life through the storms and the shoals that beset life-experience as well as into such havens of consummatory experience as enrich our human life from time to time. (Dewey, 2008, p. 389)

The philosophical search for truth is a meditative way of living out the answers it finds and the questions it asks such that they are felt, understood, and incorporated in growing wisdom; it is a gradual, not only theoretical but also emotional and practical transformation of the philosopher. (Peperzak, 1999, p. 124)

There is no essential opposition compelling us to choose between philosophy as theory and as artful life-practice. Indeed, we must not choose between them….We surely should build our art of living on our knowledge and vision of the world, and reciprocally seek the knowledge that serves our art of living. Philosophy is strongest when both its modes of practice are combined to reinforce each other as they did in ancient philosophy. (Shusterman, 1997, p. 4)

Reflection on our ways of living…has always been a vital function of philosophy….The ancient questions, "Am I living as I am supposed to live?" "Is my life something more than vanity, or worse, mere conformity?" "Am I making the best effort I can to reach…my unattained but attainable self?" make all the difference in the world. (Putnam, 2008, p. 12)

The Stoics distinguished three interrelated components of living wisely: a moral component of living ethically, virtuously, and with integrity; a psychological component of maintaining composure and tranquility in the midst of chaos and tribulation; and an intellectual component of disciplined thinking and the construction of a value-oriented understanding of the world and one's place in it.[4] The Stoics correlated these three components of well-being with the disciplines of ethics (behavior), physics (perspective), and logic (thinking), respectively, and indicated that each discipline involved both a theoretical component and an applied or lived component (Hadot, 1995, p. i24). This tradition provides us with categories of wisdom-oriented objectives for philosophy education, including precollege philosophy. Here are some objectives that might be included in those categories:

Theoretical Ethics

- To help students develop skills of interpersonal communication and to provide opportunities for them to develop empathy through learning about the values and interests of others and about their own complex relationships to their social and natural environments (Schertz, 2006; Sharp, 1993, 2006).
- To familiarize students with relevant ideas, personalities, and episodes from the history of philosophy in an age-appropriate manner as options for living well (Cam, 1994).
- To familiarize students with alternate ethical theories.
- To help students understand the procedures and develop the skills of collaborative inquiry to resolve social conflict (Gregory, 2004, 2005b).
- To provide students opportunities to reflect philosophically on the rewards and responsibilities of many kinds of interpersonal relationships and community membership.
- To provide students with opportunities to reflect philosophically on a variety of paradigms of human physical and mental health as options for living well (Gregory, 2005a).

Lived Ethics

- To help students wake up to the ethical dimension of their experiences—to recognize when issues of right and wrong, good and evil, duty, justice, and compassion arise in their experience—and to conduct ethical inquiry toward making sound ethical judgments in the course of their everyday lives (Lipman, 1987; Sharp, 1987; Sprod, 2001).

- To encourage students to cultivate particular, self-chosen habits of moral feeling and action, such as curbing appetites and egocentric passions, maintaining physical and mental health, and exercising compassion and concern for social justice, all as episodes of meaningful experience.
- To provide students with the opportunity to construct personal and collective agendas for worthwhile passionate engagements.

Theoretical Physics

- To help students understand the relationship between suffering and egotism[5] and to familiarize them with the teachings of philosophers, sages, prophets, and playwrights from a variety of traditions on this point, including, for example, Socrates, Samkya, Confucius, the Buddha, Jeremiah, Jesus, Mohammad, Epicurus, Marcus Arelius, and Aeschylus.

Lived Physics

- To provide students with the opportunity to reflect on their emotional lives and to practice emotional self-regulation (Gazzard, 2000; Lipman, 1995).
- To provide students with the opportunity to reflect philosophically on their own experiences of discontent, unrequited desire, fear, humiliation, aversion, anxiety, and other forms of suffering and on their experiences of tranquility, gratitude, empathy, reverence, and awe in an attempt to discern ways in which they contribute to their own suffering and contentment.
- To provide students with opportunities to experiment with contemplative practices, such as communal ritual (Sharp, 2007), empathic awareness (Sharp, 2006), aesthetic appreciation, present-moment mindfulness (Hadot, 1995, pp. 84–85), contemplation of nature (Hadot, 1995, p. 97), yoga (Armstrong, 2006, pp. 195–197), and other practices recommended in wisdom traditions for the cultivation of equanimity and autonomy.

Theoretical Logic

- To help students acquire the cognitive skills and dispositions of sound reasoning.
- To help students learn the concept of robust philosophical inquiry and master its constituent inquiry strategies.
- To help students learn the theory of collaborative inquiry and develop dialogical competencies.
- To help students construct stable but fallible value-oriented worldviews that will help them understand the meaning and purpose of their lives and that will both inform and be informed by their experiences.

Lived Logic

- To provide students with the opportunity to experience the enjoyment of intellectual challenge.
- To provide students with the opportunity to use their thinking and inquiry skills to solve problems that arise in their own (nonacademic) experience.
- To help students develop a critical spirit (Oxman-Michelli, 1992) to learn to avoid manipulation and otherwise achieve personal autonomy.[6]
- To help students discipline their inner dialogue (Hadot, 1995, p. 102) to acquire the disposition to engage in ongoing self-examination and self-correction of their beliefs and values (Sharp, 1996) and otherwise to become "more thoughtful, more reflective, more considerate, more reliable" (Lipman, Sharp, & Oscanyan, 1984, p. 15)—in short, more reasonable people (Lipman, 1993).

The call for contemporary education to adopt wisdom-oriented objectives is an important opportunity for philosophers to become as involved in educational policy and practice as they were at the height of the critical thinking movement in education. However, in this instance, philosophy has as much to gain as it has to offer. As Cam (2006) observed:

> Unlike many other academic disciplines, philosophers have never thought about how they might reconstruct their discipline for general educational purposes until quite recently; and being effectively cut off from any

concern with school education or education beyond the university, philosophical practice has tended to be narrowly academic and insular. (p. 37)

Many philosophers working in Philosophy for Children have argued that the work of reconstructing the discipline of philosophy in the context of precollege education should be the occasion for a broader reconstruction of professional philosophy (Cannon, 2002; Kennedy, 1999). I suggest that in particular, reinstating philosophy's wisdom-oriented objectives in precollege education could help return philosophy to its original identity as the disciplined study and practice of living well.[7]

References

Alexander, R. J. (2003). *Talk for learning: The first year.* Northallerton: North Yorkshire County Council.

Armstrong, K. (2006). *The great transformation: The beginning of our religious traditions.* New York: Knopf.

Cam, P. (1994). Dewey, Lipman, and the Tradition of Reflective Education. In Taylor, M., Schrier, H. and Ghiraldelli, Jr., P., (Eds.), *Pragmatism, Education and Children.* Amsterdam: Editions Rodopi B.V., pp. 163–81.

—. (2006). Philosophy and the school curriculum: Some general remarks. *Critical and Creative Thinking: The Australasian Journal of Philosophy in Education, 14,* 35–51.

Cannon, D. (2002). How has involvement with Philosophy for Children changed how I/we understand philosophy? *Analytic Teaching: The Community of Inquiry Journal, 22,* 97–105.

Cannon, D., & Weinstein, M. (1985). Reasoning skills: An overview. *Thinking: The Journal of Philosophy for Children, 6,* 25–26.

Dalin, G. D. (1983). Critical thinking and problem solving in the elementary school curriculum. *Analytic Teaching: The Community of Inquiry Journal, 4,* 23–24.

Dewey, J. (1933/1997). *How we think.* Mineola, NY: Dover.

—. (2008). *The later works of John Dewey. Volume 16, 1925–1953: 1949–1952. Essays, typescripts, and knowing and the known* (Boydston, J. A., Ed.). Carbondale: Southern Illinois University Press.

Dolz, J. (1996). Learning argumentative capacities. A study of the effects of a systematic and intensive teaching of argumentative discourse in 11-12 year old children. *Argumentation, 10,* 227–251.

Fisher, R. (2008a). Philosophical intelligence: Why philosophical dialogue is important in educating the mind. In M. Hand (Ed.), *Philosophy in schools* (pp. 96–104). New York: Continuum International.

—. (2008b). *Teaching thinking: Philosophical enquiry in the classroom* (3rd ed.). New York: Continuum.

Garcia-Moriyón, F., Rebollo, I., & Colom, R. (2004). Evaluating Philosophy for Children: A meta-analysis. *Thinking: The Journal of Philosophy for Children, 17,* 14–22.

Gardner, H. (2006). *Multiple intelligences: New horizons* (rev. ed.). New York: Basic Books.

Gazzard, A. (2000). What does Philosophy for Children have to do with emotional intelligence? *Thinking: The Journal of Philosophy for Children, 15,* 39–45.

Gratton, C. (2000). Precision, consistency, implication and inference. *Thinking: The Journal of Philosophy for Children, 15,* 30–37.

Gregory, M. (2004). Conflict, inquiry and education for peace. In S. N. Chattopadhyay (Ed.), *World peace: Problems of global understanding and prospects of harmony* (pp. 265–278). Calcutta: Naya Prokash.

—. (2005a, July). *Inquiry and human health.* Paper presented at Education, Peace and Justice, the XII International Conference of the International Council for Philosophical Inquiry with Children, Mexico City.

—. (2005b). Practicing democracy: Social intelligence and philosophical practice. *The International Journal of Applied Philosophy, 16,* 161–174.

—. (Ed.). (2008). *Philosophy for Children practitioner handbook.* Montclair, NJ: Institute for the Advancement of Philosophy for Children.

Gregory, M. R., & Laverty, M. J. (2009). Philosophy and education for wisdom. In A. Kenkman (Ed.), *Teaching philosophy* (pp. 155–173). New York: Continuum International.

Hadot, P. (1995). *Philosophy as a way of life: Spiritual exercises from Socrates to Foucault* (M. Chase, Trans.; A. I. Davidson, Ed.). Malden, MA: Blackwell.

—. (2002). *What is ancient philosophy?* Cambridge, MA: Harvard University Press.

Haynes, F., & Haynes, B. (2000). The development of a conceptual framework for critical thinking and problem solving K–12. *Critical and Creative Thinking, 8*(1), 15–22.

Haynes, J. (2002). *Children as philosophers.* London: Routledge Falmer.

Hyland, T. (1994). *Competence, education and NVQs: Dissenting perspectives.* London: Cassell.

Imbrosciano, A. (1993). Logic in schools. *Critical and Creative Thinking, 1*(1), 1–56.

Kennedy, D. (1999). Philosophy for Children and the reconstruction of philosophy. *Metaphilosophy, 30,* 338–359.

—. (2004). Communal philosophical dialogue and the intersubject. *International Journal for Philosophical Practice, 18,* 203–218.

Kotnik, R. (2008). Curriculum and standards: Intercultural enculturation. Paper presented at Philosophie der Interkulturalität [Philosophy of Interculturality] conference, University of Graz, Austria.

Kuhn, D., Shaw, V., & Felton, M. (1997). Effects of dyadic interaction on argumentative reasoning. *Cognition and instruction, 15*(3), 287–315.

Lim, T. K. (2003). Introducing Asian philosophy and concepts into the community of inquiry. *Thinking: The Journal of Philosophy for Children, 16,* 41–44.

Lipman, M. (1987). Ethical reasoning and the craft of moral practice. *The Journal of Moral Education, 16,* 139–147.

—. (1991). *Thinking in education.* Cambridge, England: Cambridge University Press.

—. (1993). Unreasonable people and inappropriate judgments. *Critical and Creative Thinking, 1,* 10–18.

—. (1995). Using philosophy to educate emotions. *Analytic Teaching: The Community of Inquiry Journal, 15,* 3–10.

—. (1998). The contributions of philosophy to deliberative democracy. In D. Owens & I. Kucuradi (Eds.), *Teaching philosophy on the eve of the twenty first century* (pp. 6–29). Ankara, Turkey: International Federation of Philosophical Societies.

Lipman, M., & Sharp, A. M. (Eds.). (1978). *Growing up with philosophy.* Philadelphia: Temple University Press.

Lipman, M., Sharp, A. M., & Oscanyan, F. S. (1980). *Philosophy in the classroom* (2nd ed.). Philadelphia: Temple University Press.

Lipman, M., Sharp, A. M., & Oscanyan, F. S. (1984). *Philosophical inquiry: An instructional manual to accompany Harry Stottlemeier's discovery* (2nd ed.). Upper Montclair, NJ: Institute for the Advancement of Philosophy for Children.

Matsuoka, C. (2004). Mindful habits and Philosophy for Children: Cultivating thinking & problem-solving in children. *Thinking: The Journal of Philosophy for Children, 17,* 54–55.

Mercer, N., Wegerif, R., & Dawes, L. (1999). Children's talk and the development of reasoning in the classroom. *British Educational Research Journal, 25*(1), 95–111.

Morehouse, R. and Williams M. (1998), Report on student use of argument skills, *Critical and Creative Thinking, 6*(1), 14–20.

Murris, K. (2008). Autonomous and authentic thinking through philosophy with picture books. In M. Hand & C. Winstanley (Eds.), *Philosophy in schools* (pp. 105–118). New York: Continuum International.

Noddings, N. (2005). *Happiness and education.* Cambridge, MA: Cambridge University Press.

Nystrand, M., Wu, L., Gamoran, A., Zeiser, S., & Long, D. A. (2003). Questions in time: Investigating the structure and dynamics of unfolding classroom discourse. *Discourse Processes, 35*(2), 135–200.

Osberg, D., & Biesta, G. (2008). The emergent curriculum: Navigating a complex course between unguided learning and planned enculturation. *Journal of Curriculum Studies, 40,* 313–328.

Oxman-Michelli, W. (1992). *Critical thinking as "critical spirit."* Montclair, NJ: Institute for Critical Thinking Resource Publications.

Peperzak, A. T. (1999). *Reason in faith: On the relevance of Christian spirituality for philosophy.* New York: Paulist.

Pollack, G. (2007). Philosophy of education as philosophy: A metaphilosophical inquiry. *Educational Theory, 57,* 239–260.

Putnam, H. (2008). 12 philosophers—and their influence on me. *Proceedings and Addresses of the American Philosophical Association, 82*(2), pp. 101–115.

Reznitskaya, A. (2005). Empirical research in Philosophy for Children: Limitations and new directions. *Thinking: The Journal of Philosophy for Children, 17,* 4–13.

Schertz, M. (2006). Empathic pedagogy: Community of inquiry and the development of empathy. *Analytic Teaching: The Community of Inquiry Journal, 26,* 8–14.

—. (1996). Self-Transformation in the Community of Inquiry. *Inquiry: Critical Thinking Across the Disciplines 16*(1), pp. 36-47.

—. (1987). Pedagogical practice and philosophy: The case for ethical inquiry. *Analytic Teaching: The Community of Inquiry Journal, 7,* 4–7.

—. (1993). The ethics of translation. *Critical and Creative Thinking, 1,* 10–17.

—. (2006). The face of the other. *Thinking: The Journal of Philosophy for Children, 18,* 43–47.

Sharp, A. M. (2007). The classroom community of inquiry as ritual: How we can cultivate wisdom. *Critical and Creative Thinking, 15,* 3–14.

Shipman, V. C. (1983). Evaluation of the Philosophy for Children program in Bethlehem, Pennsylvania. *Thinking: The Journal of Philosophy for Children, 1*(1), 37–40.

Shusterman, R. (1997). *Practicing Philosophy: Pragmatism and the Philosophical Life.* New York: Routledge.

Slade, C. (1989). Logic in the classroom. *Thinking: The Journal of Philosophy for Children, 8,* 14–20.

Soter, A., Wilkinson, I. A. G., Murphy, P. K., Rudge, L., Reninger, K., & Edwards, M. (2008). What the discourse tells us: Talk and indicators of high-level comprehension. *International Journal of Educational Research, 47,* 372–391. doi: 10.1016/j.ijer.2009.01.001

Splitter, L. (1986). On thinking for yourself. *Thinking: The Journal of Philosophy for Children, 6,* 23–24.

—. (1988). A guided tour of the logic in Harry Stottlemeier's discovery. *Analytic Teaching: The Community of Inquiry Journal, 8,* 71–86.

Splitter, L., & Sharp, A. M. (1995). *Teaching for better thinking: The classroom community of inquiry.* Melbourne: Australian Council for Educational Research.

Sprod, T. (2001). *Philosophical discussion in moral education: The Community of Ethical Inquiry.* New York: Routledge Falmer.

Sternberg, R. J. (1999). Schools should nurture wisdom. In B. Z. Presseisen (Ed.), *Teaching for intelligence* (pp. 55–82). Skylight Training and Publishing: Arlington Heights, IL.

—. (2003). *Wisdom, intelligence, and creativity synthesized.* New York: Cambridge University Press.

van der Leeuw, K., & Mostert, P. (1987). Learning to operate with philosophical concepts. *Analytic Teaching: The Community of Inquiry Journal, 8,* 93–100.

Walton, D. (1998). *The new dialectic: Conversational contexts of argument.* Toronto: University of Toronto Press.

Weinstein, M. (1988). Reason and critical thinking. *Informal Logic, 10,* 1–20.

Willingham, D. T. (2007). Critical thinking: Why is it so hard to teach? *American Educator, 31*(2), 8–19.

Notes

1. See "IAPC Timeline" at
    http://cehs.montclair.edu/academic/iapc/timeline.shtml (accessed October 22, 2008).
2. *Thinking: The Journal of Philosophy for Children* (Montclair, New Jersey: Institute for the Advancement of Philosophy for Children, 1979 to present);

Analytic Teaching: The Community of Inquiry Journal (LaCrosse, Wisconsin: Viterbo University, 1981 to present, online at http://www.viterbo.edu/analytic); *Critical and Creative Thinking: The Australasian Journal of Philosophy for Children,* renamed *Critical and Creative Thinking: The Australasian Journal of Philosophy in Education* (Federation of Australasian Philosophy in Schools Associations, 1993 to present); and *Childhood & Philosophy: A Journal of the International Council of Philosophical Inquiry with Children* (2005 to present, online at http://www.filoeduc.org/childphilo).

3   In this regard, Howard Gardner (2006) lamented that "especially in the United States, with its focus on quantitative markers and its cult of educational efficiency...the most important subject matters are those that lend themselves readily to such assessment, like mathematics and science. In other content areas, value is assigned to the aspects that can be efficiently assessed (grammar rather than voice in writing; facts rather than interpretation in history). Those disciplines that prove most refractory to formal testing, such as the arts, are least valued in the uniform school" (pp. 170–171).

4   Hadot (1995) summarized these components as "a complete transformation of his representations of the world, his inner climate, and his outer behavior" (pp. 85–86). "What is needed is the immediate transformation of our way of thinking, of acting, and of accepting events. We must think in accordance with truth, act in accordance with justice, and lovingly accept what comes to pass" (p. 229).

5   As Hadot (1995) explained, "In the view of all philosophical schools, mankind's principal cause of suffering, disorder, and unconsciousness were the passions: that is, unregulated desires and exaggerated fears. People are prevented from truly living, it was taught, because they are dominated by worries. Philosophy thus appears, in the first place, as a therapeutic of the passions" (p. 83).

6   Thus, Hadot (1995) asserted that "on this level, we are no longer concerned with theoretical logic—that is, the theory of correct reasoning—rather, we are concerned not to let ourselves be deceived in our everyday lives by false representations" (p. 192).

7. Earlier versions of this essay were presented at the international symposium *Philosophy, Philosophy Are You There? Doing Philosophy with Children,* November 28, 2008, at University of the Aegean, Rhodes, Greece, and published in *Farhang Journal, 69,* 157–174 (Iranian Institute for Humanities and Cultural Studies, Tehran, reprinted with permission).

Chapter Two

Philosophical Dialogue across the School Curriculum: The Case of Mathematics

Nadia Stoyanova Kennedy
Stony Brook University, SUNY
and David Kennedy
Montclair State University

In this chapter, we explore some essential characteristics of the pedagogy of communal dialogue as manifested in the form of a community of philosophical inquiry (CPI). The CPI is understood to be an "ideal speech situation," a context for distributed and multilogical dialogue that not only represents a different model for knowledge construction and epistemology but also is an exemplary pedagogical site for a form of schooling that satisfies the criteria for the ongoing reconstruction of habit that is authentic in social democracy. In the vocabulary of complexity theory, the CPI is redescribed as an open, emergent, self-organizing system that fluctuates between chaos and stagnation and is ecological, self-organizing, nonlinear, nonhierarchical, emergent, and engaged in continual reconstruction. We argue for the use of philosophical dialogue across the curriculum and specifically in the case of the mathematics classroom. To introduce the CPI with its dialectical process of knowledge construction into the mathematics classroom is to introduce a dimension of inquiry that goes beyond inquiry within the mathematical system and does not impose prefabricated questions but invites children to pose questions of their own about mathematics concerning both its internal relations and its relation to the world. Finally, we sketch in broad strokes a curriculum that integrates communal philosophical inquiry into the traditional school content areas. Three models for organizing inquiry into disciplines are outlined: single-discipline, interdisciplinary, and whole-curriculum approaches, each of which corresponds to a more general organizational model for curriculum planning, that is, within a single classroom, between classrooms, and across the whole school.

What Is a Community of Philosophical Inquiry (CPI)?

A CPI is an intentional speech or discourse community committed specifically to the investigation of an ontological, epistemological, aesthetic, or ethical question: a finite group of people who meet in some venue or online to deliberate with one another about common, central, and contestable (CCC) concepts, such as truth, justice, friendship, gender, education, and personhood. *Inquiry* is meant as a form of deliberation that is oriented toward the discovery and/or invention of new meanings. The group may gather together to investigate concepts within disciplinary boundaries, such as mathematics (e.g., infinity), history (e.g., progress), or biology (e.g., organism), or they may be dedicated to an emergent theme structure, whereby one problematization leads to another. In all cases, they meet in the interest of experiencing some sort of reconstruction of belief through the interrogation of assumptions in the space of dialogue around which they are gathered. CPI facilitators model, coach, and intervene procedurally to clarify and coordinate the emergent structure of the collaboratively constructed argument, which develops through a series of spontaneous critical interventions, or moves, such as offering and evaluating examples, proposing counterarguments, exploring implications, classifying and categorizing, summarizing, and restating.

CPI represents something quite distinctive and more or less immediately recognizable from other kinds of group talk (although it is connected to them all) and something that involves a different kind of teacher talk, or pedagogy. These differences are not just in technique; it is not as if it shares the same model of knowledge as, say, traditional math pedagogy but just does it in an informal or student-centered way, for example. Rather, it represents a different model of knowledge and, therefore, implies a different model of teaching.

First, CPI needs to be distinguished from its precursors and alternatives. The phrase *community of inquiry* was, as far as we know, originally coined by the American philosopher C. S. Peirce, and he meant it as community of experts—scientists or professional philosophers. Pierce held that the truth is "what the community of inquiry will decide is the case in the long run" (Raposa, 1989, p. 154).

This in no way implies that there is no such thing as truth, which is a mistake that is often made by both students and teachers who first encounter CPI. Rather, Peirce's dictum may be understood to mean that indeed there is such a thing as the truth, but it can never be reached—until we reach the horizon represented by the long run, which because there is always more to the long run, we never will. This is the heart of a *fallibilist* approach to knowledge, which means that we can never be sure that we have the whole truth or the final word and that we could, in fact, be quite wrong about a number of things. It also implies an *inquiry* approach to knowledge, in that knowledge is never fully and finally accomplished but is the subject of ongoing construction and reconstruction, and a *communal* approach, which means that knowledge is actually a social phenomenon, something that we argue, deliberate, and decide to be the case together and that is in continual reconstruction through *dialogue* ("thinking for ourselves and with others"). The latter is neither groupthink nor debate and, as a process and phenomenon, has some very specific characteristics.

First, CPI aspires to be an ideal speech situation, which means that everyone has the same right to speak. Because everyone has a voice and no one voice is privileged, it is—or aspires to be—polyphonic. Even if there is an expert in the group, he or she must submit to the collective, collaborative, deliberative process. This is seldom attained in practice. However, it means that CPI is an exemplary pedagogical site for a form of schooling that satisfies the criteria for the ongoing reconstruction of habit, which is an authentic social democracy and without which political democracy is not realizable.

Second, CPI is multilogical. It operates through the expression and attempted coordination of multiple points of view, multiple styles of thinking, multiple ways of talking, and multiple experiences of the world. It is structured as dialogue, which involves seeking the truth together rather than against each other, as in the model of debate.

Third, CPI is distributed. Voice, intelligence, and thinking are distributed throughout the group. Another way of saying this psychologically rather than just cognitively is that the group that forms a CPI is a collective subject. It is one person. There is a group personality, a specific group process, a chemistry. There are contradictions to be addressed within the group just as there are within the individual. So there is a dialogue that goes on between the individual and the group, within the group, and within the individual. Roles are distributed: leader/initiator, mediator, provocateur, summarizer, logician, and restater. CPI has as the goal of a complete and equal distribution between roles that involve speaking and listening. Thus, the teacher in a CPI is a facilitator rather than an instructor, and her goal is to slowly become an equal member of the group herself; her success is measured by the extent to which her regulative function—distributing turns fairly and showing concern for the argument as a whole rather than just her individual perspective—is shared by every other member of the group. In a mature community of inquiry, each member takes the same care for the procedural and substantive processes himself; this allows the facilitator to become more philosophically—and not just procedurally—active.

Fourth, CPI is an *open, emergent, self-organizing system*, in that[7]:

1. It is *ecological*. The confrontation of perspectives that it entail leads not to a unilateral imposition of one perspective but to the transformation of the whole system to a new level of development. It leaves all elements of the ecosystem intact but different. One change within the system can transform the whole system. We may identify the system (at least on one level) as the argument: a structure of propositions, assumptions, and hypotheses in a dynamic process of reconstruction.

2. It is *nonlinear* and *irreversible* and in continual dialectical transformation. It never returns to a previous level of organization. Once we have had that conversation about justice, we will never talk about it in the same way again. The whole system can be altered by the influence of minor effects. For example, in an educational situation, the logical structures of one individual may not coincide with the logic of the whole system. What for one individual may represent merely an aspect of the current state of the system may, for another, represent an element that triggers its transformation. What seems minor for one may be the last straw for another. A system that appears to be far from transformation may reorganize in the following moment, and vice versa: a system that appears primed for transformation may hang in a state of stagnation indefinitely.

3. It is only *partially predictable*. This is different from the goal of traditional instruction, which is to be completely predictable ("At the end of the unit, the student will be able to....") Because it is only partially predictable, it is only partially controllable, or we say that it is characterized by *ambiguous control*.

4. The system fluctuates between *chaos* and *stagnation*, which are hypertrophies of levels of difference and sameness, openness and closedness, motion and rest, instability and stability, and overstimulation and understimulation. The role of the facilitator, who has ambiguous control like anyone else in the group, is to try to strike the balance. There is a paradox here, in that the goal of a dynamic system is equilibrium, which would be an equalization of energy throughout the system, or entropy. On this analogy, to achieve the ideal speech community would be to close it down; if it accomplishes its goal, it ceases to function.

5. As an ecological, self-organizing, nonlinear, nonhierarchical, and emergent system engaged in continual reconstruction, a CPI is what Vygotsky (1978) grasped and communicated for us without the language of systems. He described the process of learning as the internalization by each element of the system of the movement of the system as a whole. In other words, through the process of group dialogue, what happens *between us* is internalized so that it happens *within* each one of us. For example, if someone argues through offering an example, through analyzing an example for its relevance, through offering a hypothesis, through identifying an unstated assumption, or through seeking clarification of someone else's statement, these communicative moves are transformed through the "internal reconstruction of an external operation" (p. 56) into moves within the universe of my personal thinking. In my internal dialogue, I begin to think of examples, entertain hypotheses, seek my own assumptions, and so on. In returning to the CPI, I bring that growing critical *instrumentarium* of critical skills back to the group, where it contributes to the external operation of the conversation, thus creating a positive feedback cycle. The teacher's role is to facilitate that process.

6. In a classroom context, the discourse characteristics enumerated previously constitute an alternative learning system to the traditional model. An alternative epistemology, or set of beliefs about knowledge, implies an alternative pedagogy. For this reason, the facilitator operates differently from the instructor in a few crucial respects: she considers herself a fellow inquirer, a senior inquirer, with her students; she listens and seeks to understand her students' thinking as much as she seeks to inform that thinking; she does not have to be right all the time; she does not have to know everything; and her impulse and goal are to distribute authority rather than to consolidate it. These are the first, most essential characteristics of a pedagogy of communal dialogue.

The Problematization of Concepts
in Philosophical Inquiry

Philosophical inquiry is an inquiry into *concepts*. By concepts, we understand those assemblages of assumptions, implicit or explicit propositions, working theories, vague or precise beliefs, memories, and expectations (in Husserl's terms, *retentions* and *protensions*) gathered around a theme, such as justice, love, time, or infinity, that influence how we act and react in our dealings with the world and how we understand those actions and reactions. Concepts develop or should develop as a result of both experience and reflection. My concept of friendship, for example, emerges quite early in life, undergoes all the relational vicissitudes that follow, and influences them as well.

Ethical concepts carry a normative element, that is, they suggest how the world *should be*. Ontological or metaphysical concepts, on the other hand, reflect how the world *objectively is*, which is as elusive a question as how the world should be. Concepts invoke a kind of opening, or as Leonard Cohen described it, a "crack."[8] The crack between how it is and how it might be—between the naïve and the scientific, the individual and the universal, the subjective and the intersubjective, or the individual and the community—is where the question lies. It might be argued that this crack and the question that emerges from it is the focal point for our evolutionary potential as a species, for it is here that cognitive reconstruction and, by implication, psychological, social, and political reconstruction become possible.

The best known school curriculum in the CPI—the Philosophy for Children novels and manuals—is composed entirely of questions. This curriculum favors the novel over the textbook because the latter is a book of answers, and the former is a provoker of questions. The textbook assumes the question and thus, for the purposes of inquiry, suppresses it. As such, any question it might answer is a rhetorical one, a question to which the answer is already known. The philosophical novel, because it is a narrative instead of an expository text, makes it possible to represent the multivocal, dialogical, and nonlinear contextually situated practice of group deliberation. It can represent through character, plot and dialogue, "the way we think when we inquire," as Matthew Lipman (2003, p. 85) put it. The narrative can be constructed so that it assumes nothing or at least continually questions its own assumptions. It can dramatize the emergence of questions and the dialogue that those questions trigger. The Lipmanian manuals that accompany the novels are basically simple lists of questions about the concepts that are highlighted in the novels. Some examples follow.

On Belief[9]

- What reason do you have for believing that you are now wearing shoes?

- What reason do you have for believing that you are not dreaming?
- What reason do you have for believing that the person next to you really exists?
- What reason do you have for believing that, during the night, the sun is on the other side of the earth?
- Do you have any reason for not believing in giants?
- Do you have any reason for not believing in angels?
- Is make-believe true, false, or neither true nor false?
- Can we control what we do or do not, can or cannot, want to or do not want to, or ought or ought not to believe?
- How do you know that you are believing in the right thing?
- Is there a right thing to believe?
- Can you follow multiple beliefs?
- Can you create your own beliefs?
- Can you believe something without knowing that you do?
- Can someone tell you what to believe?
- Can someone believe for you?
- Do we need people to tell us what to believe?

On Concepts

- What do we mean when we use the word *concept?*
- Is there a difference between the way we use *concept* and *idea?*
- What is the relation between concepts and things?
- What is the relation between concepts and experience?
- Do concepts have structure? If so, must they?
- Can concepts disappear?
- Can concepts be invented?
- Are concepts collective?
- Do animals have concepts?
- Do babies have concepts?
- Are concepts only mental phenomena?
- Can two concepts be identical?
- Are concepts communicable?
- How do concepts change?

Are These Things Alive?[10]

Seaweed? The sun? A leaf? A molecule? A worm? An atom? A hurricane? A tsunami? Lightning? Thoughts? Blood? Feelings? A cell? Memories?

The concepts of belief, concept, alive, friendship, time, truth, body, play, mind, measurement, infinity, number, and order can be distinguished from other concepts in that they are CCC (Splitter & Sharp, 1995). They are common because, for example, we all—even the most brutish thug or the most individualistic loner—have a concept of friendship. They are central because how we construct them is important to how we think about our lives, and they are contestable, first because there are as many versions of them as there are people and second because they are, or ought to be, under continuous revision as a result of ongoing experience.

A CPI practiced at any age can be defined as a form of deliberative communal dialogue dedicated to the ongoing reconstruction of the CCC concepts that constitute our systems of belief. The process of reconstruction begins when a concept is problematized, and problematization begins when we see the crack, that gap in the concept where the descriptive and the normative do not meet that produces questions. Typically, that happens when we encounter some stimulus, whether text, event, or intuitive realization, that makes us see or feel the crack. Usually, CCC concepts are already problematized in our own inner lives anyway through the contradictions that emerge through experience, and we are developmentally primed for these moments.

When we engage in a CPI, the concept undergoes deconstruction; as we search together to define it, to exemplify it, and to operationalize it—to know more clearly what we mean when we use it to describe something—we discover all sorts of ambiguity and contradictions in our use of the term and that, although we all use the same term, we understand it in different ways. This new awareness of its contestability heightens our watchfulness when we use the term and acts to further problematize it. It is as if we took it apart to examine it and found that we could not so easily put the pieces back together. In our search to universalize it, we have deconstructed it, which leads us ineluctably to the common project of reconstructing it.

The process of reconstruction involves conflict, but it is a conflict of ideas, and it is conflict in the service of building on each other's ideas rather than negating or polarizing them. The practice of what Kant referred to as "thinking for oneself and with others" (Kennedy, 1999, p. 41) resists sophistic rhetoric, which is intentionally designed to manipulate and even deceive and which is the discursive coin of the public realm. It requires a certain level of tolerance of suspense because the concept, in fact, is never completely reconstructed or, if it is, is only as a provisional construct or warranted conclusion that assumes the warrants are always open to revision. As such, it represents a qualitative shift in the epistemological outlook. This new relationship to certainty and this willingness to suspend judgment indefinitely are, in fact, key epistemological bases for critical thinking (Dewey, 1898).

The critical, multilogical thinker recognizes both the importance of the concept of justice, for example, in living the good life (and thus the importance of reflecting on it and reconstructing it) and the limitation of the concept. The monological thinker tends to totalize and reify concepts and attempts to locate them outside history, culture, and context. In doing so, he avoids or refuses the appearance of the crack in the concept; this is an evolutionary that is increasingly dangerous in a multilogical word, in which multiple perspectives confront one another in a global common space. The capacity for entertaining multiple perspectives and the skills and dispositions for collaborative, dialogical deliberation are the fundamental habits that make social democracy possible.

In a CPI, the concept comes apart, and the group begins rebuilding it, session by session. It might be thought of as a communal barn-raising, except that the building will be finished only in the long run, and in our actual experience, we are continually moving, replacing, and shortening or lengthening pieces and even tearing down what we have and redesigning it. Each time we get up and walk out of a session, we take a slightly revised notion of the concept and of how concepts work with us, which we tend to reflect about in terms of our own individual experience. As we explore one concept, we tend to stumble across other concepts that seem prior to the one we are reconstructing. We might find that in working on the concept of justice, we find that we have to define person, and this might lead us to remark on whether justice can be applied to animals. This might lead us to reflect on the similarities and differences between animals and humans, which might, if the question of whether animals think arises, prompt us to deliberate on what we mean by thinking, then on how language works, and so on. In other words, a CPI curriculum is inherently emergent and rhizomatic with interlinking and recursive multiple strands. The term *rhizomatic* is taken from Deleuze and Guattari (1987) and, in contrast to the hierarchical, linear, vertical, and rootlike mode of knowledge building, is a conception of knowledge that grows more like a network of rootstocks. A rhizomatic curriculum can be entered at any given point and branches toward building new meanings that link it to other related concepts. As such, it not only provides a model for the development of curriculum in other school content areas, such as history, art, and literature, but also offers a way of introducing the practice of CPI in those content areas.

Philosophical Inquiry across the Curriculum: The Case of Mathematics

The majority of CCC concepts are present not just in philosophy class but also in science, math, and all the way across the content areas. Some, such as measurement, equality, and fact, obviously appear in more than one school content area, and others emerge in the specific context of the discipline. In fact, it should be no surprise that an ensemble of certain concepts, such as those mentioned previously (fact, measurement, and equality), underlie the school curriculum. In this sense, philosophy—or at least philosophy understood as the ongoing reconstruction of concepts—is actually implicitly and potentially present in every class that we teach. All that is necessary for it to emerge as a discourse in a discipline is to identify the set of CCCs that inform the discipline and to develop sets of questions for inquiry, texts designed to trigger questions, or both. It is even possible to use the standard textbook as a framework. We could take, for example, a set of CCCs in science—organism, life, measurement, fact, experiment, nature, environment, matter, energy, cause, hypothesis, theory, and so on—assign them to those chapters of the textbook in which they figure most obviously, and take them as a guide to practicing a CPI once a week in science class. In this way, we add a philosophy of science component to the science curriculum itself. Once students become adept at spotting CCCs, which typically happens extremely quickly, they themselves can identify them in the textbook and thus approach the textbook critically as a narrative rather than an exposition of the truth.

The case of mathematics is complicated by the fact that the phrase *community of inquiry* has been in use in math education for over 20 years with various meanings, and although none of them are clearly philosophical, all have capitalized on the potential of collaborative thinking and communication in working with students on solving mathematical problems (e.g., see Boaler & Humphreys, 2005; Goos, 2004; Lampert, 1990; Schoenfeld, 1989). In math education, the term usually refers to a setting for mathematical practice in the classroom that engages the learning community in doing mathematics collaboratively. Most documented research, however, portrays a mathematical community of inquiry as collective work, with or without a facilitator, on well-defined mathematical problems, where students are in a position to ask practically oriented questions aimed at solving specific mathematical problems.

For example, in an elementary mathematics classroom, a mathematical task, such as "find a number that is the sum of 26 and 38," is typical, and some questions that students are likely to ask are "what is the right answer to this problem?" or "is 64 the correct answer?" The current reform movement in mathematics calls for an inquiry approach to math teaching and for the development of conceptual mathematical understanding coupled with more flexible procedural fluency in problem solving (NCTM, 2000). This requires a major change in instructional and learning approaches and a different attitude toward doing mathematics on the part of teachers and students. A narrow understanding of such a change is usually verbalized as a switch in emphasis from approaching a problem with the sole objective of obtaining a product or answer to approaching it for the sake of the problem-solving process itself. That is, the concern for the right answer should be replaced by a care to explore different possible ways of answering the question and, in many cases, to investigate different possible representations of the situation that might lead to different methods of solving the problem.

For example, a teacher in a reformed math classroom might pose different questions to the math task discussed previously, such as "What are some different ways of answering the question?" or "Emily, did this: $(20 +6) + (30 +8) = (20 +30) + (6 +8) = 50 + 14 = 64$. Is this method correct? Why or why not?" Alternatively, "Sam did this: $(26 + 4) + (38 - 4) = 30 + 34 = 30 + 30 + 4 = 64$. Is this correct? Why or why not? In what way is Emily's method different from Sam's method?" These are questions that call for the comparison, reflection, and evaluation of someone's argument or idea on the part of the students, but they also imply a situation in which students are participating in an inquiry led by the teacher, which is mainly based on the teacher's questions. However, such an approach does position the participants as insiders to the realm of mathematics, which is here understood as a system of principles and rules. With this model, students are expected to know those rules that are foundational to the system and to tackle problems as instances of those rules. As such, students engaged in this kind of mathematical practice could be said to be doing and talking mathematics.[11]

From an epistemological point of view, this sort of conceptual understanding and procedural fluency in mathematics is not enough to build up flexible knowledge in students unless this knowledge is connected with previous knowledge and with real mathematical experience, that is, with the experience of using and reflecting on the use of mathematics in the world. Beyond procedural fluency, philosophical inquiry allows and encourages a search for meaning in mathematical concepts that have not traditionally been offered for discussion in school mathematics. It also offers students the possibility of questioning mathematics as a system: its uses, its power and limitations, and its existential value. In other words, if we want students to develop flexible knowledge of and about mathematics, the process of construction has to be accompanied by the constant deconstruction of previously constructed concepts and by a process of reconstruction that integrates new information.

To introduce CPI, with its dialectical process of knowledge construction, into the mathematics classroom, is to introduce a dimension of inquiry that goes beyond inquiry *within* the mathematical system and that does not impose prefabricated questions but invites children to pose questions of their own about mathematics, both in its internal relations and in its relation to the world. In contrast to the first approach of doing and talking mathematics, this involves a discursive positioning that is outside the mathematical system and thus leads us to talk about mathematics. One major avenue for such inquiry is, as we argued previously, through the problematization of the CCC concepts in mathematics through critical, communal dialogue.

However, there is a distinction to be made between types of CCC concepts in mathematics that is not necessarily present in other disciplines. We may classify them as first- and second-order concepts. Concepts, such as number, infinity, and certainty, may be classified as fully contestable. Others, such as function, proportion, and algorithm, although they are certainly common and central, cannot comfortably be classified as contestable. Rather, they are descriptive terms for operations and tools that make up a sort of syntax of mathematics. Rather than be problematized, they can be instantiated in nonmathematical contexts; this leads to our ability to understand their use more clearly within the universe of math.

For first-order concepts, questions like those listed next lead to the process of deconstruction and reconstruction.

The Nature of Numbers

- Do numbers exist in nature?
- What is number?
- Is mathematics a language? If so, what are numbers?
- What can be written in numbers?
- Are numbers and letters different and, if so, how?

- Why, when you break a bowl into two equal halves, is it not a bowl anymore, but when you divide a number in half, it is still a number?
- What does the number zero mean?

In an ideal situation, a discussion plan, such as this one, is compiled from students' questions and then added to by the facilitator to deepen or refine it.

A second-order concept is not quite so easy to problematize. For example, although there is no generally accepted formal definition of *algorithm,* a common informal definition might be "a finite sequence of well-defined instructions for completing a task." In cases such as this, the problematization of the concept may be located in the spaces between different students' definitions, interpretations, and understandings. It may also arise from an examination of the differences between the use of the concept in our everyday life and the way in which it is used in mathematics. One may inquire, for example, whether algorithms are recognizable in psychological and sociological contexts; for example, do we think algorithmically in our everyday activities? Are there subconscious or unconscious algorithms that guide or underlie events, such as arguments or shopping expeditions? Is an unconscious algorithm an algorithm at all or something else? Is there a difference between algorithms in experimental science and algorithms in mathematics? Is a mathematical formula an algorithm? Does the use of any algorithms require mathematical reasoning, and if it does, what kind of reasoning does it require? These questions lead to what may be described as a kind of conceptual boundary work that acts not only to resolve any ambiguity, vagueness, and misunderstanding in our understanding of the concept and its use but also to bring to light the relation between this concept and other related concepts, such as automatization and thinking in general. Our expectation is that after exporting the concept into other contexts and examining it there, we profit by increased understanding when we import it back into the universe of mathematics.

Philosophical math inquiry with children often oscillates between two major overarching themes: (a) the issue of the presence and role of mathematics in the world, whether the focus on the world be physical, psychological, social, economic, epistemological, ontological, or something else, and (b) the nature of mathematics as a universe or a language and how we know and understand mathematics. Students usually start with questions that concern the first theme, which is a testimony to the implicit and inherited idea of the power and importance of mathematics. The following are examples of some questions related to the first theme that were brought up by students in a recent discussion: Could you measure without numbers? Would time be felt differently without numbers? Would we age if we did not know numbers? Would math be possible without numbers? Would the world be chaotic without numbers? Would there be time without numbers? Could we track anything without numbers? Some of the questions that follow exemplify the ones brought up by the students that were related to the second theme: Where do numbers come from? Are numbers alive? Were numbers invented or discovered? If numbers were invented, why? Do plants and animals understand numbers? If so, what is the difference between the human understanding of numbers and the animal understanding of numbers? Can the body count? Can we know numbers without symbols? Do things come with a specific number?

The goal of such questions about numbers is a marriage of mathematical and philosophical inquiry, in which they feed each other and empower students to build an active conceptual nexus, where a mathematical concept is not just an isolated idea or practice but has rich connections with personal experience, informal knowledge, and other disciplines. Philosophical inquiry integrated into math classes offers a larger inquiry space that is not artificially divided by subject walls and promises the development of a dispositional set that is likely to be carried with them when students leave school. Philosophical inquiry offers students the possibility of establishing different relationship with mathematics, whereby they no longer think of it as cold, unquestionable, remote, and inaccessible to all but the "gifted. They are empowered by virtue of questioning mathematics and are no longer willing to accept any answer presented as truth at its face value. As such, their inquiry into mathematics leads to one of the central virtues of CPI practice, which is the disposition, confidence, and growing capacity to think for themselves, even as they think with others.

Philosophical Dialogue across the Curriculum

Finally, we wish to sketch in broad strokes a curriculum that integrates communal philosophical inquiry into some or all of the traditional school content areas. At the very least, three models for organizing inquiry into the CCC concepts within the disciplines are possible—a single-discipline approach, an interdisciplinary approach, and a whole-curriculum approach. Each of these corresponds to a more general organizational model for curriculum planning, that is, within a single classroom, between classrooms, and across the whole school. Each can function more or less emergently; this means that the concepts are not preplanned but arise in the course of the inquiry, and more or less democratically, meaning that the concepts and the questions are generated by the students themselves with the teacher as a coparticipant.

The first model has already been discussed: a single-discipline approach will identify a group of concepts in, say, science, and through a process of shared questioning and their own deliberative dialogue, and teachers and students will develop a series of exercises, discussion plans, and activities. Those concepts may be keyed to the textbook currently in use, such that the concept of organism, for example, is explored through communal philosophical inquiry in the chapter in which it is produced and defined. This is, in fact, an invaluable strategy for demythologizing official texts and encouraging students and teachers to enter into dialogue with their epistemological assumptions rather than accept them as given. As an expository text, the textbook presents its assumptions as final and authoritative; that is, it denies that they are assumptions and states them as necessary axioms for learning. It assumes in a linear and hierarchical fashion that grasping the basics—in this case, a previously determined understanding of the concept—is necessary to construct further knowledge. To understand the concept as contestable introduces an element of deconstruction and reconstruction into the learning situation and promises the development of new meanings. When a window for the problematization of concepts through philosophical dialogue is opened, the textbook loses its status as a bearer of hegemonic, officially sanctioned knowledge and takes on a narrative status; that is, it is understood as a voice, a speaker, or an interlocutor, as conditioned by ideology, historical placement, and material conditions (like any text), with which one can enter into dialogue. Because it keeps the assumptions of the discipline in open view of students, who can stay aware of their historical and contextual character, this form of reading is fundamental to the development of critical literacy.

The second model extends the identification of concepts across disciplines and thus connects the elements of the curriculum as a whole through a network of contestable concepts. The concept of measurement, for example, can be problematized in multiple school subjects, whether science, mathematics, history, psychology, anthropology, economics, art, or music, and in fact allows the extension of student inquiry into the ruling and guiding assumptions of the process of schooling itself. This model would entail teachers and students keying the concept to the texts in the various disciplines and thus create an interweaving network of inquiry, which would encourage teachers to understand the school curriculum as a whole, to collaborate in the organization of their material, to identify readings and assign writings that connect disciplines, and even to share classroom time and space.

A third model would open the generation of CCC concepts to the whole school. The use of a central subject, either gradewide or schoolwide, is one precursor of this, but the generation of emergent philosophical themes that become the deliberative objects of the entire community, concepts, such as justice, change, technology, violence, and nature, goes beyond this in scope and participation. A concept, such as justice, can be woven through different content areas in the classroom, become the subject of whole- or part-school meetings and dialogue groups, and culminate in schoolwide action groups concerned with justice, for example, within the school community, within the larger community in which the school is set, or somewhere else on the planet. In this stage of collaborative inquiry, philosophy returns to its own disciplinary boundaries in the sense that it is no longer bound by one content area or another, but it also responds to actual, immediate instances where the concept is in play and results in real democratic action.

In fact, it is not just in collaborative deliberation that any philosophical concept undergoes reconstruction but also in lived experience and the politics of relation, and the school is the embryonic community in which habits not just of deliberation but of neighborhood, community, and planetary activism are forged. In this schoolwide model, philosophy, after it disperses itself among the disciplines, returns to the *agora,* the public space, which is its rightful place in an authentic democratic community, and deliberative communal dialogue functions as the emergent compass, the tutor, and the normative horizon of that adult collective called *school.*

References

Boaler, J., & Humphreys, C. (2005). *Connecting mathematical ideas.* Portsmouth, NH: Heinemann.

Cohen, L. (1992). Anthem. In *The Future* [Audio recording]. New York: Columbia Records.

Deleuze, G., & Guattari, F. (1987). *A thousands plateaus.* Minneapolis: University of Minnesota Press.

Dewey, J. (1898). *How we think.* Boston: Houghton Mifflin.

Gardner, H. (2006). *Multiple intelligences. New horizons* (rev. ed.). New York: Basic Books.

Goos, M. (2004). Learning mathematics in a classroom community of inquiry. *Journal for Research in Mathematics Education, 35,* 258–291.

Hadot, P. (1995). *Philosophy as a way of life: Spiritual exercises from Socrates to Foucault* (Chase, M., Trans., & Davidson, A. I., Ed.). Malden, MA: Blackwell.

Kennedy, D. (1999). Thinking for oneself and with others. *Analytic Teaching: The Community of Inquiry Journal, 20,* 40–45.

Kennedy, N. S. (2007). From philosophical to mathematical inquiry in the classroom. *Childhood and Philosophy, 3*(6). Retrieved from http://www.filoeduc.org/childphilo/n6/Nadia_Kennedy.htm

Lampert, M. (1990). When the problem is not the question and the solution is not the answer: Mathematical knowing and teaching. *American Educational Research Journal, 27,* 29–63.

Lipman, M. (2003). *Thinking in education* (2nd ed.). Cambridge, England: Cambridge University Press.

Lipman, M., & Sharp, A. (1984). *Looking for meaning: An instructional manual to accompany Pixie.* Lanham, MD: University Press of America.

Lipman, M., Sharp, A., & Oscanyon, F. (1984). *Philosophical inquiry: An instructional manual to accompany Harry Stottlemeier's discovery* (2nd ed.). Lanham, MD: University Press of America.

Lushyn, P. (2002). Paradoxical nature of facilitation in community of inquiry. *Analytic Teaching: The Community of Inquiry Journal, 24,* 110–115.

Lushyn, P., & Kennedy, D. (2000). The psychodynamics of community of inquiry and educational reform: A cross-cultural perspective. *Thinking: The Journal of Philosophy for Children, 15.*

Lushyn, P., & Kennedy, D. (2003). Power, manipulation, and control in a community of inquiry. *Analytic Teaching: The Community of Inquiry Journal, 23,* 103–110.

NCTM. (2000). *Principles and standards for school mathematics.* Reston, VA: National Council of Teachers of Mathematics.

Raposa, M. (1989). *Peirce's philosophy of religion.* Bloomington: Indiana University Press.

Schoenfeld, A. H. (1989). What's all the fuss about metacognition? In A. H. Schoenfeld (Ed.), *Cognitive science and mathematics education* (pp.189–215). Hillsdale, NJ: Erlbaum.

Splitter, L., & Sharp, A. (1995). *Teaching for better thinking: The classroom community of inquiry.* Melbourne: ACER.

Vygotsky, L. (1978). *Mind in society: The development of higher psychological processes.* Cambridge, MA: Harvard University Press.

Notes

1. See "IAPC Timeline" at http://www.montclair.edu/cehs/academics/centers-and-institutes/iapc/timeline/ (accessed October 22, 2008).
2. *Thinking: The Journal of Philosophy for Children* (Montclair, NJ: Institute for the Advancement of Philosophy for Children, 1979 to present); *Analytic Teaching: The Community of Inquiry Journal* (LaCrosse, WI: Viterbo University, 1981 to present, online at http://www.viterbo.edu/analytic); *Critical and Creative Thinking: The Australasian Journal of Philosophy for Children,* renamed *Critical and Creative Thinking: The Australasian Journal of Philosophy in Education* (Federation of Australasian Philosophy in Schools Associations, 1993 to present); and *Childhood & Philosophy: A Journal of the International Council of Philosophical Inquiry with Children* (2005 to present, online at http://www.filoeduc.org/childphilo).
3. In this regard, Gardner (2006) lamented that "especially in the United States, with its focus on quantitative markers and its cult of educational efficiency…the most important subject matters are those that lend themselves readily to such assessment, like mathematics and science. In other content areas, value is assigned to the aspects that can be efficiently assessed (grammar rather than voice in writing; facts rather than interpretation in history). Those disciplines that prove most refractory to formal testing, such as the arts, are least valued in the uniform school" (pp. 170–171).
4. Hadot (1995) summarized these components as "a complete transformation of his representations of the world, his inner climate, and his outer behavior" (pp. 85–86). "What is needed is the immediate transformation of our way of thinking, of acting, and of accepting events. We must think in accordance with truth, act in accordance with justice, and lovingly accept what comes to pass" (p. 229).
5. As Hadot (1995) explained, "In the view of all philosophical schools, mankind's principal cause of suffering, disorder, and unconsciousness were the passions: that is, unregulated desires and exaggerated fears. People are prevented from truly living, it was taught, because they are dominated by worries. Philosophy thus appears, in the first place, as a therapeutic of the passions" (p. 83).
6. Thus, Hadot (1995) asserted that "on this level, we are no longer concerned with theoretical logic—that is, the theory of correct reasoning—rather, we are concerned not to let ourselves be deceived in our everyday lives by false representations" (p. 192).
7. The following system characteristics were drawn from Lushyn (2002) and Lushyn and Kennedy, (2000, 2003).
8. Leonard Cohen (1992) in the song "Anthem" sang, "There's a crack in everything," to which he added, "That's where the light gets in."
9. Adapted from Lipman and Sharp (1984) with the addition of questions posed by seventh-grade students at the Montclair Cooperative School.
10. Adapted from Lipman, Sharp, and Oscanyon (1984) with additions and deletions by the authors.

11. See Kennedy (2007), in which I distinguished three ways of practicing mathematical inquiry in the classroom: doing and talking mathematics, talking about mathematics, and talking about doing mathematics.

CHAPTER THREE

FROM ARTS VENUES TO PERCIPIENCE TO POETIC THINKING TO POETRY WRITING IN THE COMMUNITY OF INQUIRY

CHRISTOPHER PARKER
MONTCLAIR STATE UNIVERSITY

Theory suggests that the mind is a muted instrument without symbolic notation. One might think that a symbolic language tool, such as poetry, would, therefore, be used to help cultivate the thoughts of children in schools. However, several say that this may not be the case at all. In this chapter, I explore the possibility of using the visual arts and then poetry as an entrance to philosophical inquiry within a community of inquiry (CI) with school children. To reach the poetical, I explore the use of regional art venues as cultural, archival resources for fostering percipience. This is done to enter into the aesthetic and immutable via poetic thinking to cultivate this thinking into language and the other somatic effects of poetry. This poetry may then be used to foster inquiry within a CI. I do not cover the curriculum of using a CI approach but focus rather on the philosophy and theory of percipience, poetic thinking, and the poetry writing path.

Several theories of the powerful interplay of thought and language may suggest that the mind is a muted instrument without the feature of symbolic notation (Britton, 1970; Moffet, 1968; Tremmel, 1992; Vygotsky, 1962). One might think, in turn, that a symbolic language tool, such as poetry, would be employed to help cultivate the thoughts of children in schools. However, several suggest that this may not be the case at all. In fact, within the active curriculum of teaching thinking and writing, lessons that include the writing of poetry are very hard to find. Chomsky (2006), citing Schlegel, called the function of creative imagination in any aesthetic effort "poetical" (p. 90). Still, poetic thinking, thinking regarding any aesthetic experience or creation, is scarcer (Greene, 2001; Halliburton, 1981; McCarthy, 2004; Robinson, 2001; Tremmel, 1992).

Artistic thinking and its expression are at a distance from most mainstream school curricula; similarly, poetic thinking and writing are on the outskirts of any center of focus (Greene, 1978, 1988, 2001; McCarthy, 2004; Robinson, 2001; Tremmel, 1992). Primarily, it seems that poetic thinking and writing have hardly a foot in the door past early grammar school (Tremmel, 1992). This was confirmed for me by my own experience working in the arts in New Jersey schools for the past 25 years, through discussions with my colleagues (R. Carnevale, personal communication, 2005; Doty, personal communication, 2006; Niccolletti, personal communication, 2008), and through many state documents on the subject (Pinzolo, 2008; Schmid, 2008).

This may be because the perceived knowledge acquisitions that appear to be related to poetry are associated with learning that rests far away from the central focus of most language arts curricula (Tremmel, 1992). Moreover, this may be because the main foci of language arts are concept, critical thinking, solutions, and analysis. One wry wrench in the paradigm is that language arts has been removed far enough from its aesthetic origins to be officially stripped of its arts badge (Greene, 1978, 1988; McCarthy, 2004; Robinson, 2001; Tremmel, 1992). It turns out that those concerned with middle and secondary school students' poetic thinking and writing are simply scarce poets who come to teach and not researchers, testers, or perhaps even teachers (McCarthy, 2004; Robinson, 2001; Tremmel, 1992).

In education, art remains the subordinate curriculum. However, much literature highlights how poetic thinking may be an undivided participant of all thinking (Alexander, 1992; Applebee, 1978; Bosch, 1998; Bruner, 1996; Burns, 1989; Dewey, 1980, 1997; Donaldson, 1978; Fleckenstein, 1999, 2003; Gardner, 1988; Greene, 1988; Heidegger, 1971; Jacob, 1922; Jakobson, 1985c; Kant, 1952; Lakoff, 1987; Langer, 1953; Lipman, 1980; Makkreel & Rodi, 1985; Martin, 1975; Robinson, 2001; Stewart, 1995; Szondi, 1986; Tremmel, 1992).

This paradigmatic resting point of poetry as subordinate may have something to do with the fact that in Piaget's broad theory of pedagogy, there is basically no account of poetic thinking and writing (Tremmel, 1992). Even citing others himself, Vygotsky (1962) suggested that poetry is simply inseparable from music, whereas the predominant elements of prose are thought and language. Still, Osborn (1971) said, "if education can aid in the cultivation of aesthetic percipience, the major part of its task has been achieved" (p. 28).

Another challenge is that poetic thinking may be difficult to evaluate objectively, and this may be a reason that it is only on the periphery of school curricula. It is difficult to assess because it is composed mostly of personal involvement, which is, therefore, not standardized (Bonnett, 1991).

In Western European cultures, some suggest that analytic thinking and writing are privileged as they seek a scientific truth or technical facts. This seems to be a rife habit of mind in the West (Arendt, 1978; Polanyi, 1962; Tremmel, 1992). However, the division between poetic writing and thinking and academic writing and analytic thinking may not be a division at all because poetic thinking is a feat of language and has a part in analysis (Tremmel, 1992). What is more, through poetry, we may help develop "an ineffable flush of energetic excitation...spur[ing children]...to think beyond habitual limits" (Shusterman, 1997).

Still, in a more open educational ecosphere, this might suggest a useful difference between dialogue and monologue; poetry insists on a dialogue, sonically and somatically, and prose may serve as a monologue medium with its emission of ideas and ordinary conversational parole. However, an overriding theoretical dependency on Piaget is not Piaget's problem but rather the limitation of the thinking habits of those in educational leadership (Tremmel, 1992).

In this chapter, I explore the possibility of using the visual arts and then poetry as an entrance into philosophical inquiry within a community of inquiry (CI) with school children. However, to reach the poetical, I first traverse the use of regional art venues as cultural, archival resources to foster percipience. This is done to enter into the aesthetic and immutable via poetic thinking to cultivate this thinking into the language and other somatic effects of poetry. This poetry may then be used to foster inquiry within a CI. However, I do not discuss here a curriculum using this approach in a CI, but rather, I focus on the philosophy and theory of the percipience, poetic thinking, and poetry writing path.

The CI has been explained in much of the Philosophy for Children (P4C) literature (Lipman, 2003; Lipman, Sharp, & Oscanyan, 1980). However, for the purposes of this chapter, let it suffice to say that a CI has a structure and rules that prevent it from haphazardness. A CI also usually follows a democratic approach to inquiry (Lipman et al., 1980). In essence, a CI attempts to fulfill the need to know reality in the best way. Whereas the individual is unable to reach reality sufficiently, a CI follows inquiry in a communal manner. In this way, Raposa citing Peirce suggests the individual with the group may determine what he or she believes, at the time, to be a reasonable case of truth (Raposa, 1989).

What Can the Arts Actually Do for Children's Education?

Although conflicting theories may be a restriction of the arts in education, recent research suggests that early involvement in arts activities may actually enhance cognitive skills. For instance, performance within groups may help children to develop higher levels of motivation and improve performance elsewhere (Gazzaniga, 2008). This suggests that a CI might serve as an opportunity for this development. Furthermore, experience developing music through composition may help students further manipulate information (Jonides, 2008). I discuss later the fact that poetry does contain its element of music and may be another way for children to grow in the area of language manipulation. Other recent research indicates that correlations may exist between the rhythm, meter, and rhyme of poetry and music and early literacy and phonology (Dunbar, 2008). Also, some research suggests that the manipulation of semantics may also improve memory (Posner, Rothbart, Sheese, & Kieras, 2008).

However, perhaps more importantly, Gazzaniga (2008) suggested that research on how the arts improve cognition may be life affirming, in that we may learn how to learn, think about thinking (e.g., Lipman, 1980, 2003), and improve the fecundity of our lives. In particular, the art of writing poetry may be not just a mode of life but also a pivotal device for developing the self; in other words, poetry is life affirming as part of the art of living (Shusterman, 1997).

To take action that might merit much positive attention toward the arts and cognition and its mixing of presentation and the discursive, Gardner (1988) suggested that philosophy and education should act in concert with students, teachers, poets, and other artists. The concept of art, others have affirmed, should be an important part of education in collaboration with math, science, geography, and history. That is, if it properly occupies a space in the curriculum, art may help us view the world from a different perspective and may serve as a bridge to other disciplines (Hanks, 1971).

Why is It Important?

Because we aspire to satisfy the significance of our existence, the aesthetics of our being may be a metaphysical imperative (Alexander, 1992). Theoretically, aesthetics consists of the assemblage of abridgements of earnest suggestions that are to be heeded in various ways for the many features of a piece of art (Weitz, 1956). In fact, Dewey's (1997) metaphysics, according to Alexander, is an array of caring ontology and thinking creatively about a world in a quest for its own end of the story, the closure of the aesthetic, and the completion of its action. This metaphysics requires us to see the light through nature and a creative democracy (Alexander, 1992). With the aesthetic experience as an opening to philosophical dialogue, one might ask, as Shusterman (1997) posed, "Is improved experience, not ordinary truth…the ultimate philosophical goal and criterion?" (p. 157).

Through the creative center residing in an individual, reality and self may coalesce into a creative product (Bosch, 1998; Pascal, 1929). Furthermore, action taken to generate other creative products may occur when the creative is plaited with the actual (Alexander, 1992). However, the degree of our successful creative manufacturing requires some measurement of perceiving and judging our product.

Our scale of perception, however, tips back and forth between the linguistic exigencies of memory and creativity itself (Bosch, 1998).

The creative product for the purposes of this chapter may be a poem produced by what I will call the *child poet/philosopher,* that is, a child within a CI group who has generated poetry and then uses it within a CI dialogue to open more philosophical inquiry.

What Is the Poem?

Art is presented via a particular medium, which could be film, web sites, dance, sculpture, painting, or poetry. Poetry then is a medium. The basis of the poetry medium is language with language or, as Chomsky (2006) called it, "an expression of the human mind" (p. 90). This means that poetry is not a product of nature. As a result, poetry may have an otherwise unlimited framework with which to play. In fact, poetry may be constructed recursively; this means that each poem may lead to another entirely new poem (Chomsky, 2006). For the poetic creative act and for others, there is a need for the cognitive tools of intention and imagination. However, the intentional will of the utterance of the poem does not take precedence over the poet's imagination, as it is a tool bearing a more adaptable impetus (O'Brien, 1993). However, where does this imagination originate? O'Brien seemed to suggest that Aristotle (2000) in *De anmima III.3* found imagination to be a pure output of sensory perception.

Assemblage of Parts

A poem as creative product may be an assemblage of imaginative intellectual possibilities. It might contain highlighted facts or data, such as colors, names, movement verbs, or historical information. However, these data are only broken pieces until they are assembled and collaged into a complete whole, a poem (ew 3.8–10).

Ingredients are assembled into a sort of soup of language. Then, the oral roux of poetry, with a recipe of phonology and grammar, sets forth a broth of flavorful, elaborate correspondences. These recipes of language, however, like cultural cuisine, may appear bequeathed through generations without a conscious realization of the rules of the ethnic chef who controls this soup (Fleckenstein, 2003). Even without a recipe, theorists may be inching closer to knowing how the human mind uses language creatively (Chomsky, 2006), such as poetry. One question remains: What does someone know about language that in turn, allows that person to work with language and create a poem? There may be no reason to believe that a recipe of the rules of such language may be brought to consciousness. Introspectively, it may be possible for an experienced poet to build a limited collection of results through experimentation and study. This may lead, at least aesthetically, to an understanding of some elements of the assimilation of sound and meaning. Still, this would be only superfluous knowledge. There seems to be no theory yet to even suggest that the poet may unearth the subconscious terrain of principals and rules that formulate the sonic evocation of meaning (Chomsky, 2006).

The Venue to Perceive

At this juncture, let us turn to the percipience of a work of art that may be in a venue, such as an art museum. In this case, we will look at one of the Monet's Water Lilies series paintings (Monet, 1997). As we imaginatively behold water lilies, we may let our minds wander while observing water lilies in a pond in a new way. We may enter into what Kant (1952) called the "aesthetic experience." We may let our minds travel through a broad range of secondary meanings of water lilies in a pond (Blocker, 2005).

For instance, we may think of how quiet the lilies are in the pond seem, especially in a museum and perhaps in actuality; how even though it is often complete with slime, algae, and insects, the pond water seems glasslike and clean at a glance; and how the pond water, though a staple of life formation, takes second fiddle to the life that floats on top of it. We may also think how we do not see a horizon or even a shore line, perhaps like a focused child exploring the lilies. Finally, we may see how this painting, even without a shore line, is complete and whole (Blocker, 2005; Marceau, 1997).

Moreover, in the absence of an existing definition, we may be able to float through many possible meanings associated with the pond lilies in a "reflective judgment of taste" (Blocker, 2005, p. 32). What is more, the idea or poem that follows might express an aesthetic idea in which the mind uses creative imagination to activate reasoning (Blocker, 2005; Marceau, 1997). This is because coming to greet us as old friends—even though our experience with them may not be long—certain works of art, such as Monet's Water Lilies series, seem to supplicate our attention (Osborne, 1971). Subsequently, the perception of a work as an integrated entity is what gives it aesthetic value (Maquet, 1990). Still, developing an appreciation of art is a type of skill. Calling it a skill means that it is not just a choice through a personal penchant or an esteem for the imagery and form (Osborne, 1971).

In fact, Aristotle (2009) suggested that images are just the precursor, the required standing point for deliberate thought. However, more recently, Fleckenstein (2003) suggested that even some contemporary neuroscientists see imagery as our memoir of identity or as adhering to the human soul (p. 12). Furthermore, without imagery, we do not have the ability to generate textual meaning at all (Fleckenstein, 2003). This is because there would be no meaning in a text when there is no imagery present.

Moreover, presumably included in the progression of perception is the abstract (Bosch, 1998). This implies that perception of a painting requires more than a listing of the color and forms observed if the art is to be identified as an "act of knowledge" (Bosch, 1998). In the end, language and sensation compose perception (Bosch, 1998). However, if such language is not accessible to the perceiver, the perceived possession simply evanesces (Bosch, 1998). To maintain the percipience so that we do not, as Shakespeare suggested, "lose possession of that fair thou ow'st," the child poet/philosopher may need to coagulate the language and write a poem "So [that] long as men can breath, or eyes can see/So long lives this, and this gives life to thee" (Shakespeare, 2008). *Thee* here is the perceived possession. Percipience is the art and power to perceive keenly, to cite the immutable, and to receive the imagery ready for metaphor.

Moreover, when we first see a work of art, we may experience a quiescence of the moment. This inarticulate juncture must be acknowledged. Only then can we go to work querying for something directly, which may, in turn, liberate us from quietude, unshackling our "language machine," as Chomsky (2006) might have called it. This allows the child poet/philosopher to cipher a sentence; this then dockets an artifact of art as "eternal lines" (Shakespeare, 2008).

Still, our perception receptors themselves are remarkably ephemeral. So, as mentioned, perception is a dissipating feat requiring a foundational *raison d'être* more like tent pegs than cinderblocks. In other words, to support our percept, we may seem to mortar in some language acquired from the common wonted optical acquisitions of our art experience. However, in actuality, we raise only a temporary tent that sways in the ephemeral zephyr and is supported by a poetic patois that articulates the astonishment and effect elicited by our percept.

Perception then is acquired through a procured language but then avidly looks for its own new language (Bosch, 1998). Rorty, cited by Shusterman, further suggested that we do not warrant the language to which we are already accustomed but rather modify our language use with something new (Shusterman, 1997), so the process of perception includes the development of a new poetic perceptory patois of sorts.

Langer (1942, 1953), also attempting to identify distinctions that seem to limit curricula, pointed out the believed difference between two types of symbols, which she called *discursive* and *representational.* These are often considered to be two different plateaus. However, to cross the great notch between them, Applebee (1978) suggested that rather than simply ensuring the Piagetian model of more objective and analytic thinking, it might be important to take the subjective poetic route as well. This might help one to evoke a full-fledged view instead of an only fractional view point when only one method is pursued (Applebee, 1978). In other words, to reach wholeness, the skills of Piaget's mature thinker should blend with the aesthetics of poetry and its thinking (Applebee, 1978; Tremmel, 1992; Vygotsky, 1962). Shusterman (1997) also seemed to ask if it was necessary that the practical be in contradistinction with the aesthetic.

Fleckenstein (2003) went on to speak of a similar logic dualism, the formation of an amalgam. The "corporeal logic of the image and the discursive logic of word [are in] circular play" (p. 12); she called this *imageword.* Imageword, according to Fleckenstein, also includes the "ecological system of meaning produced by that circular dynamic" (p. 12). Still, logic may not be able to actually intone a parlance to explain grace, cadence, form, astonishment, or ardor. These are, however, indispensable elements of poetry (Lipman, 1980) and perhaps even rise above the limits of logic. Plus, without posing as the antitheses of logic, poetry may evince a sense of truth and connote meaning in a privileged manner (Hamrick, 1989).

Logic, others suggest, can hope to come to a true understanding only if it is dissolved into the poem itself. This means that the poem subsumes a logic of existence as the very product of its creative process (Adorno,

1961). This dual motif travels through the poem from beginning to end. The motif is further enmeshed within the two hemispheres of myth and nature. All of the poem's declarations about poetry and its poets then emit from the poem with the "logic peculiar to metaphor" (Szondi, 1986).

Also, a dialogue roused by the poem may further unpack this logic. The phonetic structure of a poem then may serve as a step into an inquiry dialectic, which may be richer in its discussion depth and thus allow for further thought topics (Jakobson, 1978).

This ecosystem's circular dynamic leads to the development of the child poet/philosopher into a type connoisseur for whom a true sense of appreciation is acquired in the process of perception, which Osborn (1971) called *connoisseurship*. Perceiving and discerning the merits inhabiting a piece of art is one part of this connoisseurship. However, proffering our discernment of the text of others (Osborne, 1971) and its amalgamation into our own "eternal line to time" is part of connoisseurship as well. Still, as discussed, the experience seeks its own new language. However, this new poetic dialect, the opening sentence perhaps of dialogue instigation, forms from its many parts as a kind of skittish Yiddish. That is why we need the cognitive indigenous chef of form to blend the roux and for the sound of language to cure the two epoxy chemicals, presentation and discourse.

However, I first examine the notion of the seduction of perception through works of art. The seduction begins because we expect faithfulness from art at a gallery or museum venue (Bosch, 1998). One reason for this faithfulness may be that the venue is a sacred place, a strong link between nature and its cultural art manifestation (Dewey, 1980; UNESCO, 2005). Faithfulness may then lead to analysis. Then, the nascent exclamations evoked and processed with effort allow the poet to preserve a sensation that, according to Bosch, may lure one to some subsequent inquiry (p. 33). Perceiving that a work has aesthetic qualities may be then an act of seduction (Bosch, 1998). That may be because perceiving art is a two-step process of reflexion and reflection: reflexion because what we look at, listen to, or touch comes from within us and returns to its origin and reflection because pondering then turns perception into a contemplative seduction (Bosch, 1998). The somatic experience is a powerful participant here.

In this chapter, I have discussed the need to solidify the evanescence of perception. Bosch (1998) went on to suggest that in holding onto that aesthetic, seductive embrace, we may, in turn, scuffle to mumble a phrase or other expressive sonic utterances, which may give latency to it leaving. In other words, if we quickly articulate something about the seduction, it may linger (Bosch, 1998). However, this may be the first step for the child poet/philosopher in developing further questions regarding the experience.

Staying Online

The perception is fleeting, so to capture the vanishing wraith that we see just briefly, we need our own linguistic canvas of paper. In this way, like an artist's rendering of the evanescent bigfoot or UFO of perception, we can typographically sketch a concept into words until our poems, like social lapidaries, hew our thoughts into inquiry (Bosch, 1998). However, as Bosch said, if we do not foster a figure for the ghost of notion, it will jell into the platitudinous phrases that require much less effort than the maintenance that our pegged tent of the ephemeral requires. A work of art may then be seen as a Campbell's soup can, a customary image stuffed into the pile in the crowded garage of everyday modern life (Warhol, 1962). However, even the poetry of platitude may begin a dialogue or an inquiry.

Together

Epoxy glue is made of two different chemical compounds. They come in separate containers when purchased. The user then mixes equal portions of the two together in some kind of container. This allows for a rapid curing process, which makes the epoxy a very strong solidifier and adhesive. The somatic impact of art and the distanced words that do not quite cure our perceptions may need to be blended into a new compound to fill the empty spaces before curing. Our garden variety vocabulary, then, needs another element. the poetry of metaphor and music, which in turn, blends more with the visual and imitated somatic, which may include sonic evocations.

The bodily attraction to a subject, or somatic seduction, then turns from pleasure to emotion to language and from sensual emotional language to poetry; this may sustain such a somatic seduction in song (Bosch, 1998). The written poem then endures for the somatic, emotional, seductive moment of perception. As such, time "grow'st" and so does the perceiver/poet grow personally (Bosch, 1998; Shakespeare, 2008); this opens the fan to waft a wider wind of dialogical forensics with others' points of view, histories, and perspective of the world.

The Poets

Still, another challenge is that we may perceptually miscue pictures or images as common icons. By doing so, we may board an everyday rail by dropping common linguistic tokens into the turnstile of ideas (Bosch, 1998). As a result, we may travel nowhere new fast. This may be one reason why Jacob (1922), citing Ruskin, classified poets into four orders.

First, there are poets without feeling. These poets may truly see. Secondly, seeing untruly are poets who have strong feelings but whose thinking is not of the same magnitude. Third are poets who are strong human beings. However, this third group nonetheless yield to even stronger influences. Finally and rarest is the poet that sees the unimaginable and inconceivable. Are they prophetically inspired? (Jacob, 1922) or are the language and the poem speaking for them?

However, the indistinct lingual blink is only that, and without an explanation, our perception of an object—which may be a picture, a movement, a sound, or a sense of touch—is woefully incomplete (Bosch, 1998). However, an explanation may be difficult to achieve. This may be because, as Shusterman (1997) suggested, the perception of a thing is in part a noncognitive experience. In other words, the percipience of it may be "simply had but not known" (p. 161). In fact, the qualities of the thing, an objectification, are reached, and that is done in part with language (Shusterman, 1997).

Still, in perceiving the art, the child poet/philosopher may begin to only ramble through the garden variety common works. This is our first response in maintaining the seduction of our senses (Bosch, 1998).

The Art of Perception

However, there remains a vacuity between the perceived somatic and the art. In linguistic terms, perceptions essay a talk that in turn, possesses a language of its own and which continues to be cultivated (Bosch, 1998). After the child poet/philosopher scrambles for the first sentence, Bosch suggested that the second sentence is not as arduous to draft. She added that if we strive on, "our words will sustain our glance" (p. 43) at the work of art, just as even the first glance stirs us to cocoon the occasion in woven words.

Degas once asked Mallarme why he could not write the poems when he has so many ideas. Mallerme replies that poems are not made of ideas but of words (Valery, 1936).

Archiving Seduction

In chapter 14 of *Harry Stottlemeier's Discovery,* Suki and Anne visit an art venue, The Frick Collection in New York City. Suki is recognized for her poetry in this and other P4C novels. Still, at the Frick, Suki moans that until it was explained to her by Anne, she saw paintings only as pretty things, much like jewelry (Lipman, 1985).

On the other hand, Degas once complained that even though as a painter he had ideas, he was still unable to address them in poetry (Jakobson, 1985d). This may be because, in essence, poetry is the poetic metamorphosis of normal oral discernment and the junction of sonic structure and meaning within language (Jakobson, 1985d). However, to get past our own disjunction, like Degas' own conflict between pictures and poetry, we must endure a period of image saturation before the need for language reemerges (Brook, 1972). After that, Bosch (1998) suggested that we "look aloud" as a way of mastering perceiving in the first place. Still, in an attempt to list certain artistic elements that appear to influence our appreciation of a piece, we may find that such a listing is insufficient to articulate our aesthetic appreciation. On the other hand, the list might be of use in exploring in a CI why comparable elements in other art do not affect us in the same way (Osborne, 1971).

It is through poetry that what Osborn (1971) calls the *connoisseur* may be able to describe these art qualities. In addition, Osborn's connoisseur makes extricable discernments and set impressions of reality as does this in art and in the subsequent poetry. The connoisseur also cautiously repudiates the untrue and the absent (Osborne, 1971). Through the poem of the connoisseur then, an artifact for meaning may be fixed, sustained, and transmitted (Bosch, 1998). The experience becomes a literary artifact and perhaps adds a better understanding for both the one who does the explaining and the ones receiving the explanation (Bosch, 1998), that is, the child poet/philosopher and other CI participants.

The Archive

An aspiration or direction to write a poem—having something to say— asks us to go into our busy archival garage and extract the germane facts, words, and records from other somatic dossiers (Bosch, 1998). However, we may also be asked to enter the archives of art, cultural history, and sacred places around us (UNESCO, 2005).

Szondi (1986), speaking of Schlegel, pointed out that the works of the ancients may have become only fragments but that the work of contemporaries has developed because of this fossilization. With fragments, it may be possible to look into the future because it is the shards of an object that can seed new ideas providing the first satisfaction of a thirst for aesthetic synthesis (Szondi, 1986).

A context of interrelatedness between an apotheosis and the actual is the necessary substratum to make a shard of information useful. In the case of this discussion, the shard may be a curator's card on the wall near a particular painting. This shard or fragment might serve as a window for the child poet/philosopher to take a better look at the historically abstruse. In fact, the fragment might be a tonic for a new historical ardor (Szondi, 1986) that might lead to a new element of poetic thinking. However, the broader archive may be the hermeneutics of the lending library of any interaction with a text and language, which includes the dialogue of the CI. This unmasks our CI conveyance in the lingual lake, the somatic umiak of poetry.

Forms

As discussed, forms in poetry, music, and art that depict feelings are then called *presentational.* On the other hand, academic writing and the analytic thought involved may be called *discursive* (Langer, 1953; Lipman, 1956). However, these are just the forms. Then, there are the experiences. Some experiences may utterly baffle discursive form. Even so, a type of nondiscursive experience may actually escort every one of our discursive thoughts (Shusterman, 1997). These experiences may include the otherwise ineffable moments of emotion and aesthetic percipience. Condillac, cited by Coski (2006), suggested that the feelings of a person are required participants in that person's act of reason. Feelings or emotions may be part of the immutable that is captured in poetic thinking. As a result, poetic thinking and the poetry in language may not at all be subordinate to the discursive as others have suggested (Coski, 2006).

Shusterman (1997), speaking of Dewey, suggested that even an ineffable experience, as inscrutable as it is, may be discernible introspectively. Furthermore, the ineffable inferred is nonetheless a necessary component of all our thinking (Shusterman, 1997). To help reach a symbol that projects the ineffable, Langer (1942) suggested the presentational form. These presentational forms might include elements of typographic, sonic, sensory, and ideation manifestation (Turco, 1986). The sound, meter, and cadence of poetry are technically things you feel, and the typography is something you see, as is the poet reciting a poem.

In this chapter, I focus on how the poem may introduce the reader or listener to a sensory level (Turco, 1986). To evoke this somatic of the sensory level, a poet uses any number of trope types, which are otherwise known as *figures of speech*. Certain types of tropes, constructed linguistically, play to your ear or display images or movements to your eye. Also, movement may be presented toward other inner senses, such as vertigo and the tactile stimulus of touch or temperature. In other words, tropes appeal to the listeners' or readers' inner senses by way of mind pictures and often through description or imitation. The sensory level then also seems a reasonable step from visual art and its evocations, suggestions, and imitations of poetry.

Metaphor is also one of the tropes in Turco's (1986) sensory level and is often prevalent in children's poetry (Koch, 1970, 1973). Szondi (1986) suggested that metaphor is a twofold sphere of nature and myth. However, in the end, there is logic within metaphor, which is exclusive to the metaphor. This logic is part of the existence of a good poem, which results from a productive poetic process (Szondi, 1986).

As mentioned, sometimes in percipient seduction and the thinking that we do to archive it, we encounter abstract concepts (Bosch, 1998). These are difficult to embrace with a form or structure even if it is evoked by a preconceptual structure of the initial percipience. As a result, in a situation in which there seems to be no appreciable preconceptual structure or its subsequent form, we purport such through metaphor (Lakoff, 1987). In other words, metaphor may be one tool for grasping experiences within a domain developed from any somatic equivalents (Lakoff, 1987) or the preconceptual structures they may colonize (Kennedy, 2006).

This may support Langer's (1942) suggestion that presentational forms, such as metaphor, are, in fact, the earlier foundation of the discursive. Poetry is cradled deep within language. However, the important symbol form of poetry is not discursive but rather presentational. Poetry, a presentational form, is the ancient cinderblock foundation of the discursive structure (Langer, 1953). Generating presentational symbolism, although it is markedly different from other discursive cognition, is integral to the discursive and vice versa (Langer, 1942; Tremmel, 1992). One thing to add is that the poem, like the indistinct lingual blink describing to our seducer, the seduction itself, "should describe itself in every one of its descriptions. In other words the work is everywhere and simultaneously poetry and the poetry of poetry" (Szondi, 1986, p. 62). This might, by no choice of the poet, include most or all of Turco's (1986) previously mentioned form components.

Whereas the discursive is analytic, the linear, abstract, and representational are metaphoric, perceptory, and concrete; it may be clear that poetry and poetic thinking completely take part in the reasoning of people. This has occurred through the annals of language history and in the development of the same within children. The representational and the discursive both aid in the operation of a child's experience in thought and language (Tremmel, 1992). That may mean that poetic thinking and writing should be part of the operation of the mind, in that poetry is connected to the real and emotional wellspring of being human (Tremmel, 1992).

There may even be, in the poetry inspired by art within an art venue, the subtleties of the analogous mapping of the geometry of the visual arts through a grammatical structure and perhaps even the phonology of the poem (Jakobson, 1985a). This may be initiated by what Lakoff (1987) called a *preconceptual structure.* Preconceptual structures may be embodied within and linked to original somatic experience (Lakoff, 1987). Schlegel, as cited by Szondi (1986), suggested that even anomalous poetry forms may provide the important staple fiber and preliminary etude for the generation of a universal message. The universal will foster forth as long as there is content within the form, and both have an innovative, creative kinship (Szondi, 1986). Perhaps in this way, Stewart (1995) suggested, the poet is both "agent and vessel of sense perception" (p. 36). The agent is poet, percipient, and vessel because, as Shusterman (1997) submitted, bringing an experience into language morphs both into a brand new state of affairs, which is coalesced and ineffable.

Somatically, poetry evokes. Dickinson (1940), perhaps speaking to the mind/body reception of poetry, said:

> If I read a book and it makes my whole body so cold no fire can ever warm me, I know that is poetry. If I feel physically as if the top of head were taken off, I know that is poetry. These are the only ways I know it. Is there any other way? (p. 366)

Dickinson seemed to speak to the mind/body reception of poetry. Keats' (1931) own comments on poetics suggest that sensation and somatic memory are elements of a work of imagination. On the other hand, in speaking of Leonardo da Vinci, Cobbing (1978) mentioned that da Vinci once requested that a poet hand over something kinetic and visual, not simply auditory.

The art of interpreting and the art of creatively envisaging aesthetic meaning may be done through shared activity. In fact, poetry may be the language to begin the creative discourse (Alexander, 1992), perhaps precociously within a newborn CI. The poems then process, when mixed into language, as part of a perceptivity and begin a transitional perception within the CI (Alexander, 1992). The CI inquirers may address the phenomenology of the inherent analogy or a likeness of their two-art experience: the visual and the verbal poetic. There may be a convergence of structure between the visual and the poem, which may then be addressed (Jakobson, 1985d) and open a hermeneutic outgrowth to follow further dialogue (Kennedy, 2006).

Words, such as *beauty, justice, courage,* and *happiness,* are commonly used in the P4C literature and CI discussions (Lipman, 1980, 2003; Lipman et al., 1980). However, where are their solidified definitions? Also, what about meaning? There seems to be no solid thought about that either (Arendt, 1978). This lack of the concrete for beauty, justice, and courage seems to be true for P4C professionals (Lipman, 1986, 2003; Lipman et al., 1980; Szondi, 1986). Then, how difficult must it be for children at the dawn of their thought/language development as well? Perhaps the innate nature of children is to use the more primary germs of the representational, such as poetry (Tremmel, 1992).

It would seem that the search for meaning is endeavored through poetry and prose and through philosophy (Hamrick, 1989). Feelings, details, and metaphor may slow down the process of coming to an understanding of the world. The discursive process may help this understanding speed through the process. However, something may be missing when the process is taken faster and not as a whole (Bosch, 1998; Tremmel, 1992).

The very tools used as representational symbols, Langer (1942, 1953) suggested, are forms of poetry. To confront the unacceptable, to understand the confounding, and to articulate that for which we have no words, children and their teachers need to use the representational along with the discursive and the academic along with the poetic. This may be true in the CI as well.

The Thing

The discursive attempts to glean the meaning of reality by standardizing, and thus managing it with the criterion of definition. Poetic thinking evinces the real by forming an interrelated expression of the thing with its own uniqueness (Bonnett, 1991). Poetic thinking, in other words, tries to comprehend a thing as it is and does not manipulate and categorize. Poetic thinking makes no assertion about the thing and instead is more straightforward and is affectively left as a presence in itself (Bonnett,

1991). Halliburton (1981) on Heidegger said that letting truth occur, the advent of verity of what something actually is, is the very essence of poetry.

However, there are things, and there are things. Some of the things can be works of art that appear vulgar and foster a blockage to aesthetic perceptivity. There may be at first a paradigmatic enmity for vulgarity. This may breed resistance to the attainment of an aesthetic perception thereof.

By the way, the exquisitely vulgar has its aesthete's sense as well. However, exquisitely vulgar images or language may not be the only blocks to aesthetic perceptivity. Images that are unfamiliar, idiosyncratic, or out of the box may not be allowed into the aesthetic perceptory of some because of a chosen abhorrence to our muffling comfort of the mechanical every day. Still, if a thing is uniformly vulgar, then Peirce, according to Osborne (1971), suggested that this should still be an esteem aesthetic because of its exquisite consistency.

Poetry and the Community

An in-door life is less poetical;
And out of door hath showers, and mists, and sleet,
With which I could not brew on pastoral.
But be it as it may, a bard must meet
All difficulties, whether great or small,
To spoil his undertaking or complete,
And work away like spirit upon matter,
Embarrass'd somewhat both with fire and water. (Byron, 2008)

Why would we take poetry to a CI from within the indoors to out of our personal doors to others? Perhaps because poetic thinking may be not only a way into a CI for thinkers to see the whole of a situation but also a way to strengthen the community. Poetic thinking may be an esteemed means of actually having a relationship with not only things but also other people. In relationships with people, for instance, Bonnett (1991) suggested that poetic thinking may be a natural occurrence and one that we often find preferable. Some relationship traits in particular even seem to be poetic. These might include the Eros of group involvement, or loving wholeheartedly, and addressing and responding to others as themselves rather than using or manipulating them. Of course, there is empathy as well as the poetics of group involvement.

The complete aesthetic appreciation of percipience may be aided by the expression of a discerned perception through poetry. This is because a poem created subsequent to an art viewing may, through its own aesthetic form, express a component of the original percipience (Osborne, 1971). The poem then brought to the CI table may begin another new inquiry of the art and all of its cognitive evocations, as rendered in poetry. The central value of poetry then is that it may build on the meaning of the experiences of the child poet/philosopher and the reader (Graham, 1996).

Furthermore, as with the relationship between seeing and hearing, there is a reciprocal kinship between the speaker and the listener in what Stewart (1995) called a "community of receptivity." This might encompass the historical development of conflicted subjectivities (Stewart, 1995). In other words, how a poem is received in a CI will vary. This, of course, may also affect the presentation of the poem and maybe even the formation of the creative product. Still, in a CI, through the community receptivity, we disclose what Alexander (1992) called an "eco-ecology of democratic freedom" (p. 213), which is best fostered by way of an aesthetic that is pragmatic. This means that despite tragedy and conflict in the world, we seek to repossess a collective belief in a meaningful substance of existence. The conscious quest to fulfill this desire Alexander (1992) called the "Human Eros" (p. 203). Eros also may be a CI component (Kennedy, 1994).

What you stew after the poetry experience, what product is produced, may even stir more of an evocation than the situation itself (Bosch, 1998). That, Dewey (1997) suggested, is because at the very moment of perception and experience the poet lives "moment to moment, preoccupied with the task at hand" (ew 12.18). However, later as the memories congeal into thoughts "a drama emerges," complete with a beginning, middle and climax of the encounter (ew. 12.18; Bosch, 1998). Perhaps these are philosophical stories.

Mind/Body/Text Osmosis and the Intertextual Umiak

Like a cell with a membrane and nucleus, the mind and body may be a porous entity within an intertextual swamp. Heidegger (1971) added that chafing across the regions of the earth is a chaotic but nonetheless canny colloquy of words in various modern media, which forms its own navigation of the swamp. In such a fluid mush of text, the mind/body is continually constructed and reconstructed. This Fleckenstein (1999) called "somatic mind," which allows us to incarnate our communication without one or the other, body or mind, totally dominating. Our continual, developing relationship between the carnal and the textual in part creates our somatic mind.

Without permeability to our intertextual ecosphere, we may become a voiceless collection of cells. Even within the CI ecosphere, our personal identity is a muscled manifestation, a frame of flesh, that evaporates and amalgamates by reacting to and being in context with "invisible inter-textual messages" (Fleckenstein, 1999, p. 303). Because we are somatic minds then, writing poetically will help us communicate and begin an inquiry. The tool is poetry because although we are permeable in one way, we also have no border that divides word and image, body and mind. We possess only a process of osmosis (Fleckenstein, 2003). A poem may give a framework.

Word Play

Like corporeal cognition in an interlingual lake, a big part of what helps us create a new poem is not just, according to Jung (2001), intellectual. However, to a great extent, creating something new is also a type of play. This, Jung said, utilizes the play instinct. In art, as in toys and games, we play with the objects that we love (Robinson, 2001). This seems to include language as well.

Ciardi (1975) told a related story about Auden. Auden, we are told, said that in advising young poets, he would first ask why the person wanted to write poetry. If the reply was "because I have something important to say," Auden would infer that this kid would not be successful. If, however, the answer was "because I like to hang around words and overhear them talking to each other," then the poet-to-be may have a stake at success (p. 3). That might be because this kind of playing with words is one of the rudiments of the art.

The play with words may encompass many poetry forms, and it is with these forms that the *how* of a meaning explication is generated. *How* a poem, or painting for that matter, means is *en suit* to *what* it means (Robinson, 2001). In fact, these forms help supply a framework to move creativity successfully out to play (Ciardi, 1975).

We need a field with boundaries perhaps to play. Poems may be an actual output of schematic symbols, in that the forms of the poems connote some of their meaning (Robinson, 2001). In other words, an uttered lyric incorporates a kinetic link between a declaration of the poet's will and what the utterance means somatically as well as linguistically (Stewart, 1995).

This somatic component may be part of what ties poetry directly to paintings and other art forms. This may be because in painting we garner meaning from forms as well. Certainly, we do not buy the *Encyclopedia of*

Color on ebay to research exactly what turquoise and verdant green commonly mean (Robinson, 2001). We must perceive the meaning another way. In fact, meaning may have many potentialities through aesthetic discernment. However, when these meanings come to be, creatively and cooperatively, through the art of living, then maybe we have reached wisdom (ew 3.5; Dewey, 1997).

Some Form of Play

Play in the school curriculum, of course, has its place; unfortunately, in common language, use the idea of *form,* a category of the poetic play, seems to be set far aside from the idea of substance. An example might be when we say "the *form* of the professor's colloquium talk seemed quite scattered, out of form, but the *substance* was very relevant to our interests" (Maquet, 1990). In this way, a vocal form might suggest a shallow façade. Although substance or the ever valuable content is really the important element, form may not be as important, just a trivial trick of semantics (Maquet, 1990).

However, that is how we might separate form and substance in speech. Form for painters, on the other hand, is the most important part of their aesthetic palette, not a superficial smudge. Still, as sound is to music and visual form is to painting, the metric form of poetry likewise is also not a façade, nor are its sound and typographic suggestions (Maquet, 1990).

The Type of Play

In addition to meaning in sound, there is a visual impact in written or printed poetry. Even the typography of a poem may carry meaning in its form. As art demonstrates the ocular interest of its makers as well, the poetry evoked by this art may show the concerns of the poem's maker, the child poet/philosopher. In addition, Maquet (1990) suggested that this kind of poetry form may demonstrate the "visual capacity of the beholders to perceive formal order in the varied idioms of different styles" (pp. 56–57). Of course, the typographic form may also support or supplement a form in meter, rhyme, or cadence. The visual may be proportioned aesthetically and meaningfully to the language.

Somatic

Beyond this, the "poetic delight," which is evoked through the structure of a poem's language and sound, may be of a proportion that can be a somatic precept; this may lead to further poetic action and response (Jakobson, 1985a). Hlobil (2000), speaking of Baumgaten, suggested that words are, in fact, a reality perceived through our senses, and this can thus affect the mind, perhaps in a somatic fashion. Dewey, according to Shusterman (1997), seemed to recognize art's "deep roots in life's needs and interests [by incorporating] the practical and cognitive, along with the somatic and social as contributing elements in aesthetic experience?" (p. 6). As suggested by Thomas Aquinas, "the senses delight in things duly proportioned as in something akin to them; for, the sense, too, is a kind of reason as is every cognitive power" (Jakobson, 1985a, p. 45).

Inseparable, as well, are intuition and the somatic mechanics of poetics in that each nourishes the other. As mentioned, the synergy of the meaning of such a poem is the business not what of the poem means but rather how the poem might mean (Ciardi, 1975). Ciardi suggested that no CI will concur on the precise meaning of a poem. However, what the poem means and the process thereof constitutes a discussion that might proceed with more success; this perhaps reduces some of the frustration possible in a CI. These frustrations, like little tokens of possible truth, may literally fall out of a discussion of the poetic technicalities.

The Somatic, Sonic Evocation

One technicality may be the sound of the poem. Partly, this is because language itself is composed of sound and meaning. Working as a duo, sound and meaning may have the ability to function in an infinite realm of possibility (Chomsky, 2006). The sound of some poetry may reach toward the goal of a meaning that may also emit from it. That may be partly because a recited poem is mainly a muscular maneuver. A poem and its sound forms may be a puissant sonic utterance. This may not always be true of words in print. By listening to the recited poem, we may actually occupy the gallery of noise and let the poem say itself through the body. Totally somatic, "poetry then is a physical occurrence which the body liberates" (Cobbing, 1978, p. 33), and when bodies collaborate in movement and music, the result may even touch on ritual.

If when a poet generates a poem and waves are propelled from the body as Rukeyser (1996) may suggest, whose body is it? It seems that there might be a surrogate for the poet's body. Polanyi (1993) claimed that the perception of things apart from the body serves as surrogate experiences of the body. As a result, it may seem as if their meaning is transposed away from us. This may be what Polanyi (1983) called "tacit knowledge." Within a CI, the tacit knowledge of a presented poem may be astonishing.

The Sound, Silence

Speaking of Heidegger, Halliburton (1981) suggested that what has already been spoken and what will be spoken share an inarticulate consanguinity with what is actually being spoken. This blood relationship of sorts occurs through what is, in fact, unspoken. That is because the situation of this relationship is enacted autonomously to human circumstance. The consanguinity of what was said, will be said, and is being said is, in essence, altogether unsaid. The unsaid correlates to and attains the spatiotemporal presence of language because it provides a situation for further spoken sentences of meaning (Halliburton, 1981).

Meter

The meter of a poem, the achievement of which requires part silence and part sound, may suggest meaning as well. This may be because meter carries its own structural history and its own temporal character. Meter evolves in time. Its sonic clock, by will or sonic suggestion, lets meter tend to accumulate its own parsed allusions (Stewart, 1995). In fact, the music or meter of a poem may possess its own language, purport, or meaning. However, this purport may be successfully evoked by the writer or reader at any time in the history of the poem's interception or recollection or not at all. This means that the purport of meter may not be presently noticed or even seen as missing to consciousness at any particular time (Stewart, 1995).

In *Poetics 1447.I.23,* Aristotle (2000) asserted that although the forms that may be combined into a poem are several; these elements of a poem must work in combination to form a whole (McKeon, 1947). We have explored the spoken, the unspoken, and the meter of a poem in this section. It may be that a poem then is the sum of its parts, a whole because the poem is not just its text. This may be what the schematic encoding of the poem generates (Robinson, 2001).

Discussion

I think that the literature and curriculum direction for the development of poetry from the percipience of visual arts leading to philosophical dialogue within a CI are limited. I suggest future work first on the development of a percipience curriculum to be used particularly within art galleries and museums accessible to school districts. This type of program has made a start with P4C affiliates. The Institute of Research for the Teaching of Philosophy (GrupIREF) in Barcelona, Spain, has explored philosophy through visual arts in out-of-the-classroom venues, such as the National Museum of Art of Catalonia (Bosch, 1998; dePuig, personal communication, 2008). A full curriculum for use in U.S. schools and around the world may be developed with some inspiration from Bosch and dePuig.

Second, a curriculum component of the percipience of art might then lead to a dialogue about poetic thinking further based on the recognition of this cognition in everyday life.

I suggest that poetic thinking might lead to artifact development or the preservation of percipient seduction through the writing of poetry. This may open many new windows for philosophical discussion when the poems are then used as fodder for cultivation of the CI dialogue.

I find that in my own experience with middle school students, some clear direction to move students toward the possible poetry form will open up possibilities outside the first response utterances. Although some of the forms as discussed are, according to some, indigenous to the poetic mind, learning what some of them look like up front may open up a window to this aesthetic otherwise trapped by an over focus on the discursive (Jakobson, 1985b).

Finally, with the transitional object of poetry—one step on the umiak trip across (Gazzaniga, 2008) the interlingual aqua sphere from percipience to poetic thinking to poetry writing—much of the current P4C curriculum for the development of a CI may be implemented or adapted. This somatic enterprise into the thinking mind of the child poet/philosopher may then further support and be supported by the wider views of the various CI communities within the community (Kennedy, 1994).

However, the main reason for percipience, poetic thinking, and then poetry in a CI umiak is that in addition to the swamp of the intertextual, questions of philosophy do not exist by themselves or sit there ready to be taken off the shelf like a choice purchase. Instead, the question arises through perceptions, observations, and experiences. Once a question begins to congeal after or during the process of its manifestation, expectations or their token languages may begin to hatch. These hatchling expectations are not always of the same species to all participants in a CI, particularly when there are adults in the group as well as children (van der Leeuw, 1987).

By displaying her expectations or even new ideas outside of the easily spoken language, the child poet/philosopher may enter the inquiry process. That process may then be available to the CI group through the reading of such a poem.

References

Adorno, T. W. (1961). Valerys Abweichungen. *Noten zur Literatur, 2,* 50–51, 55–56, 73, 78–59.

Alexander, T. (1992). Dewey and the metaphysical imagination. *Transactions of the Charles S. Peirce Society, 28,* 203–215.

Applebee, A. N. (1978). *The child's concept of the story. Ages two to seventeen.* Chicago: University of Chicago Press.

Arendt, H. (1978). *The life of the mind.* San Diego, CA: Harcourt Brace Jovanovich.

Aristotle. (2009). *On the soul* (J. A. Smith, Trans.). Retrieved from http://classics.mit.edu/Aristotle/soul.3.iii.html

Blocker, H. G. (2005). Kant for kids. *Arts Education Policy Review, 107,* 31–33.

Bonnett, M. (1991). Developing children's thinking...and the national curriculum. *Cambridge Journal of Education, 21,* 277–292.

Bosch, E. (1998). *The pleasure of beholding. The visitor's museum.* Barcelona, Spain: Actar.

Britton, J. (1970). *Language and learning.* Hammondsworth, England: Penguin.

Brook, P. (1972). *The empty space.* Middlesex, England: Penguin.

Bruner, J. (1996). *The culture of education.* Cambridge, MA: Harvard University Press.

Burns, G. L. (1989). *Heidegger's language, truth and poetry estrangements in later writings.* New Haven, CT: Yale University Press.

Byron, G. G. (2008). *Don Juan [If from great nature's or our own abyss]* Retrieved from http://www.poets.org/viewmedia.php/prmMID/19895

Chomsky, N. (2006). *Language and mind* (3rd ed.). Cambridge, England: Cambridge University Press.

Ciardi, J. (1975). *How does a poem mean?* (2nd ed.). Boston: Houghton Mifflin.

Cobbing, B. (1978). Some statements on sound poetry. In S. McCaffery (Ed.), *Sound poetry: A catalogue.* Toronto: Underwich Editions.

Coski, C. (2006). Emotion and poetry in Condillac's theory of language and mind. *The French Review, 80,* 157–170.

Dewey, J. (1980). *Art as experience.* New York: Perigee.

—. (1997). *The collected works of John Dewey, 1882–1953.* Retrieved from http://library.nlx.com.ezproxy.montclair.edu:2048/display.cfm?&client ID=72960&depth=2&infobase=pmdewey.nfo&softpage=GetClient42 &view=browse

Dickinson, E. (1940). A letter to Colonel Thomas Wentworth Higginson, August 1870. In M. L. Schuster (Ed.), *A treasury of the world's great letters* (pp. 365–367). New York: Simon & Schuster.

Donaldson, M. (1978). *Children's minds.* London: Fontana.

Dunbar, K. N. (2008). *Arts education, the brain, and language.* New York: Dana Foundation.

Fleckenstein, K. S. (1999). Writing bodies: Somatic mind in composition studies. *College English, 61,* 281–306.

—. (2003). *Embodied literacies. Imageword and a poetics of teaching.* Carbondale: Southern Illinois University Press.

Gardner, H. (1988). Toward more effective arts education. *Journal of Aesthetic Education, 22*(1), 157–167.

Gazzaniga, M. (2008). *Arts and cognition. Findings hint at relationships.* New York: Dana Foundation.

Graham, G. (1996). Aesthetic cognitivisim and the literary arts. *Journal of Aesthetic Education, 30*(1), 1–17.

Greene, M. (1978). *Landscapes of learning.* New York: Teachers College Press.

—. (1988). *The dialect of freedom.* New York: Teachers College Press.

—. (2001). *Variations of a blue guitar.* New York: Teachers College Press.

Halliburton, D. (1981). *Poetic thinking. An approach to Heidegger.* Chicago: University of Chicago Press.

Hamrick, W. S. (1989). Philosophy for Children and aesthetic education. *Journal of Aesthetic Education, 23*(2), 55–67.

Hanks, N. (1971). Education through art: A gateway. *Art Education, 24*(7), 10–17.

Heidegger, M. (1971). *Poetry, language, thought* (A. Hofstadter, Trans.). New York: Harper & Row.

Hlobil, T. (2000). Two concepts of language and poetry: Edmund Burke and Moses Mendelssohn. *British Journal for the History of Philosophy, 8,* 447–458.

Jacob, C. F. (1922). The psychology of poetic talent. *The Journal of Abnormal Psychology, 17,* 231–253.

Jakobson, R. (1978). *Six lectures on sound and meaning* (J. Mepham,

Trans.). Cambridge: MIT Press.

—. (1985a). Poetry and grammar & grammar of poetry. In K. Pamorka & S. Rudy (Eds.), *Verbal art, verbal sign, verbal time* (pp. 37–110). Minneapolis: University of Minnesota Press.

—. (1985b). Subliminal verbal patterns in poetry. In K. Pamorka & S. Rudy (Eds.), *Verbal art, verbal sign, verbal time* (pp. 50–68). Minneapolis: University of Minnesota Press.

—. (1985c). *Verbal art, verbal sign, verbal time.* Minneapolis: University of Minnesota Press.

—. (1985d). Yeats' "Sorrow of Love" through the years. In K. Pamorka & S. Rudy (Eds.), *Verbal art, verbal sign, verbal time* (pp. 79–110). Minneapolis: University of Minnesota Press.

Jonides, J. (2008). *Musical skill and cognition.* New York: Dana Foundation.

Jung, C. G. (2001). *Modern man in search of a soul.* London: Routledge.

Kant, I. (1952). *The critique of judgment* (J. C. Meredith, Trans.). London: Oxford University Press.

Keats, J. (1931). Letter to Benjamin Bailey 22 Nov 1817. In M. Buxtom (Ed.), *The letters of John Keats* (pp. 51–55). New York: Oxford University Press.

Kennedy, D. (1994). The five communities. *Analytic Teaching: The Community of Inquiry Journal, 15,* 3–16.

—. (2006). *The well of being.* Albany: State University of New York Press.

Koch, K. (1970). *Wishes, lies and dreams: Teaching children to write poetry.* New York: Chelsea House.

—. (1973). *Rose, where did you get that red? Teaching great poetry to children.* New York: Random House.

Lakoff, G. (1987). *Women, fire, and dangerous things. What categories reveal about the mind.* Chicago: University of Chicago Press.

Langer, S. K. (1942). *Philosophy in a new key: A study in symbolism of reason, rite, and art.* Cambridge: Harvard University Press.

—. (1953). *Feeling and form. A theory of art.* New York: Charles Scribner.

Lipman, M. (1956). The physical thing in aesthetic experience. *The Journal of Aesthetics and Art Criticism, 15,* 36–46.

—. (1980). *Writing: How and why.* Upper Montclair, NJ: Institute for the Advancement of Philosophy for Children.

—. (1985). *Harry Stottlemeier's discovery.* Upper Montclair, NJ: Institute for the Advancement of Philosophy for Children.

—. (1986). *Wondering at the world. Instructional manual to accompany*

Kio and Gus. New York: University Press of America.
—. (2003). *Thinking in education.* New York: Cambridge University Press.
Lipman, M., Sharp, A.M., & Oscanyan, K.S. (1980). *Philosophy in the classroom* (2nd ed.). Philadelphia: Temple University Press.
Makkreel, R. A., & Rodi, F. (1985). Poetry and experience. In *Wilhelm Dilthey: Selected works* (Vol. 5). Princeton, NJ: Princeton University Press.
Maquet, J. (1990). Perennial modernity: Forms as aesthetic and symbolic. *Journal of Aesthetic Education, 24*(4), 47–58.
Marceau, J. (Ed.). (1997). *Art: A world history.* New York: DK.
Martin, G. D. (1975). *Language truth and poetry.* Edinburgh, Scotland: Edinburgh University Press.
McCarthy, K. F. (2004). *Gifts of the muse. Reframing the debate about the benefits of the arts.* Santa Monica, CA: Rand.
McKeon, R. (Ed.). (1947). *Introduction to Aristotle.* New York: Random House.
Moffet, J. (1968). *Teaching the universe of discourse.* Boston: Houghton Mifflin.
Monet, C. (1997). Water lilies, 1916–19. In J. Marceau (Ed.), *Art: A world history* (pp. 487). New York: DK.
O'Brien, J. (1993). Reasoning and the senses: The humanist imagination. *South Central Review, 10*(2), 3–19.
Osborne, H. (1971). Taste and judgment in the arts. *Journal of Aesthetic Education, 5*(4), 13–28.
Pascal, R. (1929). A transition point in German romanticism. *The Modern Language Review, 24,* 302–312.
Pinzolo, K. (2008). *Arts Plan NJ.* New Jersey State Council on the Arts. Retrieved from http://www.njartscouncil.org/pdfs/ArtsPlanNJ.pdf
Polanyi, M. (1962). *Personal knowledge. Towards a post-critical philosophy.* Chicago: University of Chicago Press.
—. (1983). *The tacit dimension.* Gloucester, MA: Peter Smith.
Posner, M., Rothbart, M.K., Sheese, B.E., & Kieras, J. (2008). *How arts training influences cognition.* New York: Dana Foundation.
Raposa, M. L. (1989). *Peirce's philosophy of religion.* Bloomington: Indiana University Press.
Robinson, K. (2001). *Out of our minds. Learning to be creative.* West Sussex: Capstone.
Rukeyser, M. (1996). *The life of poetry.* Ashfield, MA: Paris Press.
Schmid, D. (2008, April). *What percentage of New Jersey grammar school and high school student have the arts as part of their*

curriculum. Paper presented at the Charting the Course. A Conference for the Advancement of Arts Education, Artists, and Arts Organizations.

Shakespeare, W. (2008). *Shall I compare thee to a summer's day? (Sonnet 18).* The Academy of American Poets. Retrieved from http://www.poets.org/printmedia.php/prmMediaID/15555

Shusterman, R. (1997). *Practicing philosophy. Pragmatism and the philosophical life.* New York: Routledge.

Stewart, S. (1995). Lyric possession. *Critical Inquiry, 22,* 34–63.

Szondi, P. (1986). *On textual understanding and other essays* (H. Mendelsohn, Trans.). Minneapolis: University of Minneapolis Press.

Tremmel, R. (1992). Making the return move: Secondary students thinking poetically and writing poetry. *Journal of Aesthetic Education, 26*(2), 17–30.

Turco, L. (1986). *The new book of forms: A handbook of poetics.* Hanover, NH: University Press of New England.

UNESCO. (2005, March; 2005, September). *International symposium: Conserving cultural and biological diversity: The role of sacred nature sites and cultural landscapes.* Paper presented at the Tokyo Symposium, United Nations University. Tokyo, Japan.

Valery, P. (1936). Commentaries de charmes. In *Variete, III.* Paris: Gallimard.

van der Leeuw, K. (1987, August). *Learning to operate with philosophical concepts.* Paper presented at the First International Conference of Philosophy for Children

Vygotsky, L. S. (1962). *Thought and language* (E. Hanfmann & G. Vakar, Trans.). Cambridge, MA: MIT Press.

Warhol, A. (1962). Big torn Campbell's soup can (vegetable beef). In J. Marceau (Ed.), *Art: A world history* (p. 640). New York: DK.

Weitz, M. (1956). The role of theory in aesthetics. *The Journal of Aesthetics and Art Criticism, 15*(1), 27–35.

Note

1. In this chapter, Dewey (1997), an electronic version of *The Collected Works of John Dewey, 1882–1953,* is cited with a URL in the references. Text citations that begin with a lowercase *ew* are followed by a numeric indicator with decimal point numbers (e.g., ew 2.173) and direct the reader to the precise online page and section numbers. This is used only for phrases directly quoted from this source. In all other cases, the citations for this particular source are made in a standard manner (e.g., Dewey, 1997).

Chapter Four

The Principle of Personal Worth and Its Implications for Education

Laurance J. Splitter
Hong Kong Institute of Education

In this essay, I articulate and defend what I call "The Principle of Personal Worth" (PPW), according to which persons have a unique but equal moral value which places them above nonpersons, regardless of how the latter may be characterized or categorized. I explain the relevance of PPW to education, providing a novel defense of a familiar construct: the classroom community of inquiry (CI). In brief, a CI is an environment in which individuals *become* persons, that is, entities of the highest moral significance regardless of the *kind* of object that they are. The essay draws on the work of several notable 20th-century analytic philosophers, including P. F. Strawson, David Wiggins and Donald Davidson.

Introduction

In this essay, I articulate and defend what I call "The Principle of Personal Worth" (PPW) and explain its relevance to education, particularly in relation to the community of inquiry (CI). A key preliminary step will be to examine just what we mean by "person," wherein I opt for a characterization that, while simple and familiar, has far-reaching implications for education. My view, somewhat paradoxically it may seem, is that the concept of *person* characterizes entities that are of the highest moral significance yet fails to demarcate or stand for a particular *kind* of entity.

The PPW states that (a) persons have a unique moral value or worth which, simply put, places them above nonpersons, regardless of how the latter may be characterized or categorized, and (b) with respect to this moral value, *all* persons are equal, that is, of equal value and worth. I clarify and elaborate on these claims under the following broad headings:

1. Persons are those familiar entities of which you, I, and all human persons are typical exemplars; but

2. There is no reason to insist either that only humans can be persons or that all humans are (human) persons.

3. Indeed, personhood as a classification among existents does not compete or clash with the concepts, whatever they may be, that demarcate particular *kinds* of entity, where a—perhaps *the*—primary function of a kind is to supply criteria of identity and existence for those objects that belong to it. In other words, personhood is not a kind in this sense.

4. *Being a person,* however, remains a classification of the utmost importance because of the specific moral, aesthetic, semantic, epistemological, and metaphysical dimensions of this concept.

5. *Nonpersons*—entities that are not persons—are less valuable than persons. In referring to nonpersons, I have in mind two types of entity:

   a. Ordinary objects, such as rocks, hi-fi systems, snakes, insects, birds, fish, and most mammals.
   b. "Supra-personal" entities, such as nations, cultures, ethnicities (or ethnic groups), corporations, clubs, gangs, and cults.

   The basic difference between the objects in these two groups is that the latter are, in some sense, *composed of* or *constituted by* persons, whereas the former are not.

6. No one person is more valuable than any other.

7. Persons are not more important than *simple groups* or *classes* of persons, where these are understood as collections that are *no greater than the sums of their parts*. Groups in this minimal sense are quite different from the "supra-persons" to which I previously referred.

8. Despite initial appearances, neither the strong individualism of the neo-liberal ("Western") stereotype, nor the collectivism of the neo-socialist ("Eastern") stereotype finds any support in the PPW.

9. The business of formal education, at least for the young, should be focused on nurturing and assisting the development of what I cautiously term "full personhood," rather than such subsidiary goals as vocational training, literacy or citizenship training, socialization and so on.

Who or What Am I?

We do not need to look far to find exemplars of personhood. You and I are among them, as are just about all members of *Homo sapiens,* with the possible exception of those who are extremely young or in a severely comatose or vegetative state. If the category of persons constituted what philosophers call a "natural kind," then we might rest content with such an ostensive definition, secure in the knowledge that nature—as uncovered via the labors of those experts we call "scientists"—will determine—if it has not already done so—the specific empirical details of what it is to be a member of that kind. However, to qualify for natural kind status, a concept must satisfy certain requirements, specifically, those that determine the conditions of identity for its members. As I shall explain shortly, the importance and moral status of those entities that we deem to be persons notwithstanding, there is *no* single natural kind that meets these requirements and that contains all and only persons. This leaves us with the obligation—and also the opportunity—to come up with a characterization of *person* that matches our need for such a concept in the first place.

Two fairly simple clues hint that the classification of persons as human beings is not a straightforward matter. The first, already noted, is that we may wish to deny personhood status to certain human beings who are at life's temporal extremes, specifically those not yet or only recently born and those who, for whatever tragic reason, are unable to function as persons (according to criteria to be elucidated below). That such individuals are human beings seems undeniable, assuming that they either were or will become members of *Homo sapiens,* for what property or characteristic could stand in the way of their remaining so? The second clue—admittedly more speculative than actual—is that there seems little reason to insist that persons *must* be human beings. Intuitively, that is, prior to agreeing on a precise characterization of personhood, Martians, robots, and computers—not to mention some higher-order, nonhuman mammals —might count as persons.

Elementary semantics teaches us that if the extensions of two concepts are different, whether in fact or in conception, then the concepts themselves must be different, that is, different in meaning. In the case of *person* and *human being*, any distinction *qua* concepts is consistent with the notion that I, you, and most of our friends and acquaintances are, at one and the same time, *both* persons *and* human beings. Yet, we may still wish to know which of these concepts, if either, is more closely associated with *who or what* I am (you are, she is). I propose that while my identity will be a function of the (natural) kind of thing that I am, my capacity for self-awareness, along with my unique moral status, will be functions of my being a *person*.

Numerous candidates stand out immediately in answer to "What am I?": a middle-aged, balding, overweight academic; a left-handed, Jewish Australian residing in Hong Kong; a social introvert with a weird sense of humor who is prone to depression; the eldest child of Jean and Leon Splitter; any combination of these; and so on. In claiming that none of these descriptive nouns or phrases counts as sufficiently *basic* (although the last one mentioned may come close!), I am *not* merely making the point that none of them uniquely instantiates me (because at least one of them does: I am certainly not the only middle-aged, balding, overweight academic around, although I might have been, but I am the only eldest child of Jean and Leon Splitter). According to the thinking of David Wiggins (2001) and P. F. Strawson (1959/1990), to whom my own views on identity and personhood owe a great deal, the claim that these terms are not basic is the denial that any of them answers the key question "*What is it?*" where the answer to this question points the way to the conditions of identity for identifying and tracing particular objects through space and time. According to these very conditions, no entity came into existence when I became middle-aged, balding, and/or overweight, just as none will cease to exist if and when I cease to have these properties (unless my ceasing to have them happens to coincide with my death).

In terms of classifying ourselves as a particular kind of entity, we usually think of: (i) something manifestly physical—a human being in the strict biological sense, a human body, even a brain, and so on—*or* (ii) something apparently nonphysical—a mind, soul, spirit, and so on—*or* (iii) something both physical and nonphysical (i.e. with both physical and nonphysical characteristics) — most notably, a person. Alternatively, we might draw attention away from what some regard as dubious metaphysical commitments by focusing, instead, on the *language* we use to describe the entities in question (a move that characterizes much of 20th-century analytic philosophy). Subject to a convenient modification suggested by Wiggins (2001), Strawson (1959/1990) famously distinguished, among the predicates or descriptors that we commonly use to describe various entities, between those that impute *consciousness* or some related mental condition (P predicates) and those that impute material or bodily characteristics (M predicates) (Strawson, 1959/1990; Wiggins, 2001, p. 195). Making the distinction in these terms highlights one crucial feature of ordinary language usage: while some predicates sit fairly comfortably on one side or the other of the "mental/physical" divide ("thinks," "chooses," "hopes for," and so on vs. "weighs 95 kg," "is located in this building," "has dark skin," and so on), others do not ("walks," "writes," "smiles," "plays the piano," and so on) (Wiggins, 2001, p. 234). Further, we confidently and familiarly use all three kinds of predicates (P, M, and borderline) across boundaries that, upon reflection, seem somewhat formidable if not impenetrable, particularly that between self-ascription and other ascription of both P and borderline predicates. For example, speakers in a given language community quite happily use terms that attribute mental states to themselves and others under the clear assumption that these words do *not* change meaning in the transition. When I attribute a headache or feeling of unbounded joy to myself, I mean the same thing that you do when you attribute these traits to yourself and also when I attribute them to you. There is a familiar epistemological puzzle here, namely, how it is that we so confidently use such terms in first-, second-, and third-person contexts when it appears that our *ways of knowing* are so different? (I do not look for bodily symptoms or any form of observable behavior to confirm my own headache, but I do so to learn about yours). Nevertheless, the so-called *object* of knowledge—that which is known—that is, the headache in this example, is the same kind of thing for both of us. I shall return to this idea later because it speaks directly to the kind of entity both *I* and *you* are. Meanwhile, a crucial clue to how we might deal with it comes from Strawson, who points out that as a matter of logic (or semantics), each one of the ordinary predicates that we use to refer to, describe, and classify objects—whether P, M, or borderline—must be meaningfully, albeit not necessarily truthfully, applied to a *range* of objects of one kind or another. We simply could not use words like "overweight," "headache," or "joy," whether in the first person case or otherwise, unless it makes sense to apply them to more than one object. I will suggest that while this "pluralist" (as opposed to singular) understanding of predication is clearly relevant to the ways in which we speak about objects in the world, it has particular significance for one category of objects, namely, ourselves as *persons*. More specifically, a *core precondition of my regarding myself as a person is that I regard myself as one among others* (i.e. *other persons*).

Strawson's (1959/1990) reflections on P and M predicates lead him to propose that the concept of *person* is conceptually and epistemologically *primitive* with respect to other concepts that might be used to answer the question "What am I?"; most famously, there is the Cartesian idea that I know myself, first and foremost, as a *thinking being* (mind) but, equally, there is the strong physicalist view that I am nothing other than a material object (e.g., my own body). It is important to understand that Strawson was not particularly concerned here with issues of ontology and identity; he did not reject the idea that minds and bodies, along with such abstract entities as *universals*, exist, but in proposing personhood as primitive, he rejected the grounds from which several notorious philosophical problems are often taken as emerging. Skepticism about "other minds," for example, cannot even be coherently expressed in his view because, to do so, we must start with an adequate conception of our own mind (i.e., the first-person case). However, such a conception, when properly understood, presupposes the idea mentioned above, that each of us must see himself or herself as one among *others*. However, in not focusing on issues of ontology, Strawson bypassed an issue of importance to my present concerns, namely, that of specifying identity and persistence conditions for the kind of thing that I am.

Where does a Strawsonian commitment to persons place us with respect to seeing ourselves as human beings (i.e., members of *Homo sapiens*)? My answer to this question, to be elaborated below, is along the following lines: we do indeed regard ourselves as persons in Strawson's sense, but equally, we regard ourselves as human beings with all the biological connotations usually given to that classification. Moreover, whether we regard ourselves as one or the other depends upon our interests: as entities with determinate identity and persistence conditions, we are human beings—or because I have strong reservations about the status of this concept as standing for a natural kind—animals, living organisms, and so on, that is, objects whose identities are carved out according to an appropriate classification in nature, supported by relevant laws, and so forth. However, as entities with a privileged moral status in the world, who are capable of self-awareness, belonging to one or more language communities, being educated, forging meaningful relationships, and so on, our interest is in ourselves as persons.

Kinds and Identity

In keeping with an analytic tradition defended by Quine (1960) among others, when it comes to ontology, *existence and identity are conceptually correlative*. To provide the conditions for one is to provide those for the other. Accordingly, we find an answer to the question "What am I?" by way of the question "What is conceptually involved in both identifying me *at* a particular time and re-identifying me *over* time?"

Wiggins (2001) insisted that for any genuine object, there is a right way of keeping track of it as a particular entity. The "track" in question is not merely facilitated but constituted by some underlying "sortal" (or kind) concept. Wiggins' well-known rejection of the relativity of identity commits him to the view that if an object seems to follow two divergent tracks whereby judgments of identity with respect to the two underlying substance concepts will also diverge, then one of these judgments and its attendant concept must give way. In the case of persons and human beings, where it seems that I may answer to both concepts, the divergence issue (leaving aside persons who are nonhumans) arises with such real-life phenomena as the human zygote, the individual in a vegetative state, and the notorious family of imagined cases involving brain transplantations of one kind or another. In his most recent treatment of the topic, Wiggins expends considerable energy in the defense of *human being* over *person* with respect to the most basic answer to the question of "What am I?" He finds support for the former because it is, in his view, a *natural kind* concept that regulates the behavior of entities that fall under it according to some appropriate set of natural laws. Elsewhere, I have cast doubt on this convenient but scientifically unsupported view concerning biological species and would argue, instead, that if there is any category of natural entity that corresponds to such a law-like framework, it is likely to be that of *living organism*. When it comes to persons, however, Wiggins adopts an increasingly pessimistic stance in which, despite his express desire "not to let go the idea of personhood" (p. 234), his discussion closes with a degree of vagueness that might be interpreted as doing just that! Bypassing the finer points of his argument, he is inclined to give up the idea that personhood is something to be discovered or encountered in the world (i.e., a natural phenomenon) in favor of treating this concept as *artefactual*, that is, engineered by us to serve our own particular needs and purposes.

Contemporary philosopher Eric Olson (1997) has also written on the issue of what kind of thing I/we am/are, coming down, like Wiggins (2001), but with greater conviction, on the biological side (we are animals!), on the grounds that whenever biological and psychological/ mental criteria appear to clash, we inevitably and intuitively resort to the former (Olson 1997). So, when the human fetus becomes an infant, then a child, adolescent, adult, and so on, it is one and the same continuant that persists through all these stages of growth. To cite two further examples offered by Olson, if the cerebrum of one individual were to be removed and placed into the head of another, no entity would go out of existence (though it would be severely diminished intellectually and emotionally) because the organism that now lacks the capacity for higher-order thought through the lack of a cerebrum—and is, therefore, no longer a person— may be said to persist according to whatever criterion of identity is associated with the kind of (material) entity that it is. So, while the entity who received the cerebrum might well *claim* identity with the original owner (claiming to have the same memories, experiences, and so on), he would be *mistaken*; some other intimate relationship, perhaps, but not identity. Likewise, when, tragically, a human being is reduced to a vegetative state as the result of an illness or accident, he persists *qua* organism, though (arguably) not *qua* person. There is no clash of identity here; there is only one persisting entity, and its identity is governed by the kind of thing that it is. On the other hand, personhood is a property or complex of properties that does not carry the burden of identity. To be a human (or Martian or robotic) person is to be a human (or Martian or robot) with certain admittedly important features, which, as these examples suggest, may come and go.

Persons

Following this line of thought, the inquiry into the nature of personhood becomes one about which properties, taken together, are definitive of personhood in the above sense, that is, freed from the burden of having to provide identity or persistence conditions. There is no shortage of well-known candidates here, including the capacity for rationality and self-consciousness, tool-making, goal-setting, and so on. However, I prefer to follow a lead provided by Donald Davidson, based on the idea of *triangulation*. Davidson's writings convey a powerful holistic understanding of the relationship between persons—as causal agents, as bearers of both mental and physical attributes, and as inquirers into meaning, truth, and knowledge—and the world in which they are situated, act, and are acted upon (a world that also contains other persons). Granted, Strawson, among many others, was also concerned with this relationship, but Davidson's focus on the relationships forged by those who seek to *interpret*, that is, make sense of, the linguistic utterances of their fellows is an important point of difference. In its simplest terms, this relationship has three key terms; hence, the notion of triangulation:

> The basic triangle of two people and a common world is one of which we must be aware if we have any thoughts at all. If I can think, I know that there are others with minds like my own, and that we inhabit a public time and space filled with objects and events many of which are…known to others. In particular I, like every other rational creature, have three kinds of knowledge: knowledge of the objective world…knowledge of the minds of others; and knowledge of the contents of my own mind. None of these

three sorts of knowledge is reducible to either of the other two, or to any other two in combination. (Davidson, 1998, pp. 86–87)

Davidson's principle of *triangulation* plays a key role in his later writings (Davidson, 1982, 1999, 2001a, 2001c). It is designed, in part, to block the Cartesian skeptic's attempt to restrict or otherwise prioritize knowledge to the first person, but Davidson also uses it to account, conceptually, for what we already know to be the case, namely, that we interpret one another's responses to certain stimuli as confirmation that we share and can communicate about a common (i.e., objective) world. Indeed, our capacity so to interpret one another—to behave inter-subjectively—constitutes what we *mean* by commonality or objectivity. Davidson (1995) asks, "concealed behind the epistemological problem, and conceptually prior to it, is: how did we come by the concept of an objective reality in the first place?" (p. 3). It is to this question that he claims the principle of triangulation provides the answer.

Claims to propositional knowledge involve assertions of belief. However, as Davidson (1999) points out, one cannot be a believer unless one has the concept of belief, which, in turn, involves grasping the distinction between what is claimed to be true and what is actually true (i.e., the concept of *error*). Where, Davidson asks, "Do we get the idea that we may be mistaken, that things may not be as we think they are?" (p. 129). Drawing on Wittgenstein's interpretation of *following a rule*, Davidson proposes "that we would not have the concept of getting things wrong or right if it were not for our interactions with other people" (p. 129). Such interaction is, first and foremost, through *language*; we share our observations and beliefs about the world with others, and we note that from time to time, these do not correlate; therefore, one of us must be mistaken.

So, we arrive at the familiar but central idea that what really demarcates personhood, regardless of whatever underlying kind conveys identity and persistence on those entities that are actually persons, is the presence of *language*. Even more specifically, Davidson (1994) follows Socrates in highlighting the importance of *speech*: "Writing may portray, but cannot *constitute,* the inter-subjective exchanges in which meanings are created and firmed. Socrates was right: reading is not enough. If we want to approach the harder wisdom, we must talk and, of course, listen" (p. 432, emphasis added).

Being a person matters, I suggest, not because it is an important indicator of our actual identities and not because it sanctions the kind of self-centered view of the world that some would defend, but because we persons, whatever our underlying form or kind, regard the complex networks of relationships that we observe and in which we participate with a combination of respect and awe. Of course, many of nature's creations participate in such networks, from the smallest of entities to the largest. However, only persons can have a *perspective* or point of view with respect to what they can observe, and each person's perspective is both unique and informed by the perspectives of those with whom they come into contact. Indeed, when I observe, whether intellectually or experientially, the perspectives of others, I am simply enlarging and enriching my perspective of those others (e.g., when I understand your point of view, I understand something new about you).

The idea that the development of personhood—becoming a person—is, in part, a matter of forming and shifting perspectives was advocated by the pragmatist philosopher G. H. Mead, whose work on social theory and education has not always received the attention that it deserves. In several illuminating papers, psychologist Jack Martin (2007a, 2007b) explains the role of Mead's theory of *perspective realism* in both personal development and education. From an early age, we learn to shift perspectives between our own and those of others with whom we interact, typically in play but later in more formal educational contexts. Beginning pre-linguistically, pre-reflectively, and in such familiar concrete situations as game playing and evolving over time to language-dependent, reflective, and deliberative activities, such as seeing an issue from a range of perspectives and displaying empathy, children construct and participate in relational networks in which their personhood is defined and developed.

Perspective-taking, as understood by Martin (2007a, p. 439), is a nonreductive, relational exercise that calls upon both the child's cognitive and imaginative capacities (while strengthening both) to grasp, share, and manipulate "significant symbols," specifically language. Importantly, the relations in question are *triangular* in nature, suggesting a clear sense of continuity from Mead to Davidson to Martin (2007a): "All perspectives have their origins in our social interactivity with others. They arise and are maintained within social, collective acts involving two or more individuals, and they focus on social, collective objects...whose meanings are shared by the participating individuals" (p. 439).

What is it about us persons that impels us to develop a perspective of the world, including, as a central component, a perspective on others who also have perspectives? Is it merely a kind of self-absorption, the urge to look both inward to our own perspectives and outward to others only for the purpose of enhancing our own? This would be disappointing as it drags us back to a narrow, self-centered notion of personhood reminiscent of Jean Jacques Rousseau's (1984) *amour propre* (my sense of self as prideful, vain and dependent on the assessment of others). As already indicated, we may opt for a more symmetric framework here based on a realization of the inter-dependence of inward-looking and outward-looking perspectives. However, this opens up a new charge akin to *amour propre,* one grounded in the asymmetric preference for persons over nonpersons, such as the patriot who insists that he is altruistic and not selfish because he regards all of his fellow countrymen, not just himself, as superior to outsiders.

The Principle of Personal Worth (PPW)

The PPW and Animals

My response to this charge is to admit to it, indeed, to embrace it. Persons *are* more valuable, morally speaking, than nonpersons. *This is just what the PPW expresses.* Their distinctive moral status derives from the deceptively simple idea that those things that possess and utilize language possess properties that render them valuable in ways that non-language users are not. Although this claim may seem irreducibly self-serving on behalf of us persons, it is, I think, irresistible. I will say why shortly, but notice that the charge of moral selfishness is somewhat mitigated when one recalls that a *person* does not characterize or define any particular *kind* of entity (once we accept that not all humans are persons and, conceivably, not all persons are humans).

Why is this claim irresistible? For one thing, it is hard to imagine any functioning society not adhering to it: I hate the idea of killing any animal, but first, if we remember that flies, worms, and other creeping creatures are animals, I do so regularly, and secondly, if faced with the unpleasant choice of running over a dog—even my child's pet—and running over a child—even my child's bullying tormentor – our moral obligation here is clear. Further, it is no accident that much of our language—indeed, of any language of which I am aware—applies to those aspects of ourselves that are not entirely physical. The point is not just that we have an endless number of terms and phrases to describe how we feel, what we think, intend, desire, and so on, but that in uttering them, we describe and discriminate among aspects of our own lives and those of others that would otherwise remain not simply mysterious or hidden but empty of all but the barest animalistic content. It may be true that some species of birds have sophisticated calls that enable them to communicate with their fellows, much as young infant humans do with their first cries and murmurings of "Mama" or "Dada," but the degree of sophistication is relative here: it does not follow that birds—who, after all, have *bird-brains*—have much mental life to speak of. Indeed, if Davidson is right, they have precisely as much mental life as they do language.

Many years before formulating his account of triangulation as outlined above, Davidson (1970/2001b) articulated and defended a thesis known as "Anomalous Monism" (AM). Put briefly, AM asserts that the discourse used to "talk about" objects belonging to the mind *qua* realm of the mental, including Strawsonian P-predicates and, indeed, the mind itself, is (i) indispensable to any linguistic community that seeks to make rational sense of the world and its place in it, (ii) not reducible to the language of physics or any other law-governed domain, and (iii) referentially opaque in the sense that in so far as that discourse carries any ontological commitments (i.e., can be understood only by reference to actual real-world entities), the ontology in question is part of physics and not part of some shadowy mental or subjective realm called "mind." According to AM, there is no ontology of the mental, in particular, no entities, such as minds, thoughts, and so on, yet we cannot make sense of the world, particularly those aspects of it that involve *us* (including the processes of perspective-sharing, as discussed above) without talking 'about' *it*." Once we embark on the task of explaining or even describing what we do in terms of *any one of* our motives, beliefs, desires, hopes, fears, goals, intentions, and so on, we are committed, semantically, to an indefinite process in which our mental states and activities, along with those of others, are bound together in ever-more encompassing networks (in simpler terms, our beliefs and other attitudes do not come one by one but in combinations that become more complex as we probe them further). This is Davidson's thesis of the "Holism of the Mental," and it is the major component in his overall argument for AM. However, by the terms of AM, these networks are neither part of the physical world [whether of macro objects (e.g., ourselves) or micro objects (e.g., neuron firings)] nor part of any mental world; the only domain in which they can function is that of *language* itself (whose networks are both syntactic and semantic and are structured by logic as well as grammar). However, languages, whether taken collectively or one by one, exist in practice through the actions of language speakers, that is, persons. Even characteristic qualities, such as rational agency, whereby we make and act on judgments based on connected systems of beliefs, goals, motives, and so on according to accepted norms of logic and rationality, are entirely dependent on language.

Persons, at least of the human variety, are biological organisms whose origins and functions *qua organisms* are increasingly well-understood.

However, if, as recent work in the philosophy of biology has proposed, it is the broad concept of *living organism*, rather than the more specific *Homo sapiens* that determines the natural kind to which we belong, then we should not expect to find something deeply theoretical, let alone *a priori,* behind the PPW, at least with respect to the comparison between persons and other organisms. We might simply note the contingent truth that we humans have larger brains than other living organisms. One writer, Peter Carruthers (2011), has made a strong case for that part of the PPW that contrasts persons with other objects—most notably, nonhuman animals (i.e., not including those entities I have labeled as "supra-persons") in terms of the idea of rational agency (albeit without any specific reference to language). The outcomes of agency are, needless to say, actions, that is, intentional events that have consequences of one kind or another, and it is "natural" (a word I use with great trepidation and only because Carruthers uses it) to judge these consequences according to certain moral standards. In Carruthers' words, "moral rules are conceived to be constructed *by* rational agents *for* rational agents" (p. 4). Drawing on the kind of *contractualist* views about morality made famous by John Rawls (1972) and Thomas Scanlon (1998), Carruthers argues that all rational agents have the same moral standing. This is because it is simply natural—in a nonmoral sense, based on our basic emotional needs—to want to protect our own individual rights and interests and because rational agency involves being committed to governing our behavior according to universal rules. Taken together, rules enshrining rights, interests, and so on, will extend to all rational agents, thereby excluding (most) nonhuman animals but potentially including other kinds of person because of something called "the veil of ignorance," a device famously adopted by Rawls in his *A Theory of Justice*, to ensure that even self-serving moral rules should always be extended to others (simply put, the veil of ignorance compels rational agents to formulate general rules *without* the kind of knowledge about themselves—their abilities, tastes, social position, life goals, and so on—that would reveal how they would fare under such rules, so no individual who is party to the process knows how he or she would fare once the veil is lifted). As Carruthers explains, "The governing intuition behind this approach is that justice is fairness: since the situation behind the veil of ignorance is fair (all rational agents are equivalently placed), the resulting agreement must also be fair" (p. 3).

Carruthers (2011) proceeds to argue for two further theses that are somewhat relevant to the PPW: nonrational humans, notably human infants and "senile old people" (equivalent to those in a terminal vegetative state; I am not sure which label is more humane), should be included in the moral net suggested above (i.e., they should have the same moral standing as other persons), and nonhuman animals should be excluded (i.e., they do not have the same moral standing and do not make "direct moral claims" on us). The relevance of these claims to the PPW is somewhat indirect because Carruthers avoids the use of the term "person" altogether preferring, instead, to refer to *rational agents*. As previously noted, human infants (and presumably fetuses) are not yet rational agents, while the senile elderly once were but are no longer. So, if rational agency is an indicator of personhood, these two groups are excluded, regardless of their moral standing. I am sympathetic to this view because the individuals in question are not full members of any language community. However, while I do not specifically disagree with Carruthers' claims about the moral standing of these two groups, his style of argument is revealing. Concerning infants and the senile elderly, his thesis is based on a basic fact about *human nature*, namely, that people care as deeply for their immediate relatives as they do about anything or anyone else; accordingly, they would insist on the same moral treatment for them as for other rational agents. By contrast, the feelings that people hold toward animals, even their pets, are not as universally deep as those held toward close relatives. Even when the attachments are significant, they are simply less strong than those we hold toward other humans (as I observed above, when considering the choice between running over a human and running over a dog). Aware that someone might insist that a Rawlsian veil of ignorance should extend to the *species* of those involved when working out the edges of our moral net, Carruthers states:

> Amongst the intuitions that a good moral theory should preserve is the belief that someone's moral standing shouldn't depend upon such factors as their age, or gender, or race. In contrast we don't (or don't all) think that species is morally irrelevant. On the contrary, this is highly disputed, with (I would guess) a clear majority believing that differences of species (e.g. between human and dog) *can* be used to ground differential moral treatment. (p. 10)

This strikes me as a curious form of reasoning. After all, Carruthers emphasizes more than once that rational agents involved in such activities as determining the boundaries of their moral nets must *not* take moral considerations into account on pain of begging the question. This is why the basic thrust of his arguments relies on what agents would *actually* choose or prefer, based on assumptions about self-interest not on what they *ought to* choose or prefer. However, in the case of species differences, he appears to revert either to a simplistic moral preference or to the brute fact that nonhuman animals lack the capacity (the language?) to complain about or veto rules that would discriminate against them. (If and only if those millions of cattle—or even just a few "spokes-cows"—could say "Please don't kill and eat us!" then it would be wrong to do so!) And here we see the depth of the conceptual difficulty in attempting to justify our most basic moral claims (such as, the PPW with respect to human persons over animals). I am asking what is it about us that makes us special, morally speaking. If we answer in moral terms, we face a charge of question-begging. However, if we answer—à la Carruthers, for the most part—in factual, nonmoral terms, we seem destined to fall short of providing a sufficiently strong *moral* warrant for the point in question.

Before reflecting on how these considerations bear on the PPW, I should complete the argument put forward by Carruthers (2011). He realizes that for most people (rational agents), the idea of, say, torturing a cat is morally repugnant. The problem is how to accommodate the moral component here over and above a feeling of repugnance because he has concluded that cats have no real moral standing. He might have appealed to the familiar refrain that condemns causing unnecessary pain and suffering to any creature, but again the question is *why* this would be wrong (especially if the perpetrators benefited from their actions in some way). Ultimately, he retreats to a position that redirects the morality involved onto the agent, not the animal: "The action of torturing a cat is wrong because of what it shows about the moral character of the actor, not because it infringes any rights or is likely to cause distress to other people." (p. 13). The cat-torturing case shows the torturers to be *cruel,* for example. He continues:

> Our duties towards animals are indirect in the following way. They derive from the good or bad qualities of moral character that the actions in question would display and encourage; where those qualities *are* good or bad in virtue of the role that they play in the agent's interactions with other human beings. (p. 14)

Carruthers (2011) cites empirical evidence gathered by various associations for the prevention of cruelty to animals that suggests that a primary reason for prosecuting the perpetrators is precisely the likelihood that they will, or would, also be cruel to other humans. Still, he is prepared to concede that most people develop such virtues as kindness and beneficence by which they classify all acts of torture as cruel or "inhumane," even though, morally speaking, there is an asymmetry: humans do, while other animals do not, have moral standing in their own right.

One more point worth noting is that Carruthers (2011) does not refer to the moral status of (our actions toward) such entities as works of art, pristine forests, and the global environment. However, we may infer from his comments regarding nonrational agents and animals that he would regard such entities as items of *private property* and, accordingly, to be acted upon in accordance with their *owners'* rights and wishes. Such an anthropocentric view of things that were in existence long before we were is quite contentious. After all, it is not clear that anyone *owns* either the world or the environment.

I remarked above that nonhuman animals, such as cats and cows, do not count as persons—even if it should turn out that they are of the same fundamental natural kind as human beings—because they lack the physiological, neurological, and, therefore, cognitive capacity to construct and use language. It is this lack that I am suggesting entails the absence of such mentalistic dispositions as rational agency (which Carruthers uses to ground his arguments) and self-consciousness (indeed, I go further and endorse the view—which I attribute to Davidson, among others—that such dispositions are, in the final analysis, linguistic in nature). If language is the salient trait behind the PPW, we may still feel challenged by the question, "What is it about language that attracts qualities of moral worth and value, especially when contrasted with entities that lack it?"

Given the difficulties inherent in basing moral worth on differences that are not moral but empirical, it might move us forward to note that judgments of *value* and *worth* are not always ethical in nature. We also make judgments that are *aesthetic* (e.g., "What a fantastic movie!" or "J.S. Bach is the greatest composer.") and judgments that are, more literally, about matters of taste (e.g., "The food served there is delicious!" or "I think crunchy peanut butter is disgusting!"). Indeed, it has sometimes been suggested that aesthetic judgments are actually of a higher order than, and may be taken as grounding, moral or ethical judgments or, taking a more Platonic idealist stance, that the two types of judgment are of equal importance. We may see this kind of move when we deliberately use such terms as "integrity," "harmony," "wholeness," "graceful," and "elegant" to bridge the ethical and the aesthetic (e.g., murder and cheating are morally wrong—albeit of different degrees of wrongness—and both upset or violate the broader integrity or balance of things in nature). Suppose then that we attempt to base the moral status of language-bearing creatures on the sheer *beauty* that is both an inherent feature of each particular language (on account of its inter-relationships, if not also its sounds, shapes, and so on) and expressible through language. Earlier, I suggested that persons are uniquely placed as both observers of and participants in networks of relationships of various kinds and that they regard these networks with a combination of respect and awe. Such regard may be understood in aesthetic, as well as moral terms.

Granted, the difficulty raised above over the idea of an ultimate ground for morality—that it must be either question-begging or irrelevant—has its correlate in the aesthetic domain as well: unless the justification of such an aesthetic judgment as that language is inherently beautiful, wonderful, awesome, and so on is proclaimed by *fiat*, it would be either aesthetic in nature or grounded in some other field; which, once again, implies either circularity or irrelevance. The resolution of such fundamental questions is beyond the scope of both this essay and my ability; suffice it to say that the search for ultimate, fundamental, or basic premises in any field of inquiry, including the philosophical realms of ethics and aesthetics, is bound to be philosophically problematic.

Whatever we may take to be the precise connection between rational agency, morality, and personhood in terms of how we are to value and respect persons vis-à-vis nonpersons, I take it that the *subjects* of such actions as valuing and respecting must be persons. Specifically, *all*—and *only*—persons are *capable* of making ethical judgments (about what constitutes right and wrong, etc.) and, accordingly, are ethically bound to do so (Olson, 1997, p. 104). Even the law, in most cases, does not excuse the actions of someone who behaves in a drunken rage, for example, on the grounds that all but the most addicted individuals make choices (to drink or not to drink, etc.) whose consequences they should be able to foresee (because they are rational agents). What I am suggesting is that persons thus categorized, are also those who are participants in language communities and, thereby, in networks of relationships with other persons (as well as with nonpersons, while in the latter cases, the relationships are necessarily asymmetric in various ways: I may talk to my cat or my doll, but it does not *really* talk back; this is also true for infants, areas of pristine wilderness, etc.). It is no coincidence then that conceptions of both language and morality make sense only under the assumption that persons construct, participate in, and see themselves as participants in *relationships* of one sort or another. I will go further and suggest that the boundaries of such relationships (or networks of relationships) are not necessarily defined by differences in language, culture, religion, or anything else. The only relevant boundary is that between persons and nonpersons. Consider the case of language first, for I am claiming that its scope and limits prescribe the boundaries of all aspects of our personhood, including rationality and morality; it is an empirical truth that we can and do (if we choose to) find ways to communicate successfully with *anyone* else (provided that we are both language users). Granted, in practical terms, language is both a unifier and a divider, but it is important to understand that in referring to the concept of language *communities*, I am pointedly *not* intending to carve up such communities along the lines of our ordinary language differences (e.g., I am not referring to the community of English, French, or Cantonese speakers). Granted, I cannot readily communicate with a native of Hong Kong who does not speak English (because I, frustratingly, cannot speak Cantonese). However, we may surmount this barrier via some mode of *translation*, be it a dictionary, a bilingual companion, or a more painstaking process of shared reflection on how each of us uses words to pick out objects that belong to the realm of our common experience. Going back to Davidson's triangulation model, according to which my understanding of my own words and concepts is tied up with my understanding of both your words and concepts and those of the external world of which we are both part, we can see that the inter-dependence of the three sides of the triangle is required even *within* a particular language community; otherwise, I could have no confidence at all that when you and I use the same words, we mean or refer to the same thing by them. In this context, the notion of persons being in relation to one another is crucial to our understanding of what a person is in a way in which it is not crucial to our understanding of what a human being is. Granted, biologists will insist that we humans, like every species to a greater or lesser degree, interact with our environments, including those around us who are also humans, but putting the point in this way suggests that the distinctive quality of our humanness is a matter of *degree*. (In fact, there are other organisms that are, by their natures, much more interactive with one another, e.g., ants and bees.) But on the view of personhood, which I hold, our interaction with others— paradigmatically, via language—is a difference in *kind*.

As with language, so with morality. Once we accept both that the framework defined by the concept of a person is appropriate for prescribing the boundaries, or limits, of those characteristics that we ascribe to persons, and that these limits are determined by the limits of language and communication, then we can—indeed, I claim, we *must*— accept that the limits of our morality, likewise extend to include all persons. The notion that specific moral rules, norms, or values apply to one specific group of persons—the term "Asian values" comes to mind here—may be challenged by the transcendent power of language. I am not necessarily committing myself here to a universal code of ethics— although I am inclined to be so committed—but to the more modest yet still far-reaching claim that once we find ways to communicate with those who are, in some ways, *different*, we may join in a dialogue in which both sides may participate, a dialogue that enables each person, in principle, to *empathize* with each other person (i.e., to attempt at least to see things from the *perspective* of the other). We may or may not come to agree on points of difference, ethically speaking (concerning the role of women, the moral status of homosexuality, the value of the collective over the individual, and so on), but you have the right to ask me to explain and/or justify my beliefs or traditions, and I, as a participant in the broad community of persons, am obliged to respond.

The PPW and Supra-persons

The idea of an interconnected network of interpersonal relationships—a network of networks—begins with the most intimate of relationships (parents, family, close friends, etc.) and extends to and beyond barriers of local community, nationhood, ethnicity, culture, religion, and all the other classifications that we apply to persons to embrace again, in principle, *all* persons, even those—if there are such—of kinds different from ourselves. However, as history has repeatedly shown, the luring power of some groups or collectives to persuade vulnerable individuals that they are not merely different from, but superior to, others is strong. By "group or collective," I mean more than a collection of individual persons; rather, a group in this strong sense is characterized by forces that imbue it with a power and status that go beyond the sum of its individual members. It may be defined by a set of specific properties or features (as with religion, ethnicity, etc.) but not necessarily so. Either way, the outcome is strict lines of inclusion and exclusion, often with devastating consequences. Once the Nazis convinced themselves and others that Jews, Gypsies, Slavs, and homosexuals were not members of the "Master Race" of "pure-blooded Aryans," the next step—absurd when you think about it—was to rule that they were also outside the realm of *persons* and, as such, could be treated as mere objects or worse. If we needed an actual argument to reveal why such a move is nonsensical, we could point out that as members of a language community, these individuals qualified as persons in the richest sense possible and could not, in any nonarbitrary sense, be excluded from the moral domain.

What then do we make of the moral value, status and worth of such "supra-persons" as nations, cultures, ethnicities (or ethnic groups), corporations, clubs, gangs, and cults? They may be constituted by persons but are greater than the sums of these constituent parts. By contrast, a group or class of persons is just that: a collection of individual persons that is *no* greater than the sum of its constituents. By the formal definition of a class, if you change one member, you replace one class with another. It follows immediately that while supra-persons can endure through long stretches of time, an ordinary group lasts only as long as its members survive as members. (It may be that a particular gang or cult will last only as long as its charismatic leader, but this is a contingent exception to the rule; cultures, religions, nations, and corporations have histories and traditions that are at least as important as any individual members, and the latter inevitably come and go over time.)[1]

I am not questioning the notion that these supra-persons exist, that they may have considerable value and worth, or that individual persons may derive great benefits from belonging to them—benefits that may include their very survival. However, I am questioning, indeed rejecting, the notion that these supra-persons have a value or worth—and here I am thinking in moral terms—that exceeds that of individual persons (whether or not those persons are their constituents). Consider, for example, the following statements:

1. "Same sex marriage would destroy the (sanctity of *the*) *family* and/or the moral autonomy of *religion*."
2. "The (harmony of the) state is more important than the (well-being of the) individuals in it."
3. "To die for one's faith or country (martyrdom) is glorious."
4. "Fiscal austerity is the only way to restore the federal budget to a surplus."
5. "It is wrong for Western families to adopt orphans from impoverished countries because it violates their cultural integrity/identity."

Each of these examples displays a clear violation of PPW, whereby the rights and well-being of one or more actual persons are subjugated to those of the broader collective. Part of the problem here is that it is often unclear exactly *what* the larger entity (supra-person) is. For example, does "the family" in Example 1 refer to an abstract institution—in which case it is hard to see how the claim could be justified other than by fiat or some kind of historical distortion (e.g., ignoring the many types of family that have existed throughout human history)—or to a majority/large/significant number of actual families – in which case the claim may, at least, submit to empirical testing? However, (a) I know of no such tests that provide any empirical support for Example 1, and (b) if *the family* here is merely a collection of individual families, then Example 1 is no longer a counter-example to PPW. It is just an implausible claim that pits the well-being of one entity against others of the same type. Much the same can be said in respect of the alleged threat to that abstract entity described here as "the moral autonomy of religion." It is common-place in many so-called democracies, including Australia and the USA, for blatant discrimination in employment, group membership, etc. (on whatever grounds, but usually relating to sexual orientation, marriage status of women with children, and so on) to be overlooked by the law if the discriminator acts in the name of religion. For example, where a public school may not refuse employment to a qualified teacher because he or she is homosexual or transgender, a parochial or religious school may do just that. If pressed, the employer may cite cases of actual or hypothetical cases of harm caused by such previous hirings, but such empirical evidence is rarely required. It is enough in the eyes of the law that the religion in question proscribes homosexuality, sex out of wedlock, etc. So, actual individuals suffer in the name of protecting an institution or tradition. It seems clear to me that in such situations, the ordinary meanings of terms like "harm," "threat," "autonomy," and "protecting" are in danger of being lost because in their most familiar usage, they apply to relationships between or among persons. As previously emphasized, where actual persons are at real risk of harm, PPW does not apply.

With regard to Example 2, while the individual that is the state (or nation) may be somewhat more well-defined than "the family," the statement in question may also reduce to one that compares large with small and rules in favor of the former. A socialist or communist state is often defended in terms of what is best—albeit in the long term—for all (i.e., for *each and every*) members of it (e.g., it is only a common love of the Motherland that stands in the way of social disintegration and a much worse situation for many more individuals). In critiquing such instances, my point is not to substitute some version of individualism for collectivism, even if the latter's violation of the PPW appears more blatant. Although collectives that become greater than the sum of their own constituent parts inevitably impose their own demands as "baggage" on their members, individualism in the socio-political sense allows and indeed encourages those who are stronger, wealthier, and more powerful to impose on those who are less so. It is hard to see how such a system could respect the second part (Part B) of the PPW, which demands equality of value and respect among all persons. Concerning Example 3, interestingly, where soldiers of Western nations are (usually) revered for serving their country, the more so if they are killed while doing so, those same nations condemn the mentality of leaders who send youngsters to die as martyrs for what they view as an alien cause. Still, dying for any cause that is not directly linked to the well-being of others is a dubious enterprise, the more so when those most directly involved have little real say in the matter. Example 4 is the oft-heard battle cry of "dry" conservatives who claim to value individual initiative but, as history has repeatedly shown, are prepared to sacrifice the well-being of those who cannot make it to the top on the altar of the "free" market. Such thinking is enabled by allowing several key assumptions to go unquestioned; for example, that such entities as *markets* and *budget surpluses* have a value or worth that outweighs that of individuals, and that these entities are given status and respectability within a discipline—in this case Economics—that has pretensions to be a genuine *science,* in which persons are reduced to figures and quantities, much as they are reduced to micro-particles within physics.

Finally, my interest in Example 5 was sparked by a conversation with a friend, who expressed the view that Westerners who adopt poor orphans from Africa or Asia are behaving imperialistically, notwithstanding their noble intentions. But, however we characterize imperialism—usually defined in terms of a desire, policy, or practice of extending the authority of one nation, culture, or even religion over that of another—, the core issue here is not whether these potential parents (some of whom, but not all, are unable to have biological children of their own) are being imperialistic (for most, this would be furthest from their minds), but whether by their actions real persons would be better off in some clear sense. When my cousin and her partner adopted an Ethiopian infant and proceeded to raise him as an American Jew, there is little doubt that they saved him from, at best, a short and impoverished life. Regardless of his subsequent desires (e.g., to find his birth parents, learn about his indigenous culture, even to spurn his acquired family and/or culture and/or religion), *that* he survives to do these things sufficiently justifies their actions.

It might be thought that those entities I have designated supra-persons ought to, at least on some occasions, be regarded as persons in their own right, precisely because they exhibit chains of communication and connectedness that are more or less linguistic in nature. Do nations, religions, corporations, gangs, cults, or even cultures qualify as persons because they have language? If so, then they should have the same moral status as other persons. It is doubtless true that the power and resilience of these groups have much to do with their capacities for communication and expression, both inwardly (among their own members) and outwardly (connecting to those outside the collective). More to the point, such entities have *histories* and *narratives*, whether oral or written, about where they have been and, perhaps, where they are and/or *should be* going. However, who are the narrators here, and what is the status of these narratives with respect to defining the essential nature of the supra-persons to which they relate? Are they just like those that ordinary persons may tell about themselves and their relationships with others? I think not. For one thing, divine revelation notwithstanding, the only plausible source of such narratives are individual persons with the power to experience, conceptualize, interpret, store, record, recall, and retell what is going on around them. Similar to ethical norms, prescriptions, and codes that may develop a status over and beyond that of any individual members, they, too, emerge from the deliberations and reflections—whether democratically conducted or not—of actual persons. Moreover, it is inevitably those individuals who hold the reins of power and authority whose voices are heard and recorded. If the entities in question are persons, they are extremely strange persons.

Could these supra-persons function according to basic principles of equality and respect, as reflected in Part B of the PPW? This would mean, for example, that nations, gangs, and corporations would not only treat other nations, gangs, and corporations as equals—something rarely seen in practice—but that they would treat *all* persons as equals, including those persons who belong to them, as well as those who do not, that is, *all* citizens, *all* gang members, *and* all members of corporations. However, this is precisely what does *not* occur. To the contrary, it is in the nature of these supra-entities that they regard themselves as having greater value and worth than their members, that is, than even the sum total of their members. It is this exalted value that distinguishes them from those groups that are merely collections or classes of individual persons.

Becoming a Person

An important consequence of the PPW, as applied to those collectives and associations that are greater than the sums of their parts (i.e. supra persons in my terminology), is that being—I prefer to say *becoming*—a person does not consist of and may not even involve being or becoming a member of one or more such collectives. Here I am rejecting a view that is more or less taken for granted in much of contemporary social science (including cultural and political studies), according to which (i) as persons, we need to have, or to secure, our *identities* (i.e., plural answers to the question "Who am I?") and (ii) these identities are provided, in some sense, by our belonging to and associating with just such supra entities as I have been discussing. To the contrary, I claim that (i) the issue of identity *per se* is irrelevant to our personhood because identity is determined by the kind of being that we are and (ii) in so far as I do have a sense of myself as a person, although that sense may be enhanced or enriched by my group associations and memberships, it does not require them and is certainly not constituted by them.

It is important to distinguish between identity and the common human—or personal—desire to *identify with* others who are like us in some way (same nationality, same religion, same neighborhood, same ethnicity, same sexuality, etc.). That these concepts are distinct is evident once we reflect that while identification is a matter of registering salient similarities, identity, taken literally, is as much about *distinctness*—that which makes me uniquely who or what I am—as it is about similarity. One likely consequence of ignoring this distinction is that individuals will characterize the so-called search for their identity as a search to identify a particular association or collective (i.e. supra-person) that most accurately "defines" them. There are two problems with this line of thinking:

1. It tempts people to commit what Amartya Sen (2006) labeled the "Fallacy of Singular Identification," whereby they regard one such association as overriding or exclusive (p. 20ff). Even conceding that the strength of one's attachment will be determined largely by socio-cultural considerations—the result of generations of oppression, persecution, existential denial, and so on—does not appear to stop some from *defining* themselves as *quintessentially* gay, Muslim, Chinese, and so on. However, as with all such supra-personal attachments, to place oneself so determinedly, so passionately, on the *inside* is, *ipso facto,* to place others on the *outside*, as fundamentally "other." Sen's point is that we will find it much more difficult to play the "inside/outside" game if we keep in mind that each of us belongs to many such groups, the more so if we consciously try to identify what we might have in common with others who are otherwise so different from us.

2. The alleged need to identify with such collectives and associations, whether one or many, is in my view overrated. The social commentator David Berreby (2005), in his fascinating study of the phenomenon of group affiliations, writes that "human kinds [including my supra-persons but also the myriad of groups that we identify with in the course of our lives] offer the joy of belonging to something larger than the little self" (p. 20). He then adds "that consistency [which characterizes much of the behavior of members of a given "kind"] makes it easy to

think of this sort of human kind as if it were a person itself—a being with thoughts, plans and feelings of its own." However, he does not seem to be aware of the dangers inherent in such "as if" assertions. As I have already noted, to classify human kinds or supra-persons *as* persons is to run the risk of accepting entities who, by definition, must always be more powerful and more influential than other persons. I prefer the sentiment echoed by the teenager who, when asked if her "Goth" all-black attire and accoutrements (hair, jewelry, etc.) reflected a problem of identity, retorted: "Not at all: I know who I am, and it is not defined by any of this stuff which I could give up tomorrow if I chose to." In so far as she identifies with a particular collective, this person believes (correctly, one trusts) that she controls her association with it, not the other way round.

I grant that, to borrow Berreby's own words, we persons need to be connected to something larger than the little self. However, this larger thing may be just a relational network of two or more persons, that is, a group or class in precisely the *non* supra-personal sense of the term. To reiterate, it is not that there is anything essentially wrong with identifying with one's nation, ethnic group, tribe, religion, and so on, *as long as* one has a prior and independent understanding of *who one is*. We may, from time to time, change our memberships and affiliations with such groups (through migration, conversion, leaving the tribe, etc.) without either the loss of identity (which I have suggested is conceptually impossible unless we cease to exist) or the *fear* of such a loss. The latter, in so far as it is linked to our reflective awareness of our sense of self, is allayed by the realization that each of us is "one among others," that is, each of us is a member of various inter-personal networks that define the course of our lives as persons.

Persons and Education

How, when, and where, we must now ask, do we begin the task of weaving ourselves into these networks? We do not do so, I suggest, by simply sitting back and accepting the consequences of belonging to those various collectives and associations that crowd in from Day 1. I was born a Jew, male, and Australian. I became an English speaker, left-handed, gay, philosophically inclined, and musical. I joined choirs, tennis clubs, youth groups, and so on. However, none of these associations can be relied upon to provide just the right sense of balance between my own sense of self and my sense of being one-among-others. Some, such as my membership in the tennis club, are too innocuous or too slight (even if cherished), while others, such as my nationality and my religion, have their own agendas as "supra-persons" (even if they, too, were cherished). No, we weave ourselves into these networks simply by being part of them, as I have previously remarked, from the most intimate to the more remote (but still *personal*).

However, something is still missing here. Put in these terms, the task of becoming a person through these expanding processes of weaving and networking leaves too much up for grabs. What is to prevent the supra-persons which inevitably include us from distorting our sense of personhood? Here, at the last, I turn to that device that is so familiar to all those involved in doing philosophy with children: the structured environment, which, in its ideal form, cultivates each individual's reflective sense of being *one among others*. I am referring to the *community of inquiry* (CI). When we speak of the CI as a crucial ingredient or determinant of personhood, such talk is—or should be—not merely rhetorical. Becoming a person involves coming to see oneself as one-among-others in relational networks, connected linguistically and ethically, where the significance of the phrase "one-among-others" is a balanced sense of equality: my awareness of my own value and self-worth is intrinsically linked to *your* awareness of my value and worth, which, in turn, is linked to my awareness of *your* value and worth and your awareness of your own value and worth. If this seems like a convoluted version of the "Golden Rule" of reciprocity, which, in one form or another, grounds just about every known normative ethical view, I concede that it is, but it also shows how reciprocity functions in the CI, given that its members are both self-aware and aware of one another in equal measure. Indeed, the link may be enlarged further by reference to Davidson's notion of triangulation, according to which not only our sense of mutual awareness of ourselves and one another but also our mutual awareness of a common world, is brought into the relational network.[2] After all, is this not what a CI is all about? The processes of learning about the world, learning about ourselves, and learning about one another are all interdependent and mutually reinforcing, and we know all too well what can happen when one of these three elements becomes imbued with too much importance: *either* the individual retreats inside her own subjectivity, unwilling or unable to form a perspective or make a judgment that is not self-centered; *or* the individual gives up her sense of self to the point where she no longer sees herself as an agent in the world of thinking and knowledge construction. Further, the second disjunction is itself a disjunction between investing the power to think, know, and understand in a more powerful "other" (usually the teacher) and reducing that power to something wholly objective and impersonal (as when learners see themselves as passive recipients of hard truths about an already-formed reality).

I should acknowledge a natural extension of Davidson's model here. It may be that the base of the triangle, namely, the link between myself and others, requires merely the existence of one other speaker with whom I can communicate (as Davidson sometimes suggests). However, a more reliable base for genuine knowledge involves a larger number of such speakers. In practice, we play off a range of assertions and beliefs as we work out which ones stand up to standards of reason, evidence, and justification. Such a range is provided within a cooperative *community* of thinkers, all of whom are inquiring after truth by way of determining, interpreting, and evaluating what is presented to them. Interestingly, while it is not clear that he intended to make the shift from a single interlocutor to a community, Davidson (2001c) writes that "a community of minds is the basis of knowledge; it provides the measure of all things" (p. 218).

In a genuine CI—or, at least, one in the process of formation—the required balance is maintained by the vigilance of its own members. For in this admittedly idealized construction, the community itself is *nothing more or beyond the sum of its parts*, bound together relationally as described above. It is, for this very reason, utterly unlike those "supra-persons" discussed earlier, which take on a status greater than the individuals who constitute them (the nation, the family, the tribe, etc.).

Finally, while it hardly needs to be said, the essential constituent of personhood (so I have maintained), namely, *language*, lies at the heart of the CI, just as it does in Davidson's metaphor of triangulation. Dialogue does far more than merely represent or communicate that which has already been thought. Dialogue provides the possibility for the community itself, that is, each and every one of its members, to *think*. As persons, we have many qualities, but if they and we are to flourish, we must pay more attention to language and urge our families, schools, and governments to do likewise.

References

Avramides, A. (1999). Davidson and the new skeptical problem. In U. M. Zeglen (Ed.), *Donald Davidson: Truth, meaning and knowledge* (pp. 136–154). London: Routledge.

Berreby, D. (2005). *Us & them: The science of identity.* Chicago: University of Chicago Press.

Carruthers, D. (2011). Against the moral standing of animals. In C. Morris (Ed.), *Practical ethics: Questions of life and death.* New York: Oxford University Press. Retrieved from www.philosophy.umd.edu/Faculty/pcarruthers/The%20Animals%20Issue.pdf

Davidson, D. (1982). Rational animals. *Dialectica, 36,* 317–328.

—. (1994). Dialectic and dialogue. In G. Preyer, F. Siebelt, & A. Ulfig (Eds.), *Language, mind and epistemology* (pp. 429–437). Dordrecht, The Netherlands: Kluwer Academic.

—. (1995). The problem of objectivity. In D. Davidson (Ed.), *Problems of rationality* (pp. 3–18). Oxford, England: Oxford University Press.

—. (1998). The irreducibility of the concept of self. In D. Davidson (Ed.), *Subjective, intersubjective, objective* (pp. 85–91). Oxford, England: Oxford University Press.

—. (1999). The emergence of thought. In D. Davidson (Ed.), *Subjective, intersubjective, objective* (pp. 123–134). Oxford, England: Clarendon. Retrieved from http://www.jstor.org/stable/20012936

—. (2001a). Epistemology externalized. In D. Davidson (Ed.), *Subjective, intersubjective, objective* (pp. 193–204). Oxford, England: Clarendon.

—. (1970/2001b). Mental events. In *Essays on actions and events* (pp. 207–225). Oxford, England: Clarendon.

—. (2001c). Three varieties of knowledge. In D. Davidson (Ed.), *Subjective, intersubjective, objective* (pp. 205–220). Oxford, England: Clarendon.

Martin, J. (2007a). Educating communal agents: Building on the perspectivism of G.H. Mead. *Educational Theory, 57,* 435–452.

—. (2007b). Interpreting and extending G.H. Mead's "metaphysics" of selfhood and agency. *Philosophical Psychology, 20,* 441–456.

Olson, E. (1997). *The human animal: Personal identity without psychology.* New York: Oxford University Press.

Quine, W. (1960). *Word and object.* Cambridge, MA: MIT Press.

Rawls, J. (1972). *A theory of justice.* New York: Oxford University Press.

Rousseau, J. J. (1984). *A Discourse on inequality* (M. Cranston, Trans.). New York: Penguin.

Scanlon, T. (1998). *What we owe to each other.* Cambridge, MA: Harvard University Press.

Sen, A. (2006). *Identity and violence: The illusion of destiny.* New York: Norton.

Strawson, P. F. (1959/1990). *Individuals: An essay in descriptive metaphysics.* London: Routledge.

Wiggins, D. (2001). *Sameness and substance renewed.* Cambridge, England: Cambridge University Press.

Notes

1. In this context, I am not referring to such biological supra-individuals as beehives and ant colonies; whatever their status, they pose no challenge, morally or politically speaking, to individual persons and are, therefore, irrelevant to the PPW.

2. Avramides (1999) provided a nice summary statement of Davidson's position here: "So, while we find that our knowledge of the world depends on the communication between persons, we also find that the communication between persons depends on our recognition that we occupy a shared world" (p. 148).

PART II:

PHILOSOPHY FOR CHILDREN IN THE SERVICE OF SOCIAL AND POLITICAL AIMS

CHAPTER FIVE

TEACHING ETHICS RESPONSIBLY: BRINGING GLOBAL AWARENESS TO THE CLASSROOM

JON ROGERS
WILLIAM PATERSON UNIVERSITY

The demographics of American classrooms have become significantly more heterogeneous and diverse over the past several generations. Moral and ethical curricula, however, have not been keeping pace with these changes. By and large, they remain entrenched within a predominantly Western analytical tradition that is becoming increasingly outdated. Many of the contemporary curriculum models that currently pass for educating students in moral and ethical matters have proven themselves to be inadequate to meet the demands of a multicultural classroom. If students are to possess global perspectives when they are considering matters of right and wrong, there must be concerted efforts toward teaching ethics in a context that is relevant to the realities of the classroom. This means that both the curricula and pedagogy need to be revised to provide cognizance of the diversified cultures, beliefs, and values that students bring with them into the classroom.

The demographics of the classroom in America are becoming significantly more heterogeneous and diverse as they have been for the past few generations. The ethics curriculum, however, has by and large retained its traditional roots despite these shifts. Specifically, what currently passes for educating students in moral and ethical matters is too entrenched in the Western analytic tradition to meet the demands of a multicultural classroom. I argue that schools fail to meet the needs of their students by not updating and adapting the ways in which they educate them in ethical and moral matters. When an educator is not sensitive to the variety of contexts from which her students come, she cannot teach ethics in a truly representative and inclusive fashion. If we want students to think on a global scale when considering questions of right and wrong, we need to make a concerted effort to teach ethics on a similar scale. I do not propose to give any kind of exhaustive account of what such an effort would entail, as it lies outside the scope of this chapter. My offerings here are limited to some thoughts about why some features are necessary for ethics education and why some of the features found in at least one of the current models are detrimental and should not be included.

Although the Western perspective is certainly a very important and influential one in ethical theory, it is also just that, a single perspective, that is, by definition too narrow and negligent to pay satisfactory attention to perspectives that lie outside of its own set of customary practices. Among those that are too commonly excluded from the curriculum design process include Asian philosophies from the likes of India and China, feminist ethics, ethics of care, the practices of empathy and mindfulness, and other postmodern European theories that do not see ethics as a necessarily rational study. I believe that these glaring absences may be addressed through the presentation of ethical matters in a more cosmopolitan manner, one that is sensitive to the variety of contexts that the students bring with them into the classroom. An awareness of the global dimensions present can play a significant role in shaping not just the content of the course material but even more importantly the procedural thinking skills that are necessary for any meaningful understanding or application of the content at hand. If we are at all concerned with developing a framework for ethical and moral education that is both relevant and useful to as many students as possible, we also ought to be concerned with how representative our approach is. This means that we can no longer afford to remain decidedly unilateral in either our pedagogy or our curriculum content. They must both become more global.

The need for discrete moral and ethics education in the schools has been evidenced in the steadily increasing calls for the public to pay greater attention to how a student's character is developed during his or formative years and to facilitate its process. However, as Tim Sprod (2001) noted,[1] it is a notoriously difficult thing to reach any kind of meaningful consensus, especially in the heavily pluralistic society of America, about just what exactly it means to be moral, much less how to effectively teach it. One of the methods for addressing this problem to achieve popularity in American schools has been to equate moral education with character education (Britzman, 2005; Ellenwood, 2007; Zara, 2000). Models of character education vary widely in their respective structuring and methodologies, but they all build upon the same foundation of a selected list of character traits serving as the ideals for which the students are taught to strive. The lists themselves also vary to some degree, but the extent of overlap between most of the character education models is such that many of the same words, such as *responsibility, pride, fairness,* and *citizenship,* invariably appear.

I believe that the idea of using character-education-based models as ethical curricula for students is a fundamentally flawed one. The problem is not that such models fail to live up to their claims of educating students in matters of an ethical and moral nature but rather that any approach to facilitating ethical and moral understanding that focuses on adherence to an objective set of criteria will fail to achieve the prime directive underlying ethics education—the application of principles. The learning and understanding of ethical or moral principles amount to nothing if a student is unable to apply them whenever and wherever the situation demands, and I believe that because of the objective nature of character education models, they are deficient at developing the thinking skills necessary for applying abstract and theoretical principles to real-world situations. I feel that such equivocations are only further begging the question because the question only shifts to asking what kinds of character traits are deemed to be moral ones. Starnes (2006) commented that most programs and those who support them typically cite lists of traits that are to be taken as the central pillars supporting character development. When it comes to educating students on how to develop such traits, however, the problem is that these terms are presented as things that are concrete, straightforward, and commonly understood between people. Teaching for any one of these characteristics—let alone all of them—does not seem to be any more of a tangible endeavor than teaching students to develop their moral sensibilities. In a recent clearinghouse report published by the U.S. Department of Education and the Institute of Education Sciences, 93 studies of 41 different character education programs were examined. Of all the 41 programs, 13 were qualified by their standards for review. The programs were reviewed on the basis of their effectiveness in teaching three different domains: behavior; knowledge, attitude, and values; and academic achievement. None of the reviewed programs demonstrated a "strong positive effect with no overriding contrary evidence" (p. 2) in all three of the domains, and only one program demonstrated this distinction in two of the three domains. Six of the thirteen programs had no discernible effect of any kind. It may well be debatable as to which particular domains of a student's abilities moral and ethical values speak, but it seems reasonable to assume that, at the least, the concept of morality involves contemplation of eudemonistic values ("the right thing to believe") and ethical concepts involve discerning how we ought to go about realizing such values ("the right thing to do"). In more succinct terms, morality involves beliefs, and ethics involves actions. These concepts correlate very closely with the domains of behavior and knowledge, attitudes, and values. If character education is being used as the means of covering the bases for moral and ethics education, so to speak, it appears that something is getting lost in the translation. My intent here is not to argue against the validity of character education at all; I do think it deserves and has its own place in the curriculum. My only point of contention is it being used to fulfill a role for which it is not designed, and I am not singling it out as being particularly egregious in its transgressions. The same problems and questions will exist when one tries to subsume moral and ethics education into any other context, whether it be education for principles, standards, manners, conduct, or goals. If we are to take the education of morals and ethics seriously, we must treat them as the distinct areas of academic and practical discipline that they are.

My belief about why all of these substitution methods will come up short in their effectiveness lies not in how they are trying to teach moral and ethical development but rather in what they are trying to teach. More specifically, the aims of such programs invariably target the teaching of content and not procedural skills. Because nailing down just what constitutes moral thinking has been demonstrated as a notoriously difficult thing to do (Beck & Murphey, 1994; Davis, 1993; Giroux, 1993; Goodman, 2006; Tappan, 2006), it should not be much of a surprise that the efforts made at trying to pick out and develop any certain set of characteristics will necessarily be, to some degree, arbitrary and biased toward the personal and professional views of the author; the confusion that inevitably results from all of the different conflicting ideas about which set of traits is the most appropriate one for students to learn.

Perhaps a better means of approaching the problem is to instead develop a pedagogy that teaches the students to develop the skills associated with making moral judgments and taking ethical actions. One of the primary advantages of this approach is that the thinking skills involved in the formation of moral judgments enjoy a greater amount of consensus (though by no means unanimous) than any particular skill or skill set does. In fact, the main point of contention surrounding procedural thinking-skills-based approaches to moral and ethics education is not so much what the necessary skills are but whether those skills are transferrable across the curriculum.

Teaching for moral and ethical development will, at best, be of limited value if what is being taught cannot be employed within a variety of different contexts. We need to know how to make judgments as they relate to the natural sciences, the social sciences, the arts, and the humanities; against various historical backgrounds; within literary works; in the conceptualization of mathematical problems; and so on. The question for those advocating the thinking-skills approach thus becomes whether there is such a thing as generic, transferrable thinking skills or whether thinking skills are inherently relative to the context of the discipline in which they are used. The debate over this question has been illustrated in the academic literature in the form of an ongoing debate about the transferability of critical thinking skills; it began in the 1980s between John McPeck and Mathew Lipman. Although the specific criteria for what constitutes critical thinking has and still does vary to some degree (Ennis, 1991; Lewis & Smith, 1993; Lipman, 2003), there remains a general acknowledgment of the importance of its inclusion in the curriculum. On one side of the debate, McPeck (1981) argued that the term *critical thinking* is an empty concept in and of itself. It has meaning only insofar as it applies to the specific context in which it is taught. Thus, there is no such thing as generic critical thinking; there is only the practice of critical thinking in some larger discipline. The ability to think critically in biology, for example, is different from the ability to think critically in history, and this ability is also different in art, reading, language, math, and so on. All an educator can hope to do is teach her students how to think critically within her own particular area of specialty.

On the other side of the debate, Lipman (2003) responded to McPeck's (1981) claims by agreeing with him that critical thinking does indeed have a relative-to-context element to it. However, there does happen to be one distinct discipline that is uniquely well suited to its development. That discipline happens to be philosophy, and the special connection that he saw between the two contributed to his designing of the Philosophy for Children curriculum, which proposes to facilitate the development of students' thinking and reasoning skills through philosophical inquiry and dialogue. Lipman defined *critical thinking* as "thinking that (1) facilitates judgment because it (2) relies on criteria, (3) is self-correcting, and (4) is sensitive to context" (p. 116). There are a large variety of topical discussions that fall under the general umbrella of philosophy (aesthetics, social and political, metaphysical, phenomenological, morality, and ethics). Most if not all of the subtopics of philosophy are related to other disciplines already in place in the general school curriculum—there is the philosophy of science and art; social and political philosophy tie in very closely with the subjects of civics and social studies; and primary reading from the history of philosophy, such as Plato's *Republic* and Camus' *The Stranger,* have a place in any upper level English literature or language arts class. It should therefore be possible, at least in theory, for teachers to engage with their students in discussions of a philosophical nature that also have direct implications for issues occurring in other courses. The underlying assumption of this theory is that the philosophy card is already in the curriculum deck so to speak, and it just needs to be drawn and played. The connections between disciplines are natural ones, and they are already in place. It becomes the teacher's job to draw out those connections and make them accessible to the students.

It makes sense to talk about philosophy as part of a school's curriculum when one considers moral and ethics education because, if it is true that philosophical inquiry and dialogue can be used as a forum for the development and practice of the skills that students can in turn transfer and apply to the rest of the curriculum, there may be some hope for the justification of moral and ethics education as discrete disciplines. It seems readily apparent that at least some aspects of philosophy make their way into other disciplines much in the same manner as mathematics shares a relationship with music, health and physical education, history, political science, and so on. What is less clear is whether every part of philosophy can be transferred over and applied to every other subject area. It is possible that some philosophical concepts only have relevancy outside of their own discipline, whereas others do not. How can we know whether morals and ethics are transferrable. If they are not, does this hurt the argument for including them in the school curriculum? It is my belief that this question misperceives the nature of moral and especially ethics education (the latter of which I hereafter give special consideration), and as such, the question of transferability is ultimately an irrelevant one.

As stated earlier, ethics involves the study of right actions. Deliberating upon the appropriate course of action to take is an unavoidable part of daily life that has become entrenched in a person's automatic functions in a way similar to other perceptual and cognitive faculties, such as associating names with faces. If one has ever been at all concerned about his or her decision making enough to stop and reflect on the deliberation process and what goes into it, one has displayed an interest in ethical matters. No matter what the issue at hand happens to be, if it involves taking action, it includes an ethical component. It is difficult to think of any part of the educational process that does not aim toward and culminate in action. It would be nothing short of a nonstarter for a teacher to say that she was educating her students without having an interest in or a concern for how they act on the knowledge that they acquire and the understanding that they gain. Therefore, I believe that it is reasonable to assert that the transferability of ethics across the curriculum is not a topic of concern for educators because we can show that ethics is already an integrated component of the curriculum. The manner in which it manifests itself will indeed vary and depend on the larger context (i.e., the nature of ethical discourse will look different when the ethical considerations are brought up in a civics class, science lab, history lesson, etc.), but no matter what the context is, the nature of the discourse will always retain the same basic qualities: conceptual, normative thinking about the reasonableness of the implications and consequences resulting from a proposed course of action. Because ethics possesses the characteristics of context specificity while still retaining a substantive body of disciplinary skill specific unto itself, it deserves the same special consideration afforded to the other academic disciplines within a school's curriculum. The pluralist nature of ethical thought also requires that educators who are teaching the development of thinking skills take advantage of the value that it can add to a discussion by supplementing the content material with ideas for further investigation and imperatives for taking the discussion beyond the classroom. The expectation is that when a student learns not just the *how* of an issue but also the *why* and the *ought* of it as well, a meaningful understanding with deeply personal significance to the student can finally begin to take place.

I close with a comment and suggestion for the new direction in which we should be looking for help in making ethics education an even more viable component of the curriculum. The entire enterprise of ethics education will be lost, however, if we fail to be sufficiently cosmopolitan in our teachings. The demographics of the classroom are changing (and have been so for a while); if ethics education wants to be taken seriously, it must also adapt itself to the changing educational landscape. This means that its own curriculum must be updated to include new developments in conceptual theories, new perspectives on the old ones, and the knowledge of how to apply them to examples that are contemporary and relevant. The content materials used in social studies, history, and science are in a continual state of revision; indeed, if they were not, they would cease to remain worthwhile academic pursuits. Ethics education has admittedly stayed relatively stagnant in its development, and it does so at its own peril of obsolescence. Ann Sharp (2005), one of the primary contributors to the Philosophy for Children curriculum and a close associate of Mathew Lipman, acknowledged this lack of perspective within the ethics curriculum and within other areas of philosophical pedagogy:

> Back [in the 1970s] when we were writing the "Lisa" novel [a narrative text designed for presenting ethical ideas and problems for middle-school aged students] we knew that we were neglecting the Eastern perspectives

and the feminist perspectives and the more modern ones. We just didn't know them. And we didn't know of anyone who could do them for us. (videotape)

Neither the *Lisa* novel nor the Philosophy for Children curriculum as a whole should be taken as entirely representative of the current state of ethics education, but this comment does serve to acknowledge what is widely known as a steep bias toward the analytical traditional of philosophy that has always been synonymous with Western philosophy. Analytic philosophy is known for placing a high value upon logical thinking and rationality and for insisting upon definitions, criteria, and distinctions for analyzing concepts, ideas, and theories. Alternative ethical conceptualizations that place importance on empathy, emotion, nature, harmony, meditative thinking, and mindfulness are to greater and lesser degrees ignored, dismissed, and minimalized in traditional Western thought. The Western tradition most certainly has a place in the study of ethics; the error comes in the assumption that it composes the entirety of the study of ethics. Unfortunately for Western schools, this is precisely what the common (implicit) assumption is for ethics education. If we are concerned with teaching ethical action and the responsible initiation of social change and if we are interested in making ethics education more holistic and sensitive toward the different backgrounds of those who engage with it, we need to begin thinking about how to change our understanding of what composes ethics educational and what it can contribute to the larger curriculum in school. Otherwise, the stigmatized reputation of ethics and philosophy will continue to persist – that of an isolated, elitist discipline reserved for the intellectual indulgence of a few.

References

Beck, L. G., & Murphey, J. (1994). *Ethics in educational leadership programs: An expanding role.* Thousand Oaks, CA: Corwin.

Britzman, M. J. (2005). Improving our moral landscape via character education: An opportunity for school counselor leadership. *Professional School Counseling, 8,* 293–294.

Davis, G. A. (1993). Creative teaching of moral thinking: Fostering awareness and commitment. *Middle School Journal, 24,* 32–33.

Ellenwood, S. (2007). Resisting character education: From McCuffey to narratives. *The Journal of Education, 187*(3), 21–43.

Ennis, R. H. (1991). Critical thinking: A streamlined conception. *Teaching Philosophy, 14*(1), 5–24.

Giroux, A. (1993). Teaching moral thinking: A reconceptualization.

Journal of Educational Thought, 26, 114–130.

Goodman, J. F. (2006). School discipline in moral disarray. *Journal of Moral Education, 35,* 213–230.

Lewis, A., & Smith, D. (1993). Defining higher order thinking. *Theory Into Practice, 32,* 131–137.

Lipman, M. (2003). *Thinking in education* (2nd ed.). New York: Cambridge University Press.

McPeck, J. E. (1981). *Critical Thinking in Education.* New York: St. Martin's.

Sharp, A. (2005). *The history of* Philosophy for Children [videotape].

Sprod, T. (2001). *Philosophical discussion in moral education: The community of ethical inquiry.* New York: Routledge.

Starnes, B. A. (2006). Don't "dumb down" character education. *Education Digest: Essential Readings Condensed for Quick Review, 72*(1), 39–43.

Tappan, M. B. (2006). Moral functioning as mediated action. *Journal of Moral Education, 35,* 1–18.

Zara, E. J., III. (2000). Pinning down character education. *Kappa Delta Pi Record, 36*(4), 154–157.

Note

1. See the introductory page of Sprod (2001) for a more complete explanation of the problem with teaching moral education.

CHAPTER SIX

DIALOGIC PEDAGOGY AND ITS DISCONTENT

CHING CHING LIN
TOURO COLLEGE

The use of dialogue in the classroom, or *dialogic pedagogy,* has been considered by many educators to possess the potential to transform the classroom into a genuine learning experience. Although they are diverse in their underlying assumptions and ends in view, different schools of dialogic pedagogy concurrently stress values, such as empowerment, equality, diversity, and reciprocity. This seeming uniformity, however, tends to belie the fact that the competitive discourses within dialogic pedagogy, when juxtaposed together, give rise to conflicting claims to democracy. Although some view dialogue as the very embodiment of a democracy that mediates diverse interests within a community, there are others who warily safeguard the primacy of diversity in defiance of any form of disciplinary regime. Such apparent tension within the literature of dialogic pedagogy calls for further justification of the relatedness of dialogue and democracy: What features of dialogic pedagogy are responsible for potential democratic benefits? To what conception of democracy does each discourse of dialogic pedagogy subscribe, and how does each one fare against others? In this chapter, I provide an overview of different justifications of the link between dialogue and democracy and articulate the conflicts into which different accounts of dialogic pedagogy may have transpired. An attempt to reconcile different democratic claims of dialogic pedagogy is offered.

Conversation is the central location of pedagogy for the democratic educator. Talking to share information, to change ideas is the practice both inside and outside academic settings that affirms to listeners that learning can take place in varied time frames (we can share and learn a lot in five minutes) and that knowledge can be shared in diverse modes of speech. Whereas vernacular speech may seldom be used in the classroom by teachers it may be the preferred way to share knowledge in other settings. (hooks, 2003, pp. 44–45).

Education for democratic citizenship requires that students learn to take part in meaningful and productive discussion with people of diverse viewpoints. (McMurray, 2007, pp. 357–358).

Emerging as a new pedagogical paradigm accredited with the power to transform a classroom into a genuine learning experience, dialogic pedagogy has been hailed by many progressively minded educators as the latest beacon of hope for building democracy and civic education, (Alexander, 2005; Arber, 2000; Arce, 2004; Baker, 2005; Biesta, 1995; Blyler, 1994; Brydon, 2004; Cahill, 2007; Cruddas, 2007; DeTurk, 2006; Ghahremani-Ghajar & Mirhosseini, 2005; Gregory, 2002; hooks, 2003; Jupp, 2001; Kapellidi, 2007; Keis, 2006; Kramer, 2001; Lambert & Parker, 2006; Larson, 1999; Lensmire, 1998; Lyle, 2008; McMurray, 2007; Morrell, 2004; Sharp, 2007; Skidmore, 2006; Waller, 2005; Wertsch, 2004). The critical acclaim that dialogic pedagogy receives in the existing literature, however, tends to belie the inconsistency among competitive accounts of dialogic pedagogy in relation to democracy. Such inconsistency highlights a need to further assess the sweeping claim of the success of using dialogue as a democratic pedagogy.

To many, the alliance of dialogue and democracy seems to be self-evident. To talk is to participate, to share information; this is what is generally defined as the very characteristic of democratic behavior. For those who hold such a conviction, dialogue is the very embodiment of democracy. The coherence and credentials of dialogic pedagogy as a means of teaching democracy, however, remain to be defined and articulated, as illustrated by the inconsistencies within the literature.

This chapter is an inquiry into the purported link between dialogic pedagogy and democracy in view of the potential conflicts and tensions arising from the democratic claims of competitive accounts of the use of dialogue in the classroom. The chapter has three parts. First, there is an overview of the theoretical paradigms that inform current accounts of dialogic pedagogy with an emphasis on their differences with regard to the democratic implications of dialogue. Second, I articulate the conflicts emerging from the juxtaposition of the competitive paradigms of dialogue with regard to their respective democratic claims. Last, I compare and contrast those paradigms in light of discovered conflicts and inconsistencies in an attempt to build a coherent account of dialogue as a democratic pedagogy.

Overview

Research Question

In the existing literature of education, *dialogic pedagogy* is mostly associated with the school of Mikhail Bakhtin (Kramer, 2001; Morrell, 2004; Skidmore, 2006; Wertsch, 2004). I, however, use the term loosely as a pedagogical approach featuring dialogical interaction as an instructional tool. This chapter is an inquiry into the sweeping claim found in the existing literature about the relationship between dialogic pedagogy and democracy. The questions that guide my inquiry are as follows: What features of dialogical pedagogy are responsible for its purported democratic benefits? What characteristics of democracy does dialogic pedagogy help to induce? Given the diversity within the literature regarding the understanding of dialogic pedagogy, is it possible to have a coherent account of its relevance to democracy?

Methodology

Using the various cognates of the key word *dialogue* as a research guide (e.g., *talk, discussion, communication,* and *dialogical inquiry*) in conjunction with the words *pedagogy* and *democracy,* I came across numerous articles that bore an initial relevance to the topic. Such a research method sufficed for my current purpose because I did not want to achieve comprehensive coverage of the field, but rather I wanted to collect enough sample accounts of dialogic pedagogy to represent its diversity and coherence.

One interesting finding emerging from my survey was the promiscuous use of the term *dialogue.* Although some authors have treated the term *dialogue* as quasi-terminology, many of them use *dialogue* interchangeably with *classroom talk, discussion, communication,* and *dialogical inquiry* (Alexander, 2005; Arber, 2000; Arce, 2004; Baker, 2005; Biesta, 1995; Blyler, 1994; Brydon, 2004; Cahill, 2007; Cruddas, 2007; DeTurk, 2006; Ghahremani-Ghajar & Mirhosseini, 2005; Gregory, 2002; hooks, 2003; Jupp, 2001; Kapellidi, 2007; Keis, 2006; Kramer, 2001; Lambert & Parker, 2006; Larson, 1999; Lensmire, 1998; Lyle, 2008; McMurray, 2007; Morrell, 2004; Sharp, 2007; Skidmore, 2006; Waller, 2005; Wertsch, 2004). There is, however, a certain correlation between the theoretical paradigm upon which each article draws and its choice of words. Authors who favor dialogic pedagogy are mostly associated with Bakhtin (Kramer, 2001; Morrell, 2004; Skidmore, 2006; Wertsch, 2004), and those who opt for communication are generally associated with Habermas and dialogical inquiry with Philosophy for Children (David & Kienzler, 1999; Gregory, 2002; Hargreaves, 2003; Kennedy, 1999; O'Regan & O'Donnell, 2000).

The accounts of dialogic pedagogy discussed in this chapter were drawn from disparate theoretical sources. Each theoretical paradigm identifies different features of dialogue and has different political ends in mind with regard to the democratic benefits of dialogue. For example, although some (e.g., hooks, 2003) consider the use of vernacular language as an essential means of sharing ideas and, therefore, what primarily accounts for the democratic potential of dialogic pedagogy, others, such as Lipman, identify endeavors toward logical elucidation and critical thinking as the highest development of democratic education (Lipman, 2003; Gregory, 2002). Despite many differences among theories, one can generalize that most authors agree that social interaction unfolding in dialogue is what stimulates and necessitates both the cognitive and emotional development of children. Most authors would also agree that talk in the classroom is not just talk but structured conversations facilitated by teachers and that such interaction has profound pedagogical benefits that can be translated into democratic outcomes.

The construal of *dialogue* itself is not always in unison among different theories of dialogue. When they are put together, however, *dialogue* within the literature can indicate some of the following features:

- *Conversation:* Involving a give and take of verbal interaction and civic reciprocity.
- *Equal access:* Achieved by the setting of ground rules to ensure that each participant has an equal place in the circle of discussion. This discourages more vocal students from dominating the conversation and encourages students who normally do not speak to speak.
- *Engaged listening:* Not only listening to what other people have to say but showing interest in the identification of differences, the clarification of ideas, the deepening of perspectives, and so on.
- *Relative responsibility:* Being willing to take personal responsibility for ideas and actions. As a conversation opens one to the simultaneous existence of multiple perspectives, one must respond to the emerging tensions and decide where to stand (Kramer, 2001).
- *Recognizing differences:* Taking care not to treat identity as

predetermined in the age of the hegemony of multiculturalism. Dialogism provides a tool or position to resist the tendency to reify differences or identity.

- *Fostering voice:* Using dialogism to provide a position for young people to develop their voices. Some, however, warn against reification of the student voice by suggesting that one understands voice as emerging from a process of an active and engaged understanding of reality (Cruddas, 2007).
- *Constructivism:* Being open to the possibility that all rules can be challenged and that new ideas can be introduced but must be met with unanimous consensus.
- *Shared inquiry:* Being committed to open-ended dialogue characterized by ground rules as a respectful pursuit of "understanding about and between different individuals and groups in a common pursuit of knowledge and truth, inquiry that leads one to understand and gain insight, rather than convince someone about a particular point of view" (De Turk, 2006, p. 34).
- *Empowerment:* Associating coming to voice with the emerging critical reflection of human dignity, identity, freedom, self-determination, and so on. As bell hooks (1989) pointed out, "moving from silence into speech is a revolutionary gesture," (p. 12) and "the awareness of the need to speak, to give voice to varied dimensions of our lives, is one way [to begin] the process of education for critical consciousness" (p. 13).
- *Empathy:* Experiencing a profound connectedness revealed to us our indebtedness to others and moving us into a relationship with others.
- *Community building:* Feeling that dialogue is more than simply a source of action. As a form of action that includes talk, conversation, and deliberation, it is the basic and most essential form of participatory citizenship. It is an action in itself. "Dialogue offered the participants an opportunity to come into contact with both likeminded and unlike minded others, which allows community building, self-expression, goal articulation, explanation, and formulation of alternatives that ultimately contribute to building the public" (De Turk, 2006, p. 44).
- *Critical thinking:* Encouraging dialogue encourages an increasing awareness of the effects of social structure on knowledge, the effects of different modes of knowledge on

individuals and societies, and the linkage of knowledge and action (David & Kienzler, 1999).

Not all authors will accept these characterizations of dialogue as a whole package. Some of these features are sources of disagreement and tensions among competitive paradigms.

Given the discrepancy between the understanding of dialogue and the magnitude of its grand democratic rhetoric, a justification of the relationship between dialogue and democracy must be made in reference to such a discrepancy in understanding; that is, it should be seen as a form of defense in view of competitive understandings of the relationship in question. Such investigation into diversity and its potential contradictions in different theories of dialogue, nevertheless, is conspicuously absent in the existing literature of dialogic pedagogy. In most of the studies that I surveyed, the claim of such a link did not go far beyond mere assertion. Instead of being provided with an argument of the link in question, I found that one synonym was substituted for another, and I was circled back to where I was before. The lack of a sustained justification of the purported link of dialogue and democracy within the existing literature points to the need to dig into different theoretical paradigms of dialogic pedagogy to find further explanation of its nature.

Theoretical Resources of Dialogic Pedagogy

From the articles that I selected, I identified the following theoretical resources to which individual articles referred.

Vygotsky/Bakhtin

As part of the linguistic turn that developed in the early 20th century, Vygotsky's (1978) identification of language as a medium of learning that embodies social interaction and language learning as a key element in children's cognitive development underlines many accounts of dialogic pedagogy. In addition to Vygotsky's idea of language as cultural mediation, Bakhtin's (1981) dialogism provides an analytic tool to expose the complexity of classroom discourse. Driven by his own discontent with the monological approach of literary analysis that was dominant in his time, which viewed literary analysis as an object of scientific study and projected the researcher as an objective observer, Bakhtin sought to expose the dialogical character of language as a lived experience grounded in social exchange. Bakhtin's dialogism addresses the polyphony and multivoicedness in literary experience, which he argued was exemplified in Dostoyevsky's novels, which as a means of formulating internally persuasive discourse provide a context for the free and creative development of another's word (Bakhtin, 1981).

In the United States, the contribution of Bakhtin's (1981) dialogism consists of helping American educators see literary experience as a meaning-making process informed by the "elastic environment of others" (p.276) existing between us and the word, that is semantically open to infinite ideological possibilities:

> We have in mind first of all those instances of powerful influence exercised by another discourse on a given author. When such influences are laid bare, the half concealed life lived by another's discourse is revealed within the new context of the given author. When such an influence is deep and productive, there is further creative development of another's (more precisely, half other) discourse in a new context and under new conditions. (p. 347)

Bakhtin's acknowledgment of the presence of the other in our understanding of the world changes how American educators look at what is going on in the classroom. The corresponding task for democratic pedagogy from Bakhtin's perspective is to find ways of creating a genuine dialogic relationship with students, in and through which knowledge is constantly constructed, deconstructed, and reconstructed.

Freire/Critical Pedagogy

Freire's (1970) idea of education as a critical link in our collective struggle against oppression inspires and has given rise to a critical pedagogy that has committed itself to helping students develop a critical consciousness by examining the impacts of race, gender, and economic status on disfranchised groups. In its development, critical pedagogy has incorporated both a postmodern discourse and an alliance with theories from other critical traditions, such as feminism and postcolonial studies. Despite the significant differences existing among them, their shared vision for democracy is to "empower the powerless and transform existing social inequalities and injustice" (McLaren, 1989, p. 160).

Critical pedagogy draws upon eclectic theoretical heritages but retains the Freirean neo-Marxist premise that conceives the world as divided between the oppressor and the oppressed. With a basis in liberation and the empowerment of the underprivileged, critical pedagogy can be credited for using a variety of literature and educational resources to help students critically question their perception of self and in so doing "conscietize" the existence of the oppressive regime of power/knowledge. Rejecting what Freire (1970) characterized as the banking system of the dominant educational institutions, critical pedagogy questions the dichotomy of the teacher/student relationship and identifies meaningful teacher/student dialogue as the key mechanism in the emergence of the student's voice.

In contrast to Bakhtin (1981), critical pedagogy does not offer a thematic account of dialogue, and as such, it does not, for my purposes, make a unique contribution to helping us address the purported relationship between dialogue and democracy.

Freire's (1970) critical pedagogy, however, exposes the inadequacy of Bakhtin's (1981) dialogism as a theory of democratic pedagogy by insisting on the dialectical relationship between reflection and action, which according to Freire can be sustained in authentic teacher/student dialogue. True to his activist credentials, Freire emphasized that "to speak a true word is to transform the world" (Freire, 1970, p. 75). Freire's theory thus exposes the inadequacy of Bakhtin's dialogism as internal dialogue. Although it provides a context for formulating critical consciousness, this internal dialogue is in need of a mechanism to translate it into corresponding actions, and as we shall see later, this is what Habermas and P4C propose to provide.

Habermas

Habermas' (1984) theory of dialogue—communicative action in his terms—is built broadly upon his critique of Western rationality, which leads to its own impasse. Communicative action, an idea emerging from his extensive engagement in the discourse of modernity in decades, marks a shift from the transcendental or solipsistic tradition that defines German idealism and foundationalist epistemology. In agreement with the postmodernist critique of modernity, Habermas argued that the traditional philosophical outlook can no longer account for the simultaneous individuation and collectivization of the modern world and is inadequate for facilitating us in meeting the ethical challenges we are facing in its wake. From a postfoundationalist perspective, he maintained that knowledge cannot be reduced to either subjectivism or objectivism; rather, knowledge is intersubjective as it can arise only from the "symbolic interaction between societal subjects who reciprocally know and recognize each other as unmistakable individuals" (Morrow & Torres, 2002, p. 50). According to Morrow &Torres (2002), knowledge for Habermas is a form of inquiry that seeks a rational consensus of an ideal community of rational subjects as potential participants and a form of communication in which the participants subject themselves to the "unforced force of the better argument" (Morrow & Torres, 2002, p.50).

For Habermas (1971), the historical possibility and condition of communicative action are grounded in the emancipatory mode of knowledge. Besides being interested in using knowledge as a mode of technical control or meaning making, the human species has, as its ultimate stake, a knowledge-constitutive interest in liberating itself from all forms of societal oppression. Through his reconstruction of the Marxian ontology of praxis, Habermas considered societal oppression to consist of the inherent tension between public reason and private interests, which he proposed could be overcome by communicative action, which through its dialogical influence provides the ontological basis by which "knowledge-constitutive interest takes form in the medium of work, language, and power" (p. 313):

> The human interest in autonomy and responsibility is not mere fancy, for it can be apprehended *a priori*. What raises us out of nature is the only thing whose nature we know: *language*. Through its instruction, autonomy and responsibility are posited for us. Our first sentence experiences unequivocally the intention of the universal and unconstrained consensus. (Habermas, 1971, p. 314)

From this premise, Habermas maintained that the struggle for emancipation must take place in the formation of the public sphere, which he conceived as a space of critical discussion, open to all, where equal access to discussion and the decision-making process is vigilantly safeguarded by the mutual respect for procedural rationality that serves as a check on tyranny and domination in all forms. Recognizing that communicative action is perpetually threatened by its opposite, which can emerge in the context of manipulative, strategic action informed by self-serving interests, Habermas stressed that communicative action is embedded in the intersubjective mutuality of reciprocal understanding and a desire for shared knowledge and as such provides the possibility and foundation of authentic consensus and democratization.

P4C

Developed originally by a group of educators (Matthew Lipman, Ann Sharp, David Kennedy, Maughn Gregory, and Megan Laverty, to name a few, who continue to articulate their vision through active participation in cultural debates on larger scales) at Montclair State University, P4C is a pedagogical movement that involves teachers and students in a collaborative process of re-imagining philosophy as a form of social discourse (Kennedy, 1990, 1999). Featuring dialogical inquiry, P4C as a pedagogical approach is committed to creating a genuine learning context in which entrenched social norms or values are questioned, reasoned, deliberated, and challenged.

Drawing upon a wide range of theoretical discourses, P4C is centrally grounded in the idea of a community of inquiry (CI), which was originally conceived by Charles Peirce (1877) and which he proposed to rein in the caprice and potential tyranny of inquiry by the checks and balances of intersubjectivity. For Peirce, inquiry and community were not contradictory terms but rather supported each other. Peirce's idea of a CI received an enriched interpretation in the hands of P4C educators: the creation of a philosophical community based upon inquiry becomes a communal, dialogical event—as opposed to the privileged activity of scientists or professionals—through which different perspectives of the world are respectfully considered and critically contested. A CI teaches "ways of reasoning about the world that enhance student's ability to think critically, deliberately and imaginatively about their worlds" (Pardales & Girod, 2006, p. 303).

Peirce's (1877) idea of the CI has since been expanded by the incorporation of different discourses of dialogue, such as Buber's (1958) *I and Thou* and Gadamer's (1975) hermeneutics, by P4C educators. These theories of dialogue share the vision of prioritizing the experience of communal dialogue, which is understood not merely as a "conversation, but in David Kennedy's words, as an 'emergent, multivocal and interactive story about the world, and about persons thinking about the world'" (Kennedy, 1999, p. 339).

According to Lipman (2003), CI is the middle term or link between education and democracy and between the scientific method and democratic practices. It can help set in motion what otherwise is merely a pale apparition of a natural tendency. The democratic potential of the CI hence lies in the transformative potential of dialogue as a face-to-face lived communal event in which the lived experience of the participants is unfolded as a great narrative—the emergence of what Martin Buber called "living we" (Kennedy, 1999)—that in its irreducible multitude challenges the very pretense of authoritative voice in its various forms.

Feminist Pedagogy

Feminist educators tend to be reserved about the democratic potential of dialogue; for example, Elizabeth Ellsworth's (1994) main qualm about dialogic pedagogy was its potency to withstand the infiltration of corporate interests and its capitalistic racketeer. Her critique was in line with the traditional feminist emphasis on community building and its role in building alliances for engaged social action. Although they have recognized the importance of fostering the student's voice, feminist educators have been critical about the lack of mechanism in dialogic accounts that provides the translation of belief into action.

In agreement with its action-oriented politics, the feminist approach to dialogic pedagogy grounds its discourse in the critique of the divide between the cognitive and the affective and stresses the affective power of dialogue in fostering and building empathy, which cultivates mutual understanding and coalition building (Lambert & Parker, 2006; Waller, 2005). Through empathetic understanding and getting in touch with their own (thus far repressed) feelings, students may expand their sense of the self so that the other or otherness is welcomed rather than rejected (Wang, 2005). The somatic and psychological effects of empathy turn a loose exchange of words into a purposeful inquiry into the connectedness of human destiny.

Poststructuralist, Postmodern, Postcolonialist, and So On

Educators who are in the poststructuralist and/or postcolonialist tradition appeal to the aporia experience of the subject, without which, they argue, no genuine dialogue is possible. Understood as a predicament in the moments of dialogue, aporias create an unfamiliar momentum that cannot be reconciled or dissolved by our usual understanding and compels us to radicalize our understanding and imagination (Arber, 2000; Brydon, 2004; Wang, 2005).

An aporia is the active experience of a possibility of the impossible and defies the dichotomy of identity and difference (Wang, 2005). From this perspective, truth is not about deciding upon a set of preexisting choices but involves an act of performance that actively maneuvers between the polarized value systems imposed by the domination of certain values.

If the new arrival, who arrives is new, one must expect—without waiting for him or her and without expecting it—that he or she does not simply cross a given threshold. Such an arrival affects the very experience of the threshold, whose possibility he thus brings to light before one even knows whether there has been an invitation, a call, a nomination, or a promise. What we could here call *the arrival* is whatever or whoever, in arriving, does not cross a threshold separating two identifiable places, the proper and the foreign or the proper of the one and the proper of the other (Derrida, 1992; Wang, 2005).

The ambivalence of voice and identity entails for postcolonialists a different conception of democracy. Democracy is not so much about pursuing a mutual understanding of each other's differences because there is no such difference per se. Rather, democracy is the perpetual act of resisting any attempt to congeal one's existence into essence.

> We are no doubt permanent subjects of a language that holds us in its power.
> But we are subjects in process, ceaselessly losing our identity, destabilized by fluctuations in our relations to the other. Interpretation...is itself a revolt. (Kristeva, 1985/1987, p. 9)

Tension and Conflicts

A close look at the juxtaposition of the different accounts of the relationship of dialogue and democracy suggests some theoretical issues that underline their differences.

Among the authors of the theories of dialogue that we just surveyed, it is commonly agreed that voice always appears in the form of multiplicity. One does not just discover one's voice. Developing one's voice means the recognition of the authoritative voice in one's own. Voice in the dialogic pedagogy is always about reflecting *alterity,* the irreducible presence of the other, within the self.

However, even in the wake of postmodern politics, voice also signifies the struggle to achieve self-identity. For many, democracy is ultimately a vision of the democratization of the decision-making process that thrives on accommodating multiple demands within the society itself and actually builds upon the strength of the individual voice. It is this emergence of a social agency or subject in the process that conditions democracy and constitutes the possibility for social change. The challenge to democracy, which is also its strength, therefore lies in the building of a community that is open to all and brings all voices to this decision-making process.

Many, including democratic educators who pursue a communitarian agenda, have been cautious of this talk of unity within multiplicity. Feminists, such as bell hooks (2003) and Elizabeth Ellsworth (1994), have warned us against a faux project of community building with the pretense of democracy. Their concern was that the procedural rationality figuring in many dialogic models might belie the agenda of private interests in its technocratic impartiality. In the era of globalization, such threats seem to grow more real as we have experienced the ever-intrusiveness of state-assisted capitalization in an everyday context (Feigenbaum, 2007).

The qualm against a communitarian strain within dialogic pedagogy tends to be that it is slighted as rhetoric and touted as unwarranted caution by supporters of dialogic pedagogy, who have argued that a mechanism of self-regulation is already built into the dialogic process—as seen in the cases of Habermas (1984) or P4C (Lipman, 2003); this should suffice to alleviate such compunction (Burbules, 2000). The critics' voices, however, deserve to be taken more seriously. Despite their failure to deliver their argument in a more forceful and coherent form, they have pointed to a theoretical lacuna in the heart of the theory of dialogue, that is, a need to explain to what extent dialogue and the recognition of intersubjectivity can effectively help us in our Sisyphean struggle against societal oppression.

In particular, the discontent and reservation within the school of dialogic pedagogy echo a larger sentiment in the critical tradition in its broader sense, that is, theories that may or may not snuggly fit under the umbrella of dialogic pedagogy. For many, intersubjectivity and the mechanism of checks and balances, unfolded and sustained in the dialogic process and interactions, might be insufficient to withstand the infiltration of private interests and a corporate agenda that contribute to the sustenance of the status quo, and they may have rightly incurred skepticism against it. Foucault (1982) and Butler (1997), for example, opted to use *subjectivization* to denote the ambivalence underlining the formative process of subjectivity and to reveal the entanglement of power and knowledge. Also, Derrida (1992), with the aid of the Socratic concept of aporia, argued for an inevitability of an epistemic impasse within the development of modernity that defies any dialectic synthesis. In feminist and postcolonial literature, such a notion of radical subjectivity is often evoked to challenge the hegemony of dialogue. An apt example is Spivak's (1988) subaltern. Through the rhetoric "can the subaltern speak?," she demonstrated the dilemma of the subaltern by showing how the subaltern is inevitably trapped by the dualistic logic of the oppressive discourse that helps perpetuate the subjection and oppression (Spivak, 1988).

For theorists of dialogic pedagogy, aporia may not be an objection to the possibility of dialogical inquiry per se. As in a classical Socratic dialogue, impasse and the resulting puzzlement prompt the subject to pursue further investigation and therefore could be a critical step in moving the dialectic forward. For critics of dialogic pedagogy, however, aporia, rather than a state in passing that waits to be synthesized in the next level of dialogic movement, is something that is sustained and remains. Going back to Spivak's (1988) example, we find that the question for the subalterns is not to assert their voice, which they have come to see as a trap of the dualistic logic of power. They have settled for something more realistic, to merely delineate and reveal the trajectory of power, whose trace has defined their subjectivity.

The Coherence of Dialogical Inquiry
as a Democratic Pedagogy

The ambivalence of the voice emerging in the juxtaposition of different accounts of dialogical inquiry opposes democracy as a dialectic moving toward a never-realized unity with democracy as sustaining moments of impasse in the totalizing gaze of power. For the purpose of this chapter, the opposition, however, cannot be ignored and must be reconciled by further probes into the coherence of dialogic pedagogy as a theory.

All of the theories of dialogue under consideration share the conviction that the inundation of energy from dialogic inquiry when it is consistently applied possesses the transformative potential to subvert the authoritative voice of the signifying order. To voucher such conviction against its critics, however, we need to have an account of how the dialogic approach can effectively withstand the totalizing effects of power.

In what follows, I assess how each theory might address the voice of discontent against dialogue as form of intervention in achieving democracy as the counterposition tends to indiscriminately apply its criticism to all, despite the significant differences among the competitive theories with regard to the character of dialogue and their respective democratic potential. I focus on Bakhtin, Habermas, and the CI due to the fact that because, in comparison to others, they have developed a more defined view of the relationship of dialogue and democracy.

In contrast to Habermas (1984) and P4C (Lipman, 2003), Bakhtin's (1981) dialogue reflected a populist notion of democracy. His theory of dialogism is closely associated with his idea of carnival, an idea that he traced to the medieval times when a carnival figured as a collectivity of shared energy and periodically challenged the official function of the established social hierarchy. Bakhtin's carnivalesque dialogue was, therefore, grounded in a romanticized picture of the life world. Although it is capable of shattering the complacent facade of authority, the eruptive power of folk energy derived from a carnival can also be unconstrained and volatile and can fail to critically discern legitimate distinctions (Bakhtin, 1981).

It is difficult to conceive a populist notion of dialogue in a world infiltrated by the ever-present tentacles of capitalist control and corporate interests. The energy that we experience in, say, frenetic shopping malls or boisterous street fairs seems only to replicate the capitalist logic of reproduction. The problem of Bakhtin (1981) comes to the fore when his theory is compared to that of Habermas (1984) and the CI; both emphasize the self-regulation of dialogical inquiry. For both Habermas and P4C, dialogue cannot be just a loose banter of conversation. Dialogue should lead to the explicating of different viewpoints and the disclosure of logical and argumentative structures of discourse unfolded through dialogue. Dialogue, without being subject to the discipline of logical inquiry, would have nothing to offer in the advancing of democracy.

Procedural rationality plays an important part in both Habermas' (1984) "public sphere" and P4C's (Lipman, 2003) CI. Both agree that the respect for procedural rationality and self-constraint thus exercised is what prevents dialogical inquiry from becoming arbitrary and from disintegrating into a mere burst of bustling energy. A question, however, arises for Habermas and P4C theorists at this juncture: How do we know when procedural rationality ceases to be impartial and becomes an unwilling accomplice of special interests in its role of adjudicating democratic behaviors in daily contexts?

In the case of Habermas (1984), procedure and ground rules of communicative action are subject to the dialectic of purposive rationality and instrumental rationality. They are constantly constructed and reconstructed in light of our ongoing assessment of the measured distance between real-world situations and the idea of the public sphere. The trouble with Habermas is that his idea of the public sphere remains too abstract to guide us in our quest for an open and fair-minded inquiry. The distance between the life world and the public sphere in Habermas' theory admits so many interpretations that the very concept of public sphere may not allow us to discern whether the communicative action in which we are engaged is actually reiterating the socially oppressive logic that helps to sustain the status quo. What is lacking in Habermas' theory is a third term to bridge the universal (public sphere) and the particular (the life world).

Compared to Bakhtin's (1981) carnivalesque dialogism and Habermas' (1984) public sphere, the CI seems to offer the right dialectic of the universal and the particular. Similar to the other two paradigms, the CI is grounded in the ontological possibility of the fused horizon of our joint destiny as a human species. What separates the CI from the others is that instead of conversing with an undifferentiated crowd as in Bakhtin's carnival or the ideal rational agents that populate Habermas' public sphere, we are face to face with real people, whose very presence compels our ethical and moral conscience and informs our judgment of procedural fairness.

As a communal event, the CI provides the distance and relation at the same time, a synthesis absent in Bakhtin and Habermas. Distance keeps dialogue from disintegrating into nondiscrimination, as seen looming in Bakhtin's carnival, whereas relation anchors and embodies dialogue as a real event in the world. The CI "opens a space of transformative potential. Through its interplay, boundaries are continually being reconfigured—not just conceptual boundaries, but corporeal and affective as well" (Kennedy, 1999, p. 340).

Such a synthesis of psychological engagement and the critical distance of dialogue aptly presents itself when we compare dialogue to a play, as was famously appropriated by Gadamer (1970). According to Gadamer, a *play* in its multiple meanings is a real-life communal event arising from the real world that contains its possibility in the first place. It continues to hold a dialectic relationship with the real world. As a play unfolds, all the superficial social distinctions dissolve into an emerging sense of "we," where in its "felt collectivity," individuals come to face to face with each other as "I" and "thou." It is this duality of disinterest and interest, which are simultaneously operative in a CI, that helps it sustain its democratic promise.

Conclusion

The inconsistencies of dialogical pedagogy in the existing literature leave doubt about whether dialogue alone can effectively check aggression against humanity in all forms. Without such potential inconsistencies being addressed, skepticism lingers about the effectiveness and legitimacy of dialogue as a democratic pedagogy.

From my research, I conclude that theories from Bakhtin's and Habermas' traditions lack the critical element to give us a satisfactory account that substantiates their democratic claims of dialogue. The CI combines the strengths of both paradigms and hence better equips us to meet the theoretical demands of conceiving dialogical pedagogy as a means and tool for delivering democracy.

References

Alexander, R. (2005, July). *Culture, dialogue and learning: Notes on an emerging pedagogy.* Presented at Education, Culture and Cognition: Intervening for Growth, 10th International Conference, University of Durham, United Kingdom.

Arber, R. (2000). Defining positioning within politics of difference: Negotiating spaces "in between." *Race Ethnicity and Education, 3,* 45–63.

Arce, J. (2004). Latino bilingual teachers: The struggle to sustain an emancipatory pedagogy in public schools. *International Journal of Qualitative Studies in Education, 17,* 227–247.

Baker, B. (2005). State-formation, teaching techniques, and globalization as aporia. *Discourses: Studies in the Cultural Politics of Education, 26,* 45–77.

Bakhtin, M. (1981). *The dialogic imagination: Four essays.* Austin: University of Texas.

Biesta, G. J. J. (1995, April). *From manipulation to communication: Communicative pedagogy and the postmodern crisis of the subject.* Presented at the Annual Meeting of the American Educational Research Association, San Francisco, CA.

Blyler, N. R. (1994). Habermas, empowerment, and professional discourse. *Technical Communication Quarterly, 3,* 125–145.

Brydon, D. (2004) Cross-talk, postcolonial pedagogy, and transnational literacy. *Situation Analysis, 4,* 70–87.

Buber, M. (1958). *I and thou.* (R. G. Smith, Trans.). New York: Charles Scribner's Sons.

Burbules, N. (2000). The limits of dialogue as a critical pedagogy. *Revolutionary pedagogies.* New York: Routledge.

Butler, J. (1997). *The psyche life of power: Theories in subjection.* Stanford, CA: Stanford University Press.

Cahill, C. (2007). The personal is political: Developing new subjectivities through participatory action research. *Gender, Place and Culture, 14,* 267–292.

Cruddas, L. (2007). Engaged voices—Dialogic interaction and the construction of shared social meanings. *Educational Action Research, 15,* 479–488.

David, C., & Kienzler, D. (1999). Towards an emancipatory pedagogy in service courses and user departments. *Technical Communication Quarterly, 8,* 263–283.

Derrida, J. (1992). Interview of Jacques Derrida by Alan Montefiore. In

Jacques Derrida [Film]. Princeton, NJ: Films for the Humanities & Sciences. Transcription prepared by D. Ege'a-Kuehne & V. Hillis (1996).

DeTurk, S. (2006). The power of dialogue: Consequences of intergroup dialogue and their implications for agency and alliance building. *Communication Quarterly, 54*, 33–51.

Ellsworth, E. (1994). Why doesn't this feel empowering? Working through the repressive myths of critical pedagogy? In *The Education Feminism Reader* (pp. 300–327). New York: Routledge.

Feigenbaum, A. (2007). The teachable moment: Feminist pedagogy and the neoliberal classroom. *The Review of Education, Pedagogy, and Cultural Studies, 29*, 337–349.

Foucault, M. (1982). The Subject and Power. *Critical Inquiry, 8*(4), 777–795.

Freire, P. (1970). *Pedagogy of the oppressed*. New York: Seabury.

Gadamer, H. (1975). *Truth and method*. New York: Crossroad.

Ghahremani-Ghajar, S.-S., & Mirhosseini, S. A. (2005). English class or speaking about everything class? Dialogue journal writing as a critical EFL literacy practice in an Iranian high school. *Language, Culture and Curriculum, 18*, 286–300.

Gregory, M. R. (2002). Constructivism, standards, and the classroom community of inquiry. *Educational Theory, 52*(4), 397–408.

Habermas, J. (1971). *Knowledge and human interests*. Boston: Beacon.

—. (1984). *The theory of communicative action. Vol. 1: Reason and the rationalization of society*. Boston: Beacon.

Hargreaves, A., Margarida, F., & Thompson, M. D. (2003). Big change question: Does critical theory have any practical value for educational change? *Journal of Educational Change, 4*, 181–193.

hooks, b. (1989). *Talking back: Thinking feminist, thinking black*. Toronto: Between the Lines.

—. (2003). *Teaching community—A pedagogy of hope*. New York: Routledge.

Jupp, J. C. (2001). Rio Grande valley: Border crossing, diversity within diversity, and rethinking categorical language. *Multicultural Review, 35*, 34–41.

Kapellidi, C. (2007). The speaking subject in communication: Subjectivity and the (gendered) self. *Camling*, 112–119.

Keis, R. (2006). From principle to practice: Using children's literature to promote dialogue and facilitate the coming to voice in a rural Latino community. *Multicultural Perspectives, 8*, 13–19.

Kennedy, D. (1990). Hans-Georg Gadamer's dialectic of dialogue and the epistemology of the community of inquiry. *Analytic Teaching: The Community of Inquiry Journal, 12,* 43–51.

——. (1999, Spring). Philosophy for Children *and the reconstruction of philosophy.* Presented at the Connecticut Colloquium.

Kramer, K. (2001). Educating through meeting: Reflections on a dialogic pedagogy for teaching religious studies. *Teaching Theology and Religion, 4,* 64–70.

Kristeva, J. (1985/1987). *In the beginning was love: Psychoanalysis and faith.* New York: Columbia University Press.

Lambert, C., & Parker, A. (2006). Imagination, hope and the positive face of feminism: Pro/feminist pedagogy in "post" feminist times? *Studies in Higher Education, 31,* 469–483.

Larson, B. E. (1999, May/June). Influences on social studies teachers' use of classroom discussion. *The Social Studies,* 125–132.

Lensmire, T. J. (1998). Rewriting student voice. *Journal of Curriculum Studies, 30,* 261–291.

Lipman, M. (2003). *Thinking in education.* New York: Cambridge University Press.

Lyle, S. (2008). Dialogic teaching: Discussing theoretical contexts and reviewing evidence from classroom practice. *Language and Education, 22,* 222–242.

McLaren, Peter. (1989). *Life in schools: An introduction to critical pedagogy in the foundations of education.* New York: Longman.

McMurray, A. J. (2007). The role of discussion and dissent in creating civic understanding. *American Secondary Education, 36*(1), 49–58.

Morrell, E. (2004). Bakhtin's dialogic pedagogy. *Journal of Russian and East European Psychology, 42*(6), 89–94.

Morrow, R. A., & Torres, C. A. (2002). *Reading Freire and Habermas.* New York: Teachers College, Columbia University.

O'Regan, P., & O'Donnell, D. (2000). Mapping intellectual resources: Insights from critical modernism. *Journal of European Industrial Training, 24,* 118–127.

Pardales, M. J., & Girod, M. (2006). Community of inquiry: Its past and present future. *Educational Philosophy and Theory, 38,* 299–311.

Peirce, C. S. (1877). The fixation of belief. *Popular Science Monthly, 12*(November), 1–15.

Sharp, A. M. (2007). Education of the emotions in the classroom community of inquiry. *Gifted Education International, 22,* 248–257.

Skidmore, D. (2006). Pedagogy and dialogue. *Cambridge Journal of Education, 36,* 503–514.

Spivak, G. C. (1988). *Can the subaltern speak?* Urbana, IL: University of Illinois Press.

Vygotsky, L. S. (1978). *Mind in Society: The development of higher psychological processes.* Cambridge, MA: Harvard University Press.

Waller, M. R. (2005). Epistemology of engagement. *College Literature, 32,* 154–170.

Wang, H. (2005). Aporias, responsibility, and the im/possibility of teaching multicultural education. *Educational Theory, 55,* 45–60.

Wertsch, J. V. (2004). Postscript on Bakhtin's dialogic pedagogy. *Journal of Russian and East European Psychology, 42*(6), 50–52.

CHAPTER SEVEN

EMPOWERING THE OTHER: NEGOTIATING RACISM AND MARGINALIZATION IN A CLASSROOM COMMUNITY OF INQUIRY

LAVINA SEQUEIRA
BERGEN COMMUNITY COLLEGE

A snapshot of the U.S. classroom today showcases the vast diversity of its students. Research indicates that students belonging to ethnic populations often face discrimination and alienation because of phenotypic associations and problematic concepts, such as race, gender, and religion. In addition, existing social structures, mainstream ideologies, power, and hierarchy in the classroom contribute to the conception and their labeling as "others." The current tools used to combat marginalization and otherness are superficial without a complete evaluation and analysis of the implicit causes. The literature suggests that when issues pertaining to marginalization due to racism are broached in the educational milieu, most educators tend to maintain a morally objective distance because of a lack of understanding and training. In this exploratory chapter, I offer the solution of using the community of inquiry (CI) as an effective pedagogical tool by educators to empower all students and thereby reduce the notion of otherness through a participatory process of dialogue, inquiry, and care and enable the evolution of a caring, sustaining community within the classroom that is capable of including everyone in the inquiry process by discouraging dominant ideologies and encouraging the awareness and social consciousness of the individual. The CI, when used effectively, has the capacity to reduce student differences and feelings of marginalization.

Overview

U.S. classrooms today are becoming increasingly diverse in the racial and ethnic makeup of their student populations. A snapshot of today's classroom represents a student population in which individual ways of learning, knowledge acquisition, and meaning making are as diverse as the students themselves. Given this diversity, I believe that it is the educator's responsibility to understand how to best meet the educational needs of all students in the classroom. Some of the ways in which these educational goals can be met include acknowledging and celebrating the differences of each student, providing each student a safe, caring, and nurturing environment to be empowered, thereby securing an empowering educational milieu for all students.

As a student of Asian Indian descent, I have on some occasions experienced marginalization and alienation in the educational environment of which I am part because of my cultural ethnicity. I have felt feelings of difference, even when I have been trying to conform to the accepted norm. Although I am a representative of my ethnic culture and proud to be part of the same, I feel burdened and conflicted to be construed as the other. I often question this conflict: Am I really the other? Should I accept the label given to me by society to be fit in? Most importantly, why should I always negotiate labels to fit societal norms?

Perhaps belonging to an ethnic minority makes me more aware of the feelings of otherness, of being tolerated but never completely accepted. I acknowledge that the perception of oneself as held by others is different than the perception that one holds of himself or herself. I believe that the dichotomy of self-perception/other perception lends itself toward the maintenance of a hegemonic power structure that stratifies and divides society along socioeconomic, racial, and cultural lines. It is therefore logical to suggest that the difference, otherness and marginalization inherent in power structures become general reflections of societal practice, a norm and a reality of which we are a part. As a society, we can change this reality, provided that we as a society first and foremost are willing to acknowledge the presence of this reality, a reality that we often choose to ignore.

To be more accepting of the other, we need a community that is capable of including and sustaining everyone in the inquiry process, a community that will discourage dominant ideologies and the perceptions of the other and one that will encourage awareness and social consciousness and enable the empowerment process of the individual and society. I believe that we can envision such a change by considering the classroom to be part of an embryonic society.

A classroom is a microcosm of the larger society. Students tend to project negative attitudes and feelings toward those whom they consider to be the other. The projection of negative attitudes by some students toward others who are considered different not only hinders the learning process but also can lead to feelings of racial difference, discrimination, prejudice, and alienation and to derogatory stereotypes. Because my focus is mainly on students and their educational milieu, I propose that the community of inquiry (CI) method is one pedagogical tool that an educator can use to question dominant biases, beliefs, stereotypes, and assumptions about the other.

Through dialogue and care, which are inherent to a CI, the barriers of discrimination and alienation that some students feel can be overcome. Through mutual respect and understanding, every student will have the opportunity to learn, grow, and become effective, functioning members of a truly democratic society.

Introduction

Education is often considered to be a process that helps individuals reach their complete potential. The intent of education is not only to bring out the best in individuals but also to help them face the realities of the world. In addition, one of the important goals toward which education aspires is to help individuals make significant contributions toward the betterment of society. These are all good goals to aspire to. However, we have to ask ourselves whether the premise on which education rests as specified previously reaches its conclusion. Does education really empower and benefit all individuals? Are there equity and equality in education for students belonging to diverse cultures? Also, in relation to my original question, does education help in the acceptance and empowerment of students who are considered to be the other?

Although I may not have all the answers to these questions, I do believe that it is important for educationists and researchers alike to ponder to what extent our present system of education is actually helpful in the realization of the goals necessary for all individuals to reach their maximum potential.

Education Today

As a beginning researcher and educationist myself, I acknowledge that as important as the general consensus and understanding of education happens to be, it is far from perfect. Many educational theorists have posited that education deals with problematic concepts, such as the historic subjugation, erasure, negation, and invalidation of the histories, cultures, experiences, and identities of racial/ethnic minority peoples (Banks et al. 2001; Delpit, 1995; Freire, 1993; hooks, 1994). Others have noted that dominant societal ideologies fuel negative perceptions and stereotypes about certain individuals and cultures (Cummins, 1984; Giroux, 1997; McLaren 1994). These educational theorists have concurred that stereotyping and negative perceptions of those considered the other are part of a larger framework of issues born from problematic concepts, such as race and racism, gender, sex, and other socioeconomic inequalities. Therefore, it is conceivable that students belonging to certain ethnic cultures feel alienated and marginalized because of such negative stereotypes and hegemonic ideologies. Further, some educational theorists (Cummins, 1984; Delpit, 1995; Giroux, 1997; McLaren, 1994) have posited that student marginalization is often embedded in a culture of power and hegemonic ideologies that exists not only in society but in schools as well.

It is by recognizing the uniqueness of every student that educators can begin not only to understand their marginalization but also to find ways to enable and empower each and every student in their care (Banks, et al. 2001; Freire, 1993; hooks, 1994; Nussbaum, 2004). Empowerment is possible if the student is afforded a voice (Freire, 1993). One way to empower a child is through the process of inquiry and dialogue. Through the process of dialogue and inquiry in a classroom, I hope to envision the possibility of affording each and every child a voice and discouraging feelings of otherness, marginalization, and alienation.

Although dominant perceptions of diverse cultures and individuals are many, in this chapter, I focus on the concepts of racism, racial identity, and difference and their contributions toward feelings of otherness. Further, I consider whether the issues of racism and otherness can be overcome in schools and in classrooms that incorporate a CI approach toward teaching and learning. For the purposes of this chapter, I refer to the CI as a pedagogical method and a tool that enables educators to practice effective teaching and learning methodologies that lead to possible student self-actualization and empowerment. Within the classroom context, educators and students co-construct meaning through dialogue and decision making based on informed, critical, caring, and creative reasoning (Lipman, 2003; Splitter & Sharp, 1995). Working with this assumption, I posit that the incorporation of the CI approach to teaching and learning helps in the understanding of issues of racism, discrimination, otherness, and marginalization. In addition, I discuss possible ways in which these problematic issues that inhibit learning can be overcome.

In the succeeding sections, I explore the concept of the CI as a democratic, inquiry-based teaching/learning pedagogical method and an educational tool that when used appropriately, in time will enable educators and students to be critical and caring individuals.

Inquiry-Based Learning

As a philosophy and a methodology, inquiry-based learning draws from the work of John Dewey (1916). Dewey noted that learning based on inquiry is an experience shared by the members who are actively engaged in its process. The process of inquiry is driven and shaped by a shared understanding of the ideas, beliefs, and experiences of the participating members, who in this case are the educators and their students. Through the process of exploration, discourse, and dialogue, all participating members become active co-constructers in meaning making and in the creation of knowledge (Dewey, 1916). According to Dewey, learning takes place because of the active collaboration of all its members. Similarly, a CI incorporates the properties of inquiry-based learning. In a CI, learning takes place because of the active participation and collaboration of all its members. Through this approach, I believe that challenges felt by marginalized students can be effectively addressed.

CI

Researchers, such as Matthew Lipman, Ann Sharp, and Laurance Splitter, believe that a functioning CI produces individuals who are better thinkers and caring members of society and are willing to accept differences and at the same time are not afraid to subject various conflicts in ideas and beliefs to reasonable scrutiny; this enables them to be critical, creative, and caring thinkers (Lipman, 2003; Splitter & Sharp, 1995). With this view, the conversion of a classroom to reflect the salient characteristics of a CI becomes an appropriate medium for tackling personal, social, and moral issues that confront society (Splitter & Sharp, 1995). In a working CI, it is possible to imagine a dialogical inquiry process in which all students will eventually overcome their limited perspectives and come together to be co-constructers of meaning making; this will enable them to be empowered to collectively and collaboratively create knowledge.

Both Dewey (1916) and Lipman (2003) noted that such dialogical inquiry helps students to consider their present perspectives, past experiences, and reasons for holding onto certain positions and ultimately to find their voice and collectively envision a democratic future. Through shared experiences, dialogue, and discourse, students begin to learn and value one another and begin to take an active role in individual learning and the construction of knowledge. Using a dialogical inquiry process, the CI approach toward teaching and learning helps in the negation of marginalization and otherness and reinforces the ideals of democracy, freedom, and equality for all its students.

As noted earlier, a snapshot of today's classroom reflects the ethnic diversity that exists in our nation. With the immigrant population projected to increase exponentially in the next decade, educators need to reflect on current educational aims and goals as well as their teaching practices to afford an empowering, democratic education for all students regardless of their backgrounds.

In the previous paragraphs, I suggested that the use of the CI approach in teaching and learning can greatly benefit educators and students. Another way that educators can provide an empowering educational milieu for all their students is to reflect on the nature and conductivity of existing classroom culture. Often, there is a culture of power that exists in classrooms. Most times, the culture of power and power relations in classrooms defines educators' and students' academic expectations and sets definite roles for the educators as well as the students. In most educational contexts, power relations tend to become coercive. Coercive power relations in a classroom tend to maintain the status quo between students and those considered the other. The voices of those marginalized are often suppressed. The suppression of voices creates not only intolerance but also a marginalization of ideas and leads to the perpetuation of ignorance and silence (Delpit, 1995; Freire, 1993). These kinds of situations may lead to conformity, which threatens the freedom of individual expression. Educationist Jim Cummins (1984) posited that educators must challenge the coercive power relations in their classrooms even in their nuanced forms and strive instead for collaborative power relations. This classroom climate will enable students to be engaged and involved and will allow for the identification of perceptions, beliefs, and structures that inhibit the learning process. Understanding others' perspectives will help foster independent critical thinking and negate marginalization. Linda Darling-Hammond (1997) posited that for a truly democratic education to take place, all students regardless of their background have to be educated in ways that ensure independent and critical thinking.

As noted earlier, many problems stemming from the existing culture of power in the classroom could possibly affect self-esteem and learning and thus lead to feelings of otherness. In the next section of this chapter, I discuss the effects of these issues on students belonging to minority ethnic cultures and the possibility that they can be overcome in a classroom CI.

Racism and Otherness

The concept of racism involves beliefs, attitudes, institutional arrangements, and acts of individuals that unfairly classify other individuals or ethnic groups because of phenotypes or cultural affiliations (Banks et al., 2001; Banton, 1998; Essed, 1991; Smedley, 1998). In addition to the unfair classification of people, racism is characterized by an individual's or group's conduct of words or practices that provide advantage or disadvantage to some individuals or groups because of their color, culture, or ethnic origin (Banks et al., 2001; Banton, 1998; Helms, 1990; Smedley, 1998). Racism implicitly presumes that relationships between groups are unequal and undesirable, wherein one group is being oppressed by the other group or the oppressor.

Society today is not a homogeneous group of people. The presumption that unequal relationships exist between various groups rests on the fact that some individuals who belong to a minority ethnic culture are considered inferior and are therefore stigmatized and marginalized. Individuals who belong to an ethnic minority culture are also expected to completely assimilate into American culture. The justification lies in the Eurocentric positionality that suggests that one culture is superior to the other and that those living on the fringes must assimilate to be accepted. In other words, individuals and cultures that deviate from the supposed norm are stigmatized, marginalized, and made to feel as the deviant or the other. Society needs to understand that the process of assimilating is often painful and fraught with struggles. Gibson (1988) noted that it may take decades or even generations before the complete assimilation of ethnic cultures into mainstream American society takes place. Therefore, to consider one as different or as the other solely on the basis of race, ethnic culture, or even immigrant status is ignorance at its best.

One of the problems that most individuals of diverse ethnic cultures face and that makes them feel as the other is racism. A look at the various social relations and structures of society shows the subliminal permeation of racism at all levels of organization. Many theorists, researchers, and educationists (e.g., Banks et al., 2001; Delpit, 1995; Freire, 1993; Gibson, 1988; Giroux, 1997; hooks, 1994; McLaren, 1994; Smedley, 1998) have posited that the categorization of individuals and cultures due to race is dangerous because racial categories tend to oversimplify and mask important individual, cultural, and ethnic differences. Many multiculturalists and educational theorists have noted that the ultimate goal of racism is to maintain a status quo in society by establishing a permanent hierarchal structure that is based on difference and power (Banks et al., 2001; Freire, 1993; Giroux, 1997; Gibson, 1988; hooks, 1994; Smedley, 1998). Banks et al. (2001) and Nussbaum (2004) noted that racism creates a hierarchy among humanity, and those considered the objects of racism and difference are denigrated to lower levels of humanity. In other instances, racism is conceptualized from a minority/majority perspective, in which the minority is mostly likely to be the oppressed group.

Therefore, Helms (1990) contended that attempts made thus far to improve the racial climate in the United States have been "theoretical, sparse and superficial at best" (p. 205). Further, Essed (1991) noted that racism has become embedded in everyday practices and tends to be taken for granted and accepted as the norm. Genuine attempts need to be made to understand racism and feelings of otherness. This will involve not only the reevaluation of individual attitudes (in this case of the educator and students) but also the analysis of how society functions and the taken-for-granted positions and norms held by society.

Schools: Racism and Otherness

It has been acknowledged that the increasing diversity in U.S schools today presents many challenges and obstacles to educators in effectively educating all students. Most of the challenges faced by educators and students involve the understanding and valuing of the identity of the students and their empowerment rather than their marginalization. Students who speak of reduced feelings of self-esteem and feelings of difference often feel marginalized because of current educational structures and practices. Therefore, as noted before, as major building blocks of society, the school and the educational system need to reexamine their aims, objectives, and goals to allow for the empowerment of all students. Further, current educational policy needs to be reviewed and reconceptualized to reflect the rich diversity of all individuals residing in the United States.

In a classroom setting, negative attitudes toward students who are different with respect to cultural ethnicity lead to feelings of difference and otherness. Often, as bell hooks (1994) observed, when the issue of race or otherness is broached in the curriculum, it is invariably treated with reference to students of color. Students belonging to different ethnic cultures feel marginalized as they feel that other students may perceive them with indifference and in other cases disgust. Martha Nussbaum

(2004) posited that the emotion of disgust plays a major role in understanding others. In her book *Hiding from Humanity,* Nussbaum talked at length about the relationship between disgust and an emotional need for innate superiority:

> We need a group of humans to bound ourselves against who will come to exemplify the boundary line between the truly human and basely animal. If those quasi-animals stand between us and our own animality, then we are one step further away from being animal and mortal ourselves. (p. 104)

Nussbaum suggested that that in understanding others as marginalized and different, the dominant or majority group is able to distance itself even further from its own animality. She further noted that these individuals and members of marginalized groups who are considered others are relegated to a status between human and animal. She posited that:

> The discomfort people feel over the fact of having an animal body is projected outwards onto vulnerable people and groups. These reactions are irrational, in the normative sense, both because they embody an aspiration to be a kind of being that one is not, and because, in the process of pursuing that aspiration, they target others for gross harms. (p. 74)

This other construction, as Nussbaum noted, has damaging effects to those who are considered the other. Although applied to a different context, this 'other' construction can be applied to individual students, educators, and the learning environment. It can generate tension, which in turn can distort cultural understanding and the genuine transaction of empowering knowledge. Negative attitudes often disenfranchise the educational experience of all students. Where students of color or minority students are concerned, such negative and stereotypical attitudes disempower and devalue the identity of the student.

These marginalizing and racist ideologies create a toxic educational milieu. They set children who are different, most likely children of color, children belonging to minorities, and children of immigrants, apart from mainstream society. These students who feel marginalized and discriminated more often than not have fewer opportunities to make their voices and experiences heard. For these students, schools can come to be perceived as restrictive and as places that propagate racial oppression and perpetuate feelings of being the other (Freire, 1993; Giroux, 1997; hooks, 1994).

The process of schooling becomes problematic when children who are culturally different are expected to set aside their views, perceptions, and cultural values to fit the societal norm. Often these marginalized students set aside their cultural views and ways of being to succeed in school. Where academic achievement is concerned, students who experience feelings of marginalization, difference, and racism (feelings of being the other) talk of having reduced levels of self-confidence and feelings of insecurity or failure (Banks et al., 2001; Delpit, 1995; Giroux, 1997; hooks, 1994). Further, researchers, such as Banks et al. (2001) and Delgado (1995), have posited that racism, difference, and the associated feelings of being the other affect not only one's own self-perception but also how one is perceived and treated by others. These feelings directly affect one's identity of perceived self.

In addition, the perception of the other creates student unrest and division in the classroom. As noted earlier, Cummins (1984) and Giroux (1997) posited that such negative attitudes lead to power structures in the classroom in which some students are privileged over others. This classroom climate is the opposite of that bred by the democratic principle of equality and the right of all students to be treated fairly. In addition, educators and students are often responsible for unconsciously nurturing such differences and divisions. On a structural level, theorists note that schools and school districts serving children of color are likely to have fewer resources allocated to them and much lower teacher expectations (Delgado, 1995; Delpit, 1995; Giroux, 1997; hooks, 1994). According to Shor (1992), such attitudes of educators, students, and administration in schools create divergent perceptions of reality. He stated that without the nuanced deconstruction of perceptions of race and otherness, we cannot understand their effects and the role that they play in marginalizing students.

However, Nussbaum (2004) offered a ray of hope. She stated that as difficult as it may be, it is quite possible to teach children not to react with disgust to people who are considered to be different. According to Nussbaum, a healthy identity should rest not on feelings of superiority over others or the need to compete against those who feel marginalized but rather on seeing oneself as unique, as important, as someone with immense potential. She noted that all students deserve a chance at a good education regardless of their diversity, their cultural ethnicity, or their minority status. She noted that genuine attempts must be made by educators and the educational system to provide a quality learning environment for all students; this will produce individual growth and self-actualization by allowing empowering educational experiences for all students.

With this goal in mind, programs must be designed for an education that nourishes students' feelings of self-worth, individuality, value, and integrity. We as a society need to understand that concepts of racism and otherness are part of a system that society has created. This means that we as a society have the ability to change the system, to transform it, and someday to totally eradicate the issues that problematize the system. Educators, particularly in classrooms, must play important roles in student resistance practices (Giroux, 1997). Schools could be restructured not only as places where students learn but also as places where educators can learn from their students (Dewey, 1916; Stigler & Hiebert, 1999); this will, therefore, create an empowering educational milieu.

In summary, embracing difference is extremely consequential for those who feel marginalized because of factors of race, difference, and otherness. Banks et al. (2001) and Giroux (1997) noted that in drawing attention to differences, individuals and students risk being ghettoized or stigmatized. On the other hand, many refuse to acknowledge that racial differences and feelings of otherness exist because that would mean the acknowledgment of other races and cultures as inferior. As Delpit (1995) and hooks (1994) pointed out, a society that ignores race is hardly race-blind because that would mean that difference is ignored and subconsciously reproduced through culture, power, and hegemonic ideology. In acknowledging differences, we as a society acknowledge that negative perceptions and hegemonic ideologies of certain cultures and individuals do exist. Only through critical inquiry can we begin to question common assumptions, socially constructed images, and the major role that education can play in celebrating diversity and helping in student empowerment.

Valuing Otherness: The Role of Educators

Negotiating the issue of racism and otherness can be challenging for any educator. As noted in previous sections, the impact of racism is direct in school classrooms as it leads to the categorization, creation, and acknowledgement of hegemonic power structures within the classroom. Such creations of majority/minority subcultures in the classroom tend to marginalize those students who are considered the other. As they do in society, power structures in the classroom work to maintain the student status quo and the hierarchal order among students of different cultures. Cummins (1984) noted that this classroom atmosphere and inherent power structure contribute to various student behavioral abnormalities and deviant behavior. They also give rise to a host of ideological perceptions and stereotypes. hooks (1994) observed that students of color generally do not feel safe in the classroom. She therefore maintained that educators must relearn how to teach diversity in their classrooms.

In an overview of research into ethnicity and education in Australia, Partington (1998) noted that teachers can indirectly encourage racism in this day and age when there is an enormous amount of negativity directed toward those belonging to diverse ethnicities. These attitudes have strong implications for education. Further, according to Ira Shor (1992):

> If we do not teach in opposition to the existing inequality of races, classes, and sexes, then we are teaching to support it. If we don't teach critically against domination in society, then we allow dominant forces a free hand in school and out. (p. 347)

It is entirely possible that educators subconsciously perpetuate negative attitudes toward those who are considered the other. Educators may be unsure and possibly apathetic toward improving relations with those students who feel marginalized in the classroom. Many educators admit that they are ill-equipped to educate the diverse students in their classroom. However, I do believe that educators would acknowledge that improving the classroom culture is indeed important.

As an educator myself, I understand that an educator's views are shaped by student classroom participation. I further acknowledge that some marginalized voices are often silenced and drowned in the cacophony of other dominant voices. Still, I believe that with effective training and constant practice, educators can begin to understand every student's perspective in the classroom, accurately diagnose student needs, motivate them, and provide them with the necessary encouragement that they require to succeed. By practicing proper self-corrective thinking, an educator can be one of the foremost proponents of effective cross-cultural understanding. This understanding implies that educators must respect and build upon the cultural strengths and characteristics that students bring with them into the classroom (hooks, 1994). In addition, educators should not minimize differences but rather should encourage students to be their authentic selves (Freire, 1993). According to hooks (1994), the classroom must be a democracy, a place where all students feel safe in participating and sharing the responsibility for contributing toward the learning that takes place.

In addition, educators must remember that students cannot be isolated from their identity. Understanding others' views and perspectives can be difficult. As Delpit (1995) noted:

> We all interpret behaviors, information, and situations through our own cultural lenses; these lenses operate involuntarily, below the level of conscious awareness, making it seem that our own view is simply "the way it is." (p. 151)

Still, I believe that educators are in a unique position that enables them to foster and facilitate the inquiry and dialogue necessary to accept change open-mindedly in their classroom. An educator's pedagogical practice repertoire must include terms, such as *participatory, learner-centered,* and *democratic learning* (Shor, 1992). Educators who engage in an active, critical, and self-reflective learning process help to empower not only the students but also themselves (Freire, 1993; Giroux, 1997; McLaren, 1994; Shor, 1992).

If we as educators recognize the cultural differences and diversity of students as strengths rather than as problems, I truly believe that we are well on our way toward creating a more equitable democratic society. Toward this important goal, I believe that the educational curriculum today should consist of a pedagogy that encapsulates a common source of personal and individual expectations, student sensibilities, and educator evaluations. In addition, this pedagogy must consider the culture, history, and diversity of all students. What is needed, therefore, is a teaching approach that is capable of engaging all students intellectually, creatively, and critically. As educators, we need an educational language that questions difference, marginalization, and existing power structures between students and focuses on the distribution of the cultural equity and capital of all students.

Therefore, training educators to use the CI approach will help them understand their students' multiple perspectives and diverse ways of understanding. If all students' contributions are valued, regardless of their background, each individual will have equal access to a truly democratic education.

Overcoming Racism and Otherness in a CI

As discussed previously, the key description marking a CI is a group/social setting of students who use dialogue and discourse to inquire into problematic and sensitive concepts, such as racism, difference, marginalization, and otherness, by using, to the best of their ability, thinking that is creative, critical, central, and caring (Lipman, 2003). Each member/student is supported and considered an integral member of the community, and each is encouraged to pursue thinking that is creative, wherein new ideas are sought out and students are expected to give relevant reasons for the positions that they take (Lipman, 2003; Splitter & Sharp, 1995). Lipman (2003) noted that dialogue is intrinsic and vital for a CI to work as dialogue makes thinking a deliberate and self-conscious process. Further, Lipman noted that students have to be reasonable when subjecting a view to a critique as it allows for the accommodation of all competing behaviors and beliefs.

Also necessary to the thinking process is the individual's social disposition toward other students. Reasonableness is a social disposition; a reasonable person learns to respect others and is prepared to take others' feelings and views into account (Splitter & Sharp, 1995). Through the CI approach, the classroom can be designed to reinforce students' potential for reasonableness (Splitter & Sharp, 1995). As noted previously, students who experience racism and otherness often internalize negative self-images and find themselves hating themselves and their identities. This is partially due to the fact that society rewards those who assimilate. Through dialogue and discourse, the students engaged in a CI are transformed and empowered by the authentication of each and every perspective, by which every view is valued and each voice is respected.

There are many inspiring stories about overcoming marginality, racism, and otherness that can be used as perfect examples for understanding empowerment, authenticity, and the power of one's voice. These stories have been largely ignored in mainstream curricula because they expose a system of privilege and challenge societal power structures, hierarchy, and meritocracy. If appropriately used, such inspiring stories can help students in all settings to learn about stereotypes and absorb assumptions of superiority, marginality, and otherness. With the use of stories and books with a multicultural base, dialogue and inquiry can be stimulated to understand issues, such as racism and marginalization. For example, the Children's Book Press has some wonderful stories that affirm and validate a child's identity and culture. Philosophical stories, such as The Thinking Stories series published by the Institute for the Advancement of Philosophy for Children, help stimulate dialogue and inquiry. These stories are age appropriate and can be included in any language curriculum.

Often, literary work vividly portrays the experiences of being the other. I feel that such literature would be extremely beneficial in education. Even if the stories used do not deal directly with diverse cultures, they will exercise the creative imagination of the students so that they can begin to imagine different lives in different cultures in the confines of their own classroom.

Gradually, when students discover one another's views and share one another's opinions, they learn to respect one another's care and appreciate one another's perspectives (Lipman, 2003) as they begin to see diversity in the context of a larger worldview. In a CI, students learn to exercise good reasoning and judgment. They begin to explore the consequences of holding certain ideas, values, and beliefs. Learning takes place because there is a common problem or issue into which students inquire; all this is done through the cooperation and collaboration of all of the inquiring members (Lipman, 2003; Splitter & Sharp, 1995). During the learning process, individual learning horizons are broadened to look beyond the visual and focus on the person as a whole, in which their race or culture is but one part. In a CI, students begin to feel safe to be able to articulate and project their personal characteristics into the community and thereby present themselves as real people and presenting an authentic self to the community (Lipman, 2003; Splitter & Sharp, 1995).

Change is not instantaneous, nor will it happen overnight. Using the CI approach, slowly and surely all students will eventually become equal partners in constructing knowledge. As a classroom community matures, individual differences and perspectives are seen as a source of stimulation and enrichment rather than an inconvenience and disruption (Lipman, 2003; Splitter & Sharp, 1995).

Conclusion

We need a more compassionate society (Sen, 2001). This is an idea echoed by prominent political activist Amartya Sen when he wrote about helping the poor and disadvantaged. I suggest that this view of compassion could be broadened to include marginalized cultures and individuals as well. Nussbaum (2004) argued that without a more compassionate society, there could be severe limits to global progress toward equity. I believe that a compassionate citizenry is vital and crucial to attending to the needs of our diverse society.

Toward this goal, schools can play a major role in influencing the formation of students' attitudes and worldviews. Schools have a responsibility to support the cultures of all students and to teach the students to respect not only diverse values and views but also other students' perceptions and identities. This is the only way that society and schools can reduce prejudice and discrimination. Further, educators need to help their students to develop a genuine understanding and respect for cultural differences. In a classroom, there may be many differing opinions regarding racism and otherness. Many students may feel resentment toward students belonging to different cultural backgrounds. However if students learn to be accepting of other cultures, it is possible that feelings of marginalization, otherness, and racism can be successfully countered. Toward this goal, I believe that the CI pedagogical method works best. By valuing the opinions of all its members, the CI caters directly to the needs and growth of the participants as concerns are voiced and the CI endeavors to address them through the inquiry process. Thus, the classroom community provides a nurturing and caring milieu in which students feel safe to creatively and critically explore ideas that may seem strange or unfamiliar.

Engaging in such a democratic practice helps children to identify themselves as part of a group, a unified whole, as Nussbaum (2004) suggested. With this goal, education becomes "the practice of freedom, the means by which men and women deal critically and creatively with their reality, and discover how to participate in the transformation of their world" (Freire, 1993, p. 34). If we as educators take small steps within our own communities, in the schools in which we work, and in our respective classrooms to try to understand students' feelings of otherness, my hope is that one day all people in this country will arrive at one common ground where ethnicity, diversity, and difference are respected and celebrated. It all starts in a school.

References

Banks, J. A., Cookson, P., Gay, G., Hawley, W. D., Irvine, J. J., Nieto, S., Schofield, J. W., & Stephan, W. G. (2001). *Diversity within unity: Essential principles for teaching and learning in a multicultural society.* Seattle, WA: Center for Multicultural Education, College of Education, University of Washington.

Banton, M. (1998). *Racial theories.* Cambridge, England: Cambridge University Press.

Cummins, J. (1984). *Bilingualism and special education: Issues in assessment and pedagogy.* San Diego, CA: College-Hill Press.

Darling-Hammond, L. (1997). *Doing what matters most: Investing in quality teaching.* New York: National Commission on Teaching and America's Future.

Delgado, R. (1995). *Critical race theory: The cutting edge.* Philadelphia: Temple University Press.

Delpit, L. (1995). *Other people's children: Cultural conflict in the classroom.* New York: New Press.

Dewey, J. (1916). *Democracy and education.* New York: Free Press.

Essed, P. (1991). *Understanding everyday racism: An interdisciplinary theory.* Newbury Park, CA: Sage.

Freire, P. (1993). *Pedagogy of the oppressed.* New York: Continuum.

Gibson, M. (1988). *Accommodation without assimilation: Sikh immigrants in an American high school.* Ithaca, NY: Cornell University Press.

Giroux, H. A. (1997). *Pedagogy and the politics of hope: Theory, culture, and schooling, a critical reader.* Boulder, CO: Westview Press.

Helms, J. (Eds.). (1990). *Black and White racial identity: Theory, research, and practice.* New York: Greenwood.

hooks, b. (1994). *Teaching to transgress.* Education as the practice of freedom. New York: Routledge.

Lipman, M. (2003). *Thinking in education.* Cambridge, England: Cambridge University Press.

McLaren, P. (1994). White terror and oppositional agency: Towards a critical multiculturalism. In D. T. Goldberg (Ed.), *Multiculturalism: A critical reader* (pp. 45–74). Oxford, England: Blackwell.

Nussbaum, M. (2004). *Hiding from humanity: Disgust, shame and the law.* Princeton, NJ: Princeton Review Press.

Partington, G. (1998). When many worlds meet: Ethnicity and education in Australia. In J. Allen (Ed.), *Sociology of education: Possibilities and practices* (pp. 183–210). Katoomba, Australia: Social Science Press.

Sen, A. (2001). *Economic progress and health.* In D. Leon & G. Walt (Eds.), *Poverty inequality and health: An international perspective* (pp. 333–345). Oxford: Oxford University Press.

Shor, I. (1992). *Empowering education: Critical teaching for social change.* Chicago: University of Chicago Press.

Smedley, A. (1998). *Race in North America: Origin and evolution of a worldview.* Boulder, CO: Westview.

Splitter, L., & Sharp, A. (1995). *Teaching for better thinking: The classroom community of inquiry.* Melbourne: Australian Council for Educational Research.

Stigler, J., & Hiebert, J. (1999). *The teaching gap: Best ideas from the world's teachers for improving education in the classroom.* New York: Free Press.

CHAPTER EIGHT

INQUIRY-BASED PEDAGOGY AND BULLYING: ANALYZING INDICATORS OF DIALOGIC INTERACTION

MONICA B. GLINA
UNIVERSITY OF OSLO

Bullying is a serious social problem that can have deleterious effects on school children. A variety of interventions have been implemented, and research shows that the majority, which are monological in nature, have demonstrated minimal, if any, impact on counteracting occurrences of bullying in schools. A quantitative content analysis of formal, conversational strategies within classroom discourse suggests that students who participated in a community of inquiry began to internalize behaviors, such as respect, fairness, and caring. The role of the facilitator in modeling and encouraging good inquiry and empowering students to fully engage in the process so that they can practice and, ultimately, internalize dispositions, such as respect, fairness, and caring, emerged as a critical element.

Introduction

Bullying is a serious social problem that can have substantial consequences for the bully, the victim, and the bystander (e.g., Nansel et al., 2001; Olweus, 2001; Rigby, 2001; Smith & Thompson, 1991). Defined as unrelenting, willful, and malicious physical or psychological abuse that results in physical or psychological harm to the victim, the bully, and the bystander (e.g., Batsche & Knoff, 1994; Olweus, 1993a; Rigby, 1996; Twemlow, Fonagy, & Sacco, 2004), bullying involves the systematic abuse of power (Smith & Sharp, 1994) and always involves someone who is able to wield power over someone else, who is not capable of defending himself or herself (Roland & Idsoe, 2001). Because of the deleterious effects that bullying has for schoolchildren, it is critical to identify a successful intervention to prevent bullying. Empirical evaluations of existing antibullying interventions have yielded mixed results. Some studies report only modest improvements (e.g., Olweus, 1993a; Smith, Ananiadou, & Cowie, 2003; Smith, Schneider, Smith, & Ananiadou, 2004), while others fail to show any significant improvement (e.g., Rigby, Smith, & Pepler, 2004). These interventions address bullying by telling students what bullying is, what the characteristics of a bully are, and what one should do if one encounters a situation in which bullying occurs (e.g., Olweus, 1993a; Smith et al., 2004; Smith et al., 2003). The results imply that interventions based largely on a traditional instructional model in which the teacher defines terms and concepts and issues of morality are unilaterally conveyed to students may lack the qualities necessary to affect change and make an impact on the problem of bullying.

Because existing interventions have not significantly or successfully impacted the problem of bullying, I examined an instructional method that gives students the opportunity to engage in a critical, dialogic, substantive group inquiry regarding the essential issues underlying aggression, such as fairness, respect, caring, justice, and empathy, using structured philosophical dialogue. Then, I analyzed a series of dialogic indicators, which are indicative of and inherent in classroom talk. Specifically, I relied on Philosophy for Children (P4C), an educational model developed by Matthew Lipman (Lipman, 2003; Lipman, Sharp, & Oscanyan, 1980), to promote the cognitive, aesthetic, and affective development of children through teacher-facilitated group inquiry (Lipman, 2003).

The Significance of Language

As the expression of our complex humanity, language plays a vital role in our experiences with one another. According to Vygotsky (1978), individuals are social and cultural beings who develop cognitively through interactions with others as they socially construct meanings through mediation tools, such as language and signs (Wertsch, 1981). Mediation tools, which are most narrowly construed as language and include cultural systems of expression, such as writing systems and paralinguistic gestures, allow individuals to label and generate new ideas. Mediation tools are social and are at the immediate disposal of individuals, who receive them as participants in the sociocultural system in which they are generated and through which they are suffused (John-Steiner, Panofsky, & Smith, 1994). Language is the mediation tool to which Vygotsky most frequently refers, seeing it in a mutually symbiotic relationship with action. For Vygotsky, language performs two inextricably bound functions. First, it offers a mechanism by which to coordinate the actions of others. Second, rather than being a mere repository for concepts, it is a tool for thinking (Van der Veer & Valsiner, 1991). Thus, Vygotsky argues that language is a key element, and asserts that cognitive thought must move from the external to the internal.

This perspective has important implications for bullies and their victims. First, bullies use a variety of behaviors to attack their victims (Smith & Sharp, 1994); these include verbal actions, such as name-calling, malicious teasing, and threats; physical behaviors, such as hitting, kicking, and tripping; and social exclusion (Crick, 1997; Olweus, 1991; Rigby, Cox, & Black, 1997; Thompson & Sharp, 1998). Espelage, Bosworth, and Simon (2001) suggest the importance of recognizing that bullying is comprised of a continuum of behaviors employed to varying degrees by bullies. This acknowledges that low-level behaviors, such as teasing and name-calling, can cause high levels of distress (Espelage et al., 2001; Hoover, Oliver, & Thomson, 1993). Although significant in their effect on the victim and extremely common in schools, these low-level behaviors may be less easily identifiable by educators and, therefore, may be taken less seriously or ignored entirely (Craig, Henderson, & Murphy, 2000). Therefore, language can be used to create exposure to these behaviors, low-level or otherwise, which can cause injurious effects.

Students engaged in a dialogic method like P4C could benefit from a thoughtful examination of language as more than a mere repository from which certain harmful terms are strategically selected in order to inflict harm on the victim. Instead, an effective antibullying intervention would offer opportunities to actively and collectively examine malicious verbal behaviors, explore the language and its effects externally, and then internalize ideas about issues like empathy and bullying.

Research suggests that in cases where children are neglected by their caregivers (Weinhold, 2003), language as a means by which children communicate and solve problems is lacking. As a result, bullies do not acquire the ability to use language to achieve their goals and resort, instead, to aggression (Eron, 1994). In this case, the thoughtful, spoken word has become an irrelevant means of communication and has been replaced by aggressive verbal assaults and physical actions. Conversely, language as a mediating tool within the social pedagogy inherent in P4C can positively affect a child's development. By using thoughtful language instead of verbal assaults and physical actions, the bully, the victim and the bystander can learn to mediate their ideas through one another, express their concerns, articulate their arguments, and become conversant with concepts and issues of morality. Thus, language becomes a tool for effective communication and solving disagreements.

The Significance of Community

In addition to considering the significant role that language plays as a vehicle for bullying behaviors, it is worth examining the participants. Historically, researchers have suggested that bullying involves at least two participants: a victim, who is the target of frequent episodes of physical and psychological abuse, and a perpetrator, who is responsible for administering the abuse (Farrington, 1993; Perry, Kusel, & Perry, 1988). However, recent research suggests that a third participant—the bystander —plays an active role in the "social architecture" of bullying, shifting bullying from a dyadic construction (bully–victim) to a triadic construction (bully–victim–bystander) (Twemlow, Fonagy & Sacco, 2004). As participants in the same community, the bully, the victim, and the bystander each have a prescribed role and substantial effects on one another. The purpose of this research was to test the potential that participation in dialogical, community-driven inquiry has for cultivating empathy and respect as bullies, victims, and bystanders meaningfully explore the issues underlying aggression.

Cultivating empathy and respect are important goals for any antibullying intervention because of their connection to bullying. First, empirical research shows a significant correlation between low empathy and bullying (Endresen & Olweus, 2001; Jolliffe & Farrington, 2006; Sutton, Smith, & Swettenham, 1999). Eisenberg and Strayer (1987) define *empathy* as sharing the emotions of another person, and the research on empathy suggests that empathy has cognitive and affective/emotional components (Davis, 1994). The cognitive component represents an individual's ability to identify with and understand another individual's perspective. The affective/emotional component represents an individual's tendency to experience feelings of sympathy or concern for another individual (Davis, 1994). Research suggests that bullies lack empathy for their victims, have difficulty feeling compassion (Olweus, 1992), and are unable to understand and sympathize with another individual's feelings (Arsenio & Lemerise, 2001; Eisenberg & Fabes, 1998).

Second, cultivating respect should be an important goal for any anti-bullying intervention because chronic bullies exhibit a lack of respect for adults and are likely to disregard institutional rules (Batsche & Knoff, 1994). Contrary to conventional beliefs about bullying, bullies seem to exhibit little anxiety and strong self-esteem (Olweus, 1993a). There is little evidence to support the notion that their victimization of others is an outward manifestation of the negative feelings that they possess about themselves (Batsche & Knoff, 1994). These inherent characteristics make the bully a formidable threat to schoolchildren around the world (Kenny, McEachern, & Aluede, 2005; McEachern, Kenny, Blake, & Aluede, 2005).

In sum, both language and the 'social architecture' of bullying can operate as powerful vehicles for perpetrating instances of aggression. These are also two of the primary components of a pedagogical model that is dialogical (language) and community-driven (community). Philosophy for Children (P4C) is an example of one such approach. Ideally, through their participation in a dialogical pedagogy of this kind, students will internalize the dispositions that derive from engaging in inquiry, as well as the processes and procedures that drive that inquiry. For example, students can cultivate their sense of respect for others by learning to listen to the perspectives of others and valuing those perspectives even when they are incongruous with their own.

Integrating Language and Community

Philosophy for Children (P4C) is a pedagogical approach (Lipman, 2003; Lipman et al., 1980) that promotes the cognitive, aesthetic, and affective development of children through teacher-facilitated group inquiry and dialogue (Lipman, 2003). P4C uses structured philosophical dialogue not only to sharpen critical-thinking skills (e.g., Banks, 1989; Camhy & Iberer, 1988) but to cultivate a sensitivity toward and understanding of others' values, interests, and beliefs (Lipman et al., 1980).

Lipman (2003) argues that it is through philosophical dialogue that children can and should learn to arrive at their own conclusions. Lipman does not suggest that there is right or wrong answer to a specific moral dilemma. He does suggest, however, that there is a right and wrong way to *think about* moral dilemmas and that philosophy can teach children the proper techniques for engaging in exploratory dialogue with one another. Specifically, students use particular rules of inquiry, such as reasoning and concept clarification, to debate reasonably with one another as they analyze questions of morality and mediate their notions of complex issues, such as caring, empathy, fairness, and respect, through other members of the community of inquiry.

A key characteristic of P4C, the community of inquiry, functions as the arena for inquiry, dialogue, and concept exploration. The community of inquiry, as discussed by advocates of the approach, such as Splitter and

Sharp (1995), "is characterized by dialogue that is fashioned collaboratively out of reasoned contribution of all participants" (p. 336). Furthermore, it respectfully acknowledges the importance of regarding "the production of knowledge as contingent, bound up with human interests and activities and therefore always open to revision" (p. 337) and the importance of understanding that "the meanings that totally subjective experience do reveal are narrow and paltry compared to the meanings one can derive from communal inquiry" (p. 341).

Thus, P4C is a pedagogical model that is defined by the inextricable link between language and community. An instructional method, such as P4C, which is steeped in the dynamics of dialogical inquiry, community interaction, and the (re)productive evolution of ideas, could also hold the necessary transformative capacity to allow students to explore the issues underlying aggression, such as empathy and respect, in a deep and meaningful way. This dialogic approach is an alternative to many of the existing interventions, which utilize an instructional model of "knowledge transmission." These interventions, which are typically monological in nature, do not offer students the opportunity to arrive at their own understanding of concepts and, consequently, of their impact and importance. Instead, students are indoctrinated with discrete notions of right and wrong without being given the opportunity to become conversant with these ideas through inquiry and dialogue.

As an antibullying intervention, P4C would not, by definition, teach students that bullying is wrong. Instead, it would equip students with the tools of inquiry and rely on the deliberative process and a sound value system as a means to an end. Instead of being told the right answer, students would engage in rational inquiry and thoughtful and insightful dialogue to draw their own conclusions about bullying and redefine the way in which they understand it and its impact on others. Thus, P4C would help students "both understand and practice what is involved in violence reduction and peace development. They have to learn to think for themselves about these matters, not just to provide knee-jerk responses when we present the proper stimuli" (Lipman, 2003, p. 105).

Lipman et al. (1980) argue that the processes of inquiry and dialogue are insufficient; it is equally as important to demonstrate sensitivity toward, respect for, and understanding of another's values, interests, and beliefs. Although committed to the procedures of inquiry, the community is equally and simultaneously responsible for adhering to conditions, such as mutual respect, fairness, and an absence of indoctrination. Layering these attributes over the process of inquiry is vital because they help to create conditions that allow participants to explore ideas freely and without marked reservation. Thus, the technique that informs inquiry must exist in concert with caring thinking.

P4C pedagogy is consistent with Vygotsky's (1978) theoretical assertions that (1) language is the essential tool in development and (2) individuals incorporate new behavior as they engage in interpersonal relationships and social activities. Social interaction, for Vygotsky, takes on a variety of forms, from peer relationships to facilitator-moderated scaffolding, modeling, guidance, and collaboration. Vygotsky suggests that working collaboratively with peers and teachers can lead students to make more substantial progress than they would have acquired alone. As a means by which to advance students' exposure to and internalization of key behaviors, such as fairness, caring, and respect, external interaction is critical before internalization can occur.

This theoretical perspective has important implications for bullies and their victims. First, an effective antibullying intervention would offer opportunities for students to actively and collectively examine malicious verbal behaviors, explore the language and its effects *externally*, and then internalize ideas about issues, such as empathy and bullying. Thus, language becomes a positive and productive tool within the parameters of an inquiry-driven, procedurally strong community.

The preceding narrative argues for the need to investigate the potential of an instructional method that uses dialogical inquiry, such as P4C, as a bullying intervention because of the value inherent in the inquiry process and the ameliorative procedural component that drives the inquiry. This study was designed to explore the following questions:

1. What are the processes of group interaction that characterize a dialogic community?
2. How are the group processes that characterize a dialogic community different from the processes present in classrooms receiving regular instruction?

Methodology

Method

Site and Sample Selection

Students in four fourth-grade classrooms at a suburban elementary school in northern New Jersey participated in this study. I chose the fourth grade for three reasons. First, school bullying increases among children who are 10 to 14 years old (Olweus, 1993b; Whitney & Smith, 1993). Second, the P4C novels that address issues of empathy, caring, trust, respect, and friendship are targeted toward fourth graders. Third, research shows that elementary-school children are developmentally ready to participate in dialogical discussions and to engage in abstract thinking (Crowhurst, 1988; Reznitskaya, Anderson, Dong, Li, & Kim, 2008), although many educators have previously underestimated this ability in young children.

Seventy-three students in four classes participated in the study. There were 36 boys and 37 girls. The average number of students in each class was 18. The elementary school served an ethnically diverse population: 18% of the participants were Caucasian, 35% were African American, 20% were Asian, and 27% were Hispanic Latino. Sixteen percent of the participants qualified for free lunch and 7% were eligible for reduced lunch.

Design and Procedure

Two classrooms were assigned to one of two treatment conditions: P4C and the control group. Students in the P4C group participated in P4C pedagogy, while students in the control group continued with their regular instruction. Prior to this study, the elementary school had not used P4C as part of its curriculum. The treatment groups were comparable in terms of gender distribution (see Table 1). Because indicators of socioeconomic status (SES) could only be obtained for a whole grade level because of privacy issues, I was unable to provide information regarding the ethnic and SES composition of each treatment group.

Table 1. Treatment Groups by Gender

P4C Group		Group Receiving Regular Instruction	
Boys	Girls	Boys	Girls
18	19	18	18

Students in two classes participated in one of the two treatment conditions: P4C and Regular Instruction. Students in the latter treatment group continued to be taught by their regular classroom teachers, who used their usual classroom techniques and strategies. Students in the P4C group participated in eight one-hour discussion sessions using P4C pedagogy. To reduce the threat to treatment fidelity, I enlisted a highly experienced P4C facilitator to mediate the discussions in both P4C classrooms.

During the first session, the P4C facilitator introduced P4C pedagogy. This exercise set the stage for deriving philosophical questions for two discrete purposes. First, students were invited to offer questions for discussion based on the reading for a particular week. The questions that they offered were of a more general, philosophical type, which they generated using the procedure that they had learned. Second, students used the technique as a mechanism by which to both launch the inquiry and advance the dialogue.

During the second session, students began to read, aloud and as a group, chapters from the philosophical novel *Kio and Gus* (Lipman, 1982), which were selected because they exemplified issues of empathy, caring, respect, and bullying. *Kio and Gus* is part of a series of philosophical novels that comprise the P4C curriculum. Targeted toward elementary-school children, *Kio and Gus* is about a young boy named Kio who visits his grandfather one summer. During his visit, he befriends Gus, who is blind. Gus introduces Kio to the direct personal awareness that her blindness affords her and the experiences that she has.

Once students completed a chapter, they read through a discussion plan, which is "a landscape through which the group and each individual in it moves as they discuss" (Kennedy, 2004, p. 758). Then, students collectively arrived at a discussion question and participated in a group discussion based on it. This pattern of events was indicative of the agenda for each of the remaining sessions.

The readings and exercises were paced so that each group discussed the same content during each session. During the last 4 weeks, the P4C sessions became more directive in nature, with students participating in peer dialogues based on a prescribed question about bullying, empathy, fairness, justice, and power issues. Students were furnished with a discussion plan and voted on the question. Some of the questions included "What is respect?" and "What is bullying?"

Data Sources

I transcribed the third, fifth, and eighth videotaped classroom discussions for each of the four classes. These particular episodes were selected because they captured the progress of student development from the early stages of the study to the later stages of intervention. The video transcriptions were then analyzed using Quantitative Content Analysis (QCA), which Berelson (1952) originally defined as "the systematic,

objective and quantitative description of the content of communication"
(p. 18). Following QCA, each discussion was coded into distinct idea
units. I used QSR NVivo 8 computer software (QSR International, 2008)
to code the transcriptions and conduct searches of the coded data.

Data Analysis

Because P4C is a community-driven pedagogy, inquiry occurs within
the group setting. Therefore, it is important to focus on the pedagogical
procedures and strategies (inquiry) that are used in the day-to-day
classroom within the group (community). This informed my decision to
conduct a quantitative analysis of a strategically selected set of
sociolinguistic features of discourse. I chose this approach because it is
useful in capturing potential changes in general patterns that emerge in
both discourse and community.

I validated the viability of taking such an approach by conducting a
literature search on the relationship between linguistic elements and
classroom discourse. My search revealed the conversational strategies, or
coding categories, that comprised the basis for my coding system. (A
complete inventory of the codes that I used and the rationale behind my
decisions are elaborated below, and examples of coding categories can be
found in Tables 2–7.)

My methodological decision to analyze sociolinguistic elements was
also mediated by the inextricable connection between language and
learning that is inherent in Vygotsky's (1978) theory of cognitive
development, as well as the argument by sociolinguists (e.g., Gumperz,
1982; Tannen, 1989) that suggests that conversational strategies promote
interdialogical interaction and the co-construction of meaning; without
dialogical interaction, there is no meaning making.

My data-analytic decision to code sociolinguistic elements and their
impact on a concrete problem like bullying also reflects my interest in
assessing discursive practices that have the potential to redistribute power
among all members of the community. Practices that are traditionally
associated with teacher-centered classrooms focus primarily on the
transmission of knowledge from the teacher to the students, who are
viewed as passive recipients. The discursive practices associated with a
teacher-centered classroom preserve prevailing power structures because
they:

> Are understood as happenings, which essentially fall into the production
> and reproduction of social, historical and cultural life manifesting not only
> linguistic mechanisms but also devices of a different order, such as those

that reproduce ideology and contribute to maintaining existing power structures. (Haidar & Rodriguez, 1995, p. 120)

According to McCombs and Whisler (1997), this is diametrically opposed to a student-centered classroom in which the emphasis is on reflective inquiry and thinking-centered learning. The purpose of coding the sociolinguistic elements I identified is to assess the degree to which each of them is present and representative of a reflective, thinking-centered, participatory environment of shared power, which lends itself to the precipitation of meaningful concept exploration.

Coding sociolinguistic elements is also consistent with the connection that Van Dijk (1995) establishes among ideology, power, and specific dialogical features that implies the methodological, data-analytic advantage of analyzing those features. Van Dijk outlines an association between ideologies and the power dynamics that exist amongst individuals:

> Ideologies define relationships of power, which in turn also may control interaction, i.e., who has more or less access to the use of specific dialogical features, such as setting agendas for meetings, making appointments, opening and closing dialogues, turn management, the initiation, change and closure of topics, style selection and variation. (p. 31)

Van Dijk's (1995) suggestion that ideologies impact power relationships and interactions has implications for bullying, which is characterized as abuse imposed by an individual who has power over someone who is defenseless against the attack (Roland & Idsoe, 2001; Smith & Sharp, 1994). Thus, power resides at the core of all bully–victim relationships, and language is one way in which a bully can torment his or her victim. Language is also the vehicle through which students can begin to recast their ideologies about bullying, as well as the overall school culture.

A student-centered pedagogical approach, such as P4C, is consistent with a pedagogy that features power sharing by the facilitator. Power sharing can invite students to participate in the group's procedural processes, the topics (e.g., caring and fairness) that are selected by these processes, and the degree to which the topics are investigated. The facilitator can invite students to use sociolinguistic elements, such as nomination and agenda setting, to participate in group processes, thereby redistributing power amongst the community's participants. The facilitator can also incorporate sociolinguistic elements, such as exploratory talk, that feature language as a mediation tool for the co-construction of, and transition toward, a potentially fairer, more caring, and more respectful school culture.

Fairclough (2000) and Coupland (1998) argue that theories of language should be operationalized in order to advance the conceptual and theoretical frameworks of social theory. According to Fairclough:

> There is a pervasive failure amongst theorists to operationalize their theorizations of language in ways of showing specifically how language figures in social life within social research. This is partly a matter of theory stopping short—theoretical frameworks and concepts which centre language within social life are not pushed in the direction of theorizations of language itself…sociolinguistics can advance social theory. (p. 164)

Following Fairclough (2000) and Coupland (2000), I chose to code nomination, dyadic exchanges, back-channeling, and agenda setting because they have the potential to impact power relationships. The choice to code these sociolinguistic elements, which can affect the redistribution of power, manifests itself in social theory and the importance of interactions that, for example, reframe the way in which language is used; the emphasis on the importance of power relationships themselves emerges from the conceptual framework of bullying (Roland & Idsoe, 2001).

Thus, in order to assess the potential that P4C has as an antibullying intervention and to identify specific processes of dialogical interaction that distinguish P4C from traditional instruction, I implemented a methodology that enabled me to examine intersubjective dialogue (talk among participants) within a democratic community of inquiry (the P4C classroom). I examined group processes for each of the treatment groups by coding conversational strategies, such as nomination, dyadic exchanges (turn-taking), back-channeling, agenda setting, low-level questions and responses, high-level questions, elaborated meaning, and exploratory talk. These indicators of dialogical interaction can be divided into two categories that mirror the two categories I delineated in the preceding narrative: community and inquiry. Nomination, turn-taking, back-channeling, and agenda setting comprise the community category; low-level questions and responses, high-level questions, elaborated meaning, and exploratory talk constitute the inquiry category. Thus, to answer my research questions, which asked, "What are the specific processes of group interaction that characterize a community of inquiry?" and "How are they different from the processes present in classrooms receiving regular instruction?", I looked to elements that (1) derive from a theoretical framework of social cognitive theory, (2) address the fundamental issue of power in bullying, and (3) align with the conceptual underpinnings of the community of inquiry. An approach of this nature represents an analysis of the fundamental components that define inquiry within a community, such as respecting another's beliefs and listening to the contributions of others, and the ways in which certain factors, such as the elements associated with community, either help or hinder the inquiry.

Indicators of Dialogical Interaction

Throughout this narrative, I have delineated the contributions of both community and inquiry to the community of inquiry. To assess each of these dimensions, I analyzed specific indicators of dialogical interaction, which are elaborated in the sections called Elements of Community and Elements of Inquiry.

Elements of Community

Nomination

Nomination, which is categorized as an element of community, is a formal procedure used to allocate speaking opportunities in, for example, the classroom. An individual can be chosen to speak by someone else; by self-nomination (e.g., by raising his or her hand) (Sacks, Schegloff, & Jefferson, 1974); by answering a question that requires a response; or by vocal intonation, physical gestures, or facial expressions (e.g., Duncan, 1972, 1974; Wardhaugh, 1992). If the speaker forfeits the opportunity to select the next speaker, any participant may exercise self-selection and become the next speaker. If none of the participants elects to self-nominate, the primary speaker has the right to retain the role of speaker (Sacks et al., 1974). Nominations were coded by the specification of who precipitated the nomination and who received the nomination. (See Table 2 for examples of how nomination was coded.)

Nomination is a sociolinguistic element that can suggest the degree to which the facilitator shares his or her power with the students. The issue of power is integral to our conceptual understanding of bullying and must reside at the core of any pedagogical antibullying intervention. In a teacher-dominated classroom setting, the power to nominate may reside exclusively with the facilitator. However, a facilitator who shares the power to nominate other speakers is redistributing that power among all members of the classroom community.

Table 2. Nomination

Facilitator nominating a student	Example 1: "Um, another comment, T?" Example 2: "K, what is your question?" Example 3: "J, you have a question? What grabbed you?" Example 4: "M?" Example 5: "T has a question."
Facilitator prompting a student to nominate the next speaker	Example 6: "Go ahead. Pick somebody" Example 7: "You call on the next person, R."
Student nominating a student	Example 8: I (male student): "R." Example 9: M (female student): "Pick someone." Example 10: Male student: "I had his hand up." Example 11: R (female student): "I."

By sharing the responsibility for nomination with his students, the P4C facilitator, as model and mediator, accomplishes three crucial objectives. First, he introduces students to the inherently democratic practice of sharing the responsibility of nomination. Second, by inviting students to facilitate the process of nomination, the facilitator takes an important step toward redistributing the power dynamic within the group, shifting it to all members of the community. Third, he encourages them to participate in the *doing* of this practice, which, in turn, affords them opportunities to practice fair and respectful behavior. The sum total of the facilitator's actions suggests a willingness to share his power and authority with the group (Kennedy, 2004). The redistribution of power has implications for the bully–victim relationship, which is typically defined by one person who wields power over another person (Roland & Idsoe, 2001). By shifting power from himself to all members of the community, the facilitator redefines the relationship between all of the group's participants.

Dyadic Exchanges as Turn-taking

Turn-taking is the process of alternating between speakers or participants in a conversation (Sacks et al., 1974). Thornbury (2005) explains that there are two main rules for turn-taking: avoid long silences and listen when others are speaking. These rules govern who speaks when and ensures that the transition between speakers is as seamless as possible.

With respect to turn-taking, I specifically examined levels of participation and distribution of talk by coding dyadic speaking exchanges. Dyadic exchanges are turns between two speakers within a turn-taking episode. The two speakers could be the facilitator and a student or two students. (See Table 3 for examples of how turn-taking was coded.) The purpose of specifically assessing dyadic exchanges is to determine the length of the interaction between any two speakers. The length of interaction could indicate the amount of time that students spend doing engaged in *doing* good inquiry.

Table 3. Dyadic Exchanges

T × 2 (two turns)	Facilitator: "How many feet equal a yardstick, somebody?" (Turn 1) Male student: "3." (Turn 2)
T × 3 (three turns)	Facilitator: "One of these sticks represents what, H?" (Turn 1) H (female student): "One meter." (Turn 2) Facilitator. "One meter, right." (Turn 3)
T × 4 (four turns)	Facilitator: "I would like to use actually this thing that just happened between T and I as an example, right, not to try to settle it but as an example whether either of them feels that what the other person did to them is bullying. T?" (Turn 1) T (female student): "Yeah, I don't really call it bullying." (Turn 2) Facilitator: "You *don't* call it bullying?" (Turn 3) T (female student): "Cause, well, I do call it bullying, but it depends who is the person because if I don't know the person then I guess it doesn't really matter. I." (Turn 4)
T × 5 (five turns)	E (female student): "And so they will bring it out on somebody else. Facilitator: "He wants to make other people feel the same in a way. How does this example that you [R] gave us earlier….How does it…does it fit in those categories? Was that what that person what doing to you? They were trying to make you feel small?" (Turn 1) R (female student): "About me and H?" (Turn 2) Facilitator: "Yeah. Would put it in the bullying category?" (Turn 3) R (female student): "Yeah." (Turn 4) Facilitator: "Okay. E?" (Turn 5)

When one recognizes when to take a turn, signals that one wants to speak, recognizes when others want to speak, yields a turn, or signals when one is listening to another speaker, these acknowledge the individual's position within the group and his or her responsibility to the group and its members. The speaker who holds the floor needs to exercise fairness when he or she recognizes that there are others who have an equal right to speak. Thus, by sharing his or her power with the students and inviting students to practice the strategies integral to successful turn-taking, the facilitator both models and promotes practicing *doing* fairness and respectful behavior through doing good inquiry.

Empowered by the facilitator requires students to exhibit high levels of personal awareness as they weigh their turn-taking needs against the mutual trust of and respect for the group. Thus, turn-taking in the community of inquiry can translate into an important component for a successful antibullying intervention. The group process of regulating turn-taking requires that students reconcile high levels of personal awareness with mutual trust of and respect for the group.

Back-channeling

Back-channeling is the third linguistic element that I coded. *Back-channeling* conveys attention to the primary speaker (Sacks et al., 1974), to whom utterances, such as "Yeah," "Right," and "Uh-huh," are tendered by the listener without the expectation that the speaker should relinquish his or her turn (Yngve, 1970, p. 574). According to Duncan (1974), there are five types of back-channeling utterances: (1) "Yeah," "Right," and so on; (2) Sentence completion; (3) Requests for clarification (e.g., "You mean . . .); (4) Restatements (repetition); and (5) Non-verbal gestures, such as nods (excluded for the purposes of this study). Table 4 provides a side-by-side comparison of examples of each type of back-channeling utterance for each of the two treatment groups. Appendix A exemplifies three of Duncan's four categories—repetition, request for clarification, and sentence completion—working in tandem with one another.

The fourth category on Duncan's (1974) list groups restatements and repetition together. However, I coded these as two separate entities to highlight a qualitative distinction. Utterances that qualified as instances of *repetition* were a verbatim recapitulation of the original phrase, such as when the student said, "It helps calm me down," and the teacher responds, "It helps calm you down." A *restatement* was an utterance that paraphrased or recast the original statement in such a way that invited the potential for clarification if deemed necessary by the primary speaker. By

Table 4. Examples of Back-channeling Utterances from Both Treatment Groups

Type of Back-channeling Utterance	P4C	Regular Instruction
"Yeah," "Right," and so on	Male speaker: "I think that you can respect someone that doesn't respect you." FS: "Mmm, yeah."	Female student: "Whales were also hunted for their blubber." Facilitator: "Uh-huh, yeah."
Sentence completion	Female speaker: "I disagree because, like, you can care for somebody like, say, your mother died when you were 3, so your father remarried, and you absolutely hate your new mother, but when your mother is old and not exactly independent anymore, but you're an adult, you can care for them, like, you can, like, give them food and shelter, but you don't have to respect them, like, you can give somebody care." Facilitator: "Without respecting them." Female speaker: "Without respecting them."	Facilitator: "What about Marvel Comics? Their Number 1 book, how much is that worth, G?" G (female speaker): "Um, 440, 440,000." Facilitator: "Dollars good. 440,000 dollars."
Request for clarification	Facilitator: "You made a distinction between somebody you know and somebody you don't. If somebody you know does it to you, you consider it teasing. If somebody you don't, you consider it bullying. Am I right?" Female speaker: "Yeah, but someone I do know it's just like, it's really bad because she says something like the person acts really bad when you do this…."	Facilitator: "The comic books. She said they were still in their glove. What do you mean by that?"

Restatement	Male speaker: "Bullying can also be hurting other people." Facilitator: "It can also be physical." Male speaker: "Yeah."	Female student: "I'm thinking it's like a virus that can spread like germs." Facilitator: "Okay, maybe it has to do with bacteria with germs."
Repetition	Female speaker: "Well, I think respect is a feeling for somebody and one cannot force a feeling upon them unless it's….Well, nobody can force a feeling upon themselves." Facilitator: "Nobody can."	Facilitator: "Yes, D?" D (female speaker): "When I start, when I start to draw, it helps me calm down." Facilitator: "It helps you calm down."

offering the restatement as a back-channeling utterance, the facilitator indicates to the student that the floor is still his as primary speaker. This gives the student permission to correct the facilitator's understanding or simply agree with the facilitator's interpretation.

Restatement also serves as validation of the student's utterance. This act affirms for the student his or her right to voice an opinion or state a perspective. The facilitator's act also models the respectful behavior associated with listening to and valuing the ideas of others. It is important to distinguish listening to and valuing ideas from agreeing with an individual's ideas. The former do not imply the latter; however, the facilitator's ability to disclose disagreement while acknowledging the value of the contribution further reinforces the respect with which students' contributions are treated.

While a turn advances the dialogue by adding to or profoundly enhancing the content of the dialogue (Henne, as cited in Oreström, 1983), back-channeling utterances contribute minimally to expanding content exploration. The substantive value of back-channeling resides in its ability to (1) maintain smooth communication (Watzlawick, Beavin, & Jackson, 1967) and (2) signal to the speaker that the listener is engaged, interested, and intellectually and emotionally reactive (Oreström, 1983).

Oreström (1983) considers requests for clarification speaking turns because they have a substantive impact on the dialogue and are comparable to paired question/answer turns. However, Oreström (1983) (1983) suggests that other back-channeling utterances, such as the repetition of the content of a speaker's turn, do not add to the content of the dialogue. Following Lipman (2003), a dialogue manifests instability, which represents a series of arguments and counterarguments that continually propel the dialogue forward. Each turn taken by an individual is a logical, purposeful "move" to both actuate and substantively elevate the dialogue.

The distinction that Lipman (2003) draws between conversation and dialogue has significant implications for the way that back-channeling utterances can be understood within the context of P4C. Lipman argues that a *conversation* involves turn-taking that does not propel the conversation forward, while *dialogue* represents a series of arguments and counterarguments that continually propel the dialogue forward. In the context of traditional linguistic theory, back-channeling by a teacher or facilitator is a device that can encourage seamless discourse and concept exploration by participants without impinging upon that discourse or the process of exploration with characteristically didactic contributions. Furthermore, the teacher or facilitator relinquishes a certain level of power and control by (1) not dictating a prescribed understanding of an issue or topic or (2) monopolizing the dialogue. Instead, the facilitator allows students to arrive at their own conclusions by allocating speaking-turn opportunities to students and supporting them through back-channeling utterances. However, within the context of P4C pedagogy, it can be argued that all utterances, including back-channeling, that derive from doing good inquiry make a substantive contribution, which manifests itself in the way that participants learn to interact with one another. For example, if the facilitator repeats the primary speaker's statement, he overtly demonstrates the behavior associated with active and engaged listening. Furthermore, back-channeling utterances can also be viewed as the mediation tools through which students in P4C construct language. Understood within Vygotsky's (1978) theoretical framework, a more diverse and evenly distributed utilization of the variety of available utterances provides students with a richer bank of mediation tools with which to socially construct caring thinking. Therefore, I would like to suggest that all utterances are significant because they are opportunities to model acceptable social behavior.

If we reexamine the conditions that I described in the previous paragraph, the facilitator who uses back-channeling (1) encourages seamless discourse and concept exploration, (2) does not impinge upon that discourse or the process of exploration, (3) does not dictate a prescribed understanding of an issue or topic, and (4) does not monopolize the dialogue but allows students to arrive at their own conclusions and models doing good inquiry, as well as and the behaviors associated with it. These are all criteria that can contribute to redistributing power among group participants and encouraging thoughtful inquiry. Therefore, even back-channeling utterances, which have traditionally been classified as linguistically unproductive, can serve a critical function in the process of doing good inquiry. As a result, all utterances, including back-channeling utterances, were coded as turns.

Agenda Setting

Agenda setting is defined as the process by which decisions are made about what topics and issues receive priority over others. I coded agenda setting by identifying the starting point at which the process for topic selection begins. This could be signaled by utterances like, "What do you see [on the discussion plan]?" and "We're trying to think about what we're gonna talk about today. Is there a question that grabbed you?" The end of the episode of agenda setting was characterized by a shift from the process of collecting questions to the beginning of real discussion.

According to Barber (2003), agenda setting "cannot precede talk, deliberation and decision but must be approached as a permanent function of talk itself" (p. 182). Agenda setting places the power of topic selection within the purview of the students. Dewey (1997b) calls into question "instruction in subject-matter that does not fit into any problem already stirring in the student's own experience" (p. 199) and suggests that instruction for instruction's sake is a misguided practice. He proposes, instead, that inquiry should result from that which grows organically from the student's interests and experiences. Only then will the student think in a reflective and effective way. Thus, participating in something that is inherently worthwhile to the learner and is undertaken of its own accord is innately more powerful than that which is imposed on the individual (Dewey, 1997a). Agenda setting as a group process is a mechanism by which questions and concepts of interest are allowed to present themselves for prioritization by the group. This invites students to play a more active role in the discussion as they become instrumental in deciding its direction. Participants in a community of inquiry give serious consideration to topics but cannot commit to any of these until they have discussed the issues, listened to one another's perspectives, explored one another's value commitments, and balanced their needs with the needs of others. It is only by the community's commitment to engage in political talk that proposed agenda topics worthy of inquiry and dialogue can organically arise. Once the agenda is set, talk can occur, and decisions and judgments can be tested.

Elements of Inquiry

Consideration of complex topics is important because it asks students to reach beyond recalling and restating information from their knowledge cache and utilize that information to, for example, build, test, and argue for ideas. This is a much more complex cognitive exercise and cultivates students' abilities to be, for example, critical purveyors of their own ideas and legitimate evaluators of the ideas of others. Low-level questions and responses, high-level questions, elaborated meaning, and exploratory talk, which comprise the inquiry category, are attributes of discourse that can both facilitate these exercises and give students the opportunity to practice doing good inquiry.

Low-level Questions and Responses

I compared the frequency of low-level questions and responses across both treatment groups. *Low-level items* were defined as any questions or responses that could be categorized in either the knowledge category or the comprehension category of Bloom's Taxonomy (Bloom, Engelhart, Furst, Hill, & Krathwohl, 1956). (See Table 5 for examples of how low-level questions and responses were coded.)

The educational objective *knowledge* is defined by a student's ability to recall information. *Comprehension* is characterized by a student's ability to translate, interpret, or extrapolate information. Students demonstrate their level of comprehension competence by understanding and using information. The multiple knowledge questions in the third and fourth examples in Table 5 require students to recall mathematical operations. These kinds of known-answer questions are asked by teachers and are exceedingly common in traditional classroom discourse (Cazden, 2001; French & MacClure, 1981).

High-level Questions

According to Nystrand, Wu, Gamoran, Zeiser, and Long (2003), high-level questions can be characterized in two distinct ways. They engender new information, and they cannot be answered by the process of simple recall or the appropriation of prior knowledge. Understanding the relationship that the two kinds of aforementioned outcomes have with high-level questions helps to operationalize them and to understand the rationale associated with their coding. High-level questions, which are deemed as such on the basis of the new information that comprise the high-level responses that they evoked, were coded accordingly. (See Table 6 for examples of how high-level questions were coded.)

Table 5. Low-level Questions and Responses

Knowledge	
Example 1	Facilitator: "What is baleen?" (low-level knowledge question)
Example 2	Facilitator: "*Mañana* is what in Spanish?" (low-level knowledge question) Female student: "Tomorrow." (low-level response)
Example 3	Facilitator: "What do we mean by *quadruple? Quadruple* is another word for what? For what, A?" (low-level knowledge question) A (female speaker): "Four times whatever." (low-level response) Facilitator: "Four times whatever, smaller or larger."
Example 4	Facilitator: "You have three fun places to visit, three historic places, three interesting facts. How many things do you have total so far? Three, three, and three." (low-level knowledge question) Multiple students: "Nine." (low-level response) Facilitator: "Three times three is?" (low-level knowledge question) Multiple students: "Nine." (low-level response) Facilitator: "Nine plus the history of your county is?" (low-level knowledge question) Multiple students: "10." (low-level response) Facilitator: "Ten, you have 10 things. Okay."
Comprehension	
Example 5	Facilitator: "Okay, we're gonna talk about meters. A blue whale is over 30 meters. How many sticks would this be, H?" (low-level comprehension question) H (female student): "Over 30." (low-level response) Facilitator: "Over 30 because one of these sticks represents?" (low-level comprehension question) Multiple students: "One meter." (low-level response)

Table 6. High-level Questions

Example 1	Facilitator: "What do you think is causing all these children to develop allergies?" (high-level question) D (female student): "I think it's like a virus that can spread germs."
Example 2	Facilitator: "How would you define thinking?" (high-level question) E (female speaker): "I don't really know, but I know it's, if you look at something, basically, you would say what it is....Like that would be a box because it would twitch in your head that when you learned when you were little what it was and you're putting together connections that you have and that's thinking."
Example 3	Facilitator: "Should we take comics seriously? S?" (high-level question) S (female student): "I think that we should start using comics here 'cause it does help with your writing and your reading." Facilitator: "Can you explain why you think that?" S (female student): "Because you have um, say, like you don't like fiction stories and you only like nonfiction stories. And then you start reading comics, and it's like a fiction story. So you're gonna learn what they're all about, and then you'll learn how to read a comic. You'll like comic books, and with writing, you'll learn how to actually write one and see how you're writing."
Example 4	Facilitator: "T, what [question] grabbed you?" T (female student): "That animals be educated." Facilitator: "That animals be educated." T (female student): "Yes." Facilitator: "What do you think?" (high-level question) T (female student): "I think 'yes' because a lot of people enter their dogs or puppies into dog shows, and they have to...the dogs need to be educated to be able to do tricks and to roll over."
Example 5	Facilitator: "R?" R (female student): "I have more than one." Facilitator: "Okay." R (female student): "I like 'Why do we think?' 'How do we think?' 'Do we need to think?' and 'What is thinking?'" Facilitator: "You have all of those thinking questions. Do you think you could answer any of them with certainty?" (high-level question) R (female student): "I think you need to think." Facilitator: "You need to think." R (female student): "Yeah. I think you do need to think because when we add one to two, you need to think of the answer, so we need thinking...." Facilitator: "To solve problems." R (female student): "Yeah." Facilitator: "And you think we couldn't survive?" (high-level question) R (female student): "Yeah. We probably wouldn't unless someone told us the answer, but thinking is better than someone telling you the answer."

Thus, high-level questions require the respondent to derive and advance a new orientation or construct rather than extract the answer from an existing bank of knowledge. This is primarily accomplished by reasoning, which is consistent with a dialogical paradigm, rather than recall, which is indicative of a transmission model of learning. While gaining fluency with the tools of argumentation, students practice reasoning in a social setting and then internalize their ability to reason. The student learns that reasoning can be used as a way to communicate with others and appease his or her need to be heard. The reasoning skills associated with asking and responding to high-level questions are significant for an antibullying intervention. These skills could help replace instances of emotional, unreasoned reaction with reasoned reactions that take into consideration the needs and perspective of other individuals.

Elaborated Explanations

An *elaborated explanation* is defined as an opinion, position, or claim that is substantiated by no fewer than two reasons. Elaborated explanations must also occur within one student-speaking turn. The speaker is required to structure the elements of his or her argument so that it clearly communicates the speaker's stance and is comprehensible to the listener(s). Operationalized, elaborated explanations are coded as a statement or a claim plus two reasons or a claim plus a reason and evidence for the reason (Anderson, Chinn, Waggoner, & Nguyen, 1998; Chinn, O'Donnell, & Jinks, 2000; Soter, Wilkinson, Murphy, Rudge, & Reninger, 2007). (See Table 7 for examples of how elaborated explanations were coded.)

Because the original rules for coding elaborated explanations comprised frameworks that were applied to students' responses to textbook readings (Anderson et al., 1998; Chinn et al., 2000; Soter et al., 2007), instances of evidence often came from direct references to the stories themselves (i.e., "On page x, he said y."). In the case of my study, students were often responding to general, philosophical questions for which supporting evidence from the story excerpt that they read was not always available. Therefore, I took *evidence* to mean an example that supported the reason or rationale offered by the student. The third example in Table 7 is an illustration of an elaborated explanation based on a claim plus a reason plus an evidentiary example. By stating her claim, offering a reason and providing evidence, the content of R's turn qualifies as an elaborated explanation. Because the evidence provided by students in this study could not always be a textual reference, the example that R derives from a situation in her own experience serves as the evidence.

Table 7. Elaborated Explanations

Example 1: A single claim supported by two reasons	S (female speaker): "I think that we should start using comics here [claim] 'cause it does help with your writing [reason 1] and your reading [reason 2]."
Example 2: A single claim supported by two reasons	K (female speaker): "I think we should use comics [claim] because, like J said, Miss G. has comics, and in third grade, our teacher, Miss R., also had comics [Reason 1]. She had it in this, she had it, and everyone had this, um, this book. It wasn't like, it wasn't like, it wasn't like a book, it wasn't, it was like a portfolio, and it had all these, all these stories. And every day, but it wasn't, it wasn't like a comic book for, for like fun and with adventures. It actually, it actually teaches us something about the lesson [Reason 2]."
Example 3: A claim or claims plus reason and evidentiary support	R (female speaker): "Well, cursing is really bad to do [Claim 1]. And it is bullying [Claim 2]. The reason it is really bad to do [Claim 1 repeated] is because it can hurt other people's feelings [reason]. Last weekend, I think it was, I went somewhere with [someone from] a different culture, and me and H were in our room, and somebody else that H knew was saying, 'Do you hear something? I think it sounds familiar.' And that was like bullying to me and H because they pretended like we weren't even there [evidence]."

In the same way that students use reasoning skills to respond to high-level questions, students require a similar skill set to develop an elaborated explanation. Researchers (e.g., Bargh & Schul, 1980; Webb, Farivar, & Mastergeorge, 2002) suggest that elaborated explanations are opportunities for students to enhance their own understanding of concepts by explaining it to and clarifying it for others. Students mediate their ideas through one another and challenge one another's ideas and perspectives by offering alternative reasons and options for consideration. Formulating a minimum of two reasons to corroborate a claim or constructing an elaborated explanation consistent with the claim–reason–evidence format suggests another strategy for gaining a fluency with the tools of reasoning and argumentation that help students engage with and, ultimately, internalize critical reasoning skills. Students learn the socially acceptable parameters for advancing an argument. Furthermore, students learn to structure the information or the argument so that it communicates what the speaker wants to clearly communicate to the listener. These criteria can have significant implications for an antibullying intervention. For example, students who learn to posit cogent arguments that are substantiated with rational reasons may be better equipped to identify and argue against the irrationality and injustice that resides in the power relations between bullies and their victims.

Exploratory Talk

Exploratory talk is characterized by the critical, reasoned co-construction of knowledge by two or more students (Mercer, 2002; Mercer, Wegerif, Dawes, Sams, & Fernandez, 2007). Episodes of exploratory talk address a single topic, occur primarily amongst students, and proceed without any substantive interruptions from the facilitator. Any interference from the teacher needs to be weighed to determine whether or not it is procedural and, therefore, does not disrupt the talk or if it is substantive and, therefore, drives the talk, in which case the talk cannot be considered exploratory (Soter et al., 2007). Appendix B illustrates an episode of exploratory talk, which begins *after* the teacher asks the question and includes the requisite three uninterrupted student turns. In this example, the teacher's interjections are unobtrusive because they serve only to nominate the next speaker. Appendix C shows an instance of discourse that would not qualify as exploratory talk for two reasons. First, the students in this excerpt are not involved in the critical, reasoned co-construction of knowledge (Mercer, 2002; Mercer et al., 2007). Second, the facilitator almost exclusively drives the talk.

Exploratory talk allows students to consider their own arguments and weigh the validity of the arguments of others. By engaging in the critical, reasoned, co-construction of knowledge (Mercer, 2002; Mercer et al., 2007), students can explore complex concepts as they work toward an understanding of those concepts. Reflective inquiry and thinking-centered learning are characteristics of a student-centered classroom (McCombs & Whisler, 1997) and are conducive to the kind of reasoned co-construction characteristic of exploratory talk. This level of engagement and investigation can suggest the importance of acknowledging others' opinions, respecting the rights of others to be heard in a fair and equitable manner, entertaining multiple perspectives and synthesizing personal virtues, and recognizing one's responsibility to his or her community (Burgh, Field, & Freakley, 2006). According to Lipman (1988), these dispositions overtly represent a participant's commitment to and "full acceptance of the responsibility of citizenship" (p. 88).

Interrater Reliability

In order to assess the consistency in the coding of nomination, dyadic exchanges (turn-taking), back-channeling utterances, agenda setting, low-level questions and responses, high-level questions, exploratory talk, and elaborated explanations, a second rater coded the transcripts. I divided each of the 12 transcripts into two segments. I used SPSS software to randomly select 50% of 24 segments as a sample to be coded by the second rater. The second rater, a doctoral student, was trained prior to coding in two ways. First, she had the opportunity to read and request clarification on the coding rationale for each coded element. Then, I reviewed the coding rules with her and provided her with a number of transcript segments with which to practice. These practice segments were selected from among the 50% that were not part of the coding sample. The Pearson correlation coefficients estimating interrater reliability for the nine coded items are shown in Table 8. The percentage of agreement, which ranges from .91 to .99, suggests a high level of agreement between the two raters, which implies an overall consistency in the way that the coding rules were applied.

Table 8. Interrater Reliability Estimates for Coded Items

Coded Item	Pearson r
Nomination	.99
Dyadic exchanges	.92
Back-channeling	.98
Agenda setting	.99
Low-level questions	.91
Low-level responses	.95
High-level questions	.93
Exploratory talk	.93
Elaborated explanations	.91

Results and Discussion

The results, which are captured in Tables 9–13, suggest marked differences between the P4C group and the group receiving regular instruction for all of the coding categories except for exploratory talk. Overall, the data suggest that students who participate in a community of inquiry begin to manifest new behaviors characteristic of a community of inquiry, such as those associated, for example, with nomination and agenda setting. These significant findings are consistent for all of the coded categories except for exploratory talk.

In addition to analyzing particular discourse elements, I also wanted to capture the relationships between the facilitator and the students. First, the importance of teachers and peers as collaborators is theoretically substantiated by Vygotsky (1978). Second, as members of the school community, teachers are integral components of the educational setting, who can have a drastic impact on the actions taken on behalf of students. Following Vygotsky, students take their cues from teachers, who, research suggests, often do nothing in response to bullying and who perpetuate the myth through their own actions within the school's culture. For example, many teachers subscribe to the myth that bullying is a normal, acceptable occurrence; they see it as a natural part of growing up and, as a result, respond to it with indifference (Coy, 2001). Furthermore, research suggests that teachers are either ill-equipped to recognize and deal with bullying (Isernhagen & Harris, 2003; Unnever & Cornell, 2003; Weinhold, 2003) or fail to recognize it entirely (Weinhold, 2003). A marked impact can only be achieved by redefining the school culture by impacting, through classroom discourse, the power relations that exist between teachers and their students. This can be achieved by teachers redistributing their power, cultivating shared possession of the discourse, modeling dispositions for their students through their interactions with them, and providing opportunities for students to practice these dispositions.

The data suggest that the role of the facilitator appears to be inextricably linked to the degree of success that a group can achieve when habituating itself to such dispositions as caring and fairness. According to Tannen (1989), these linguistic strategies can support or compromise empowerment. The data show that modeling and empowerment permeated nomination, back-channeling, turn-taking, the commitment toward engaging higher-order concepts and the time spent on agenda setting. The following section discusses the results for each coded element.

Elements of Community

Nomination

Coding nominations allowed me to test whether distributed nomination is present as a process of group interaction in the P4C classroom, the classroom receiving regular instruction, or both. Table 9 compares the instances of nominations in the P4C group and the group receiving regular instruction. The data show that nominations in the group receiving regular instruction were generated exclusively by the teacher. Students in the P4C group, however, received 71.5% fewer nominations by the facilitator than those received by the regular-instruction group.

In addition to nominations by the facilitator, four additional categories within nomination emerged in the P4C group that were not present in the group receiving regular instruction. These categories are: the facilitator prompting a student to nominate the next speaker, one student nominating another student, one student prompting another student to nominate the next speaker, and a student nominating the facilitator. Table 9 shows how the additional categories that emerged in the P4C group are distributed.

Table 9. Instances of Nominations Across the Treatment Groups

Type of Nomination	P4C		Control	
	Number	%	Number	%
Facilitator nominating a student	35	28.5	141	100.0
Facilitator prompting a student to nominate the next speaker	37	30.0	0	0.0
Student nominating a student	44	35.8	0	0.0
Student prompting a student to nominate the next speaker	5	4.1	0	0.0
Student nominating the facilitator	2	1.6	0	0.0

The first two types of nomination—the facilitator prompting a student to nominate the next speaker and a student nominating another student— are regularly promoted by the P4C facilitator. An interesting trend emerges in the latter two actions: a student prompting another student to nominate the next speaker and a student nominating the facilitator to speak. Students seemed to appropriate and elaborate the technique used by the facilitator to distribute nominations. One student prompting another student to nominate the next speaker seems to signal that (1) the student has internalized the behavior of fairly and equitably nominating the next speaker, which has been modeled by the facilitator within the social setting, and (2) the student has taken that behavior, enhanced it, and begun to use it as part of his or her repertoire of behaviors. In the absence of a negative response from the facilitator, this behavior could eventually become a habit (Dewey, 1997a). Thus, the results suggest that nomination was present in the P4C group in a more varied sense and that students in the P4C group, who were encouraged to *do* nomination, reinterpreted their roles as nominators by changing the surface structure of the move.

This is important for P4C as a potential antibullying intervention. I have argued that engaging in, or *doing*, inquiry exposes students to the behaviors associated with it, such as listening to one another and being fair to one another. Although the study's duration was short, it can be argued that students had already begun to habituate (Dewey, 1997a) themselves to the behaviors that the facilitator modeled.

Dyadic Exchanges as Turn-taking

Table 10 shows the number and percentage of dyadic exchanges in the P4C group and the regular-instruction group. One hundred percent of the dyadic exchanges that occurred in the group receiving regular instruction had 10 turns or fewer, while the P4C group featured longer exchanges of greater variety. Dyadic exchanges with 11 turns or more emerged in the P4C group only. The data suggest that students in the P4C group had multiple and varying opportunities to practice doing good inquiry with a facilitator who is skilled at it. Following Vygotsky (1978), who argued that individual learning occurs through the internalization of behaviors exhibited by others, I contend that these opportunities allowed students in the P4C group to both observe the rules for turn-taking as modeled by an experienced facilitator and utilize them in their dyadic exchanges with the facilitator. The length of these dyadic exchanges is significant, as well, because it implies greater exposure to the rules and behaviors associated with good inquiry. This provides students with extended durations during which they can simultaneously witness, acquire, and become conversant with these mediation tools. While 34% of the turns in the P4C group could be categorized as $T \times 2$, $T \times 3$, or $T \times 4$ (two turns, three turns, and four turns, respectively), the other 66% ranged from $T \times 5$ to $T \times 31$ without instances of $T \times 16$, $T \times 22$, $T \times 23$, $T \times 24$, $T \times 26$, $T \times 27$, or $T \times 30$.

The data suggest that students in the P4C group had more opportunities than students in the regular-instruction group to construct rules within the social context. By engaging in lengthy dyadic exchanges with the facilitator, students do not merely witness but actively participate in the process of rule generation. Lengthier dyadic exchanges provide episodes that give the facilitator time to model the kinds of behavior associated with strategies, such as holding the floor during his or her turn and signaling when he or she was listening (Thornbury, 2005). Because of the length of the dyadic exchanges in the P4C group, the facilitator could lead students in both creating rules and applying them in practice.

Dyadic exchanges as a function of doing good inquiry become another mechanism by which to practice being respectful of and fair to others. Because of the dispositions that are modeled and cultivated by the rules governing turn-taking, in general, and dyadic exchanges, in particular, this process of group interaction appears to be present in a more pronounced and varied form in the P4C group than in the regular-instruction group. As in the case of nomination, individuals are required to exercise respect, fairness, and caring in recognizing the person who should be given the next speaking turn, and the facilitator provides the conditions that are conducive to cultivating these dispositions.

Table 10. Instances and Percentages of Dyadic Exchanges Across the Treatment Groups

Number of Turns	P4C		Regular Instruction	
	Number	%	Number	%
T × 2 to T × 3	23	30.0	101	71.0
T × 4 to T × 10	27	35.0	41	29.0
T × 11 to T × 31	27	35.0	0	0.0
Total	77	100	142	100

Back-channeling

Table 11 shows the number[1] of back-channeling utterances for each treatment group. Although back-channeling as a composite of its component parts is not exclusive to the P4C group, it is more evenly distributed in the P4C group than in the group receiving regular instruction. A more evenly distributed use of back-channeling in the P4C group could reflect access to a larger and more diversified arsenal of tools for mediation, which, according to Vygotsky (1978), are critical for the social construction of meaning. A larger store of tools is important for an antibullying intervention because it supplies students with alternate means of expressing themselves. Eron (1994) reports that bullies use aggression instead of language to resolve conflicts. Amassing a catalog of language tools could help bullies to begin to transition from solving problems with aggression toward using the variety of language tools at their disposal.

Table 11. Comparison of Back-channeling Utterances across the Treatment Groups

Type of Back-channeling Utterance	P4C		Regular Instruction	
	Number	%	Number	%
"Yeah," "Right," and so on	38	30.0	6	6.9
Sentence completion	15	12.0	2	2.3
Request for clarification	24	19.0	6	6.9
	Restatement		Repetition		Restatement		Repetition	
	Number	%	Number	%	Number	%	Number	%
Restatement or repetition	17	13.0	33	26.0	3	3.4	70	80.5
Total number	127				87			

The data suggest that the regular-instruction group used repetition and restatement 83.9% of the time, while the P4C group used these types of utterances 39% of the time. According to Halliday and Hasan (1976), the "sharing" of words, which is inherent in repetition (and restatement), both creates and reinforces interpersonal bonds among individuals (p. 292). Back-channeling utterances, such as repetition and restatement, can be utilized to establish and nurture mutual respect and trust among the facilitator and the students.

The P4C group featured more than five times as many instances of restatement than the group receiving regular instruction, while the group receiving regular instruction had more than two times as many instances of repetition than the P4C group. Paraphrasing students' utterances suggests that the facilitator in the P4C group acknowledges student contributions, thus ascribing a level of importance not just to what each student says but to the students themselves. If back-channeling utterances are viewed as a tool of good inquiry and doing good inquiry allows the facilitator to model behaviors, such as respect and fairness, it seems that back-channeling can be construed as a process of group interaction that manifests itself in the community of inquiry very differently than in the regular-instruction group. In the case of back-channeling, this process is not exclusive to the P4C group; it is just applied more diversely with what might be construed as an arguably different impact on the community and its participants. This can be an important component of an antibullying intervention because it recognizes and models the validity associated with the perspectives of others.

I have made an argument for considering all aspects of back-channeling as significant because, as a function of good inquiry, they contribute to the social dimension, or community aspect, of group interaction. There is, however, one aspect of back-channeling over which it is important to cast a critical lens. Utterances, such as "Yeah," "Right," and "Uh-huh," are intended to impart from the listener to the speaker a level of attention (Sacks et al., 1974). These utterances are themselves somewhat suspect because it is entirely conceivable and, thus, important to recognize that an inattentive or preoccupied listener could utter "Yeah," "Right," and "Uh-huh" just as easily as one who is genuinely engaged in the discourse. Although there was a marked disparity between the number of "Yeah," "Right," and "Uh-huh" utterances in the P4C group (38) and the group receiving regular instruction (6), it is difficult to determine whether they are the products of listeners who are immersed in the speaker's turn or apathetic to it. As I suggested at the beginning of this section, analyzing all aspects of back-channeling as a whole gestalt allows for the use of "Yeah," "Right," and "Uh-huh" utterances as a means of triangulation rather than an individual metric.

Agenda Setting

Students in the P4C group spent an average of 10.96 minutes on agenda setting, while the students in the regular-instruction group did not spend any time on this process. This could be explained by referring, once again, to the traditional classroom model, which requires teachers to satisfy an entire complement of instructional directives. This precludes teachers from relinquishing the task of agenda setting to the students, and this is reflected in the data.

Instructional obligations may also dictate the responsibility that a teacher can or may be willing or able to share with his or her students. However, inviting students to participate in agenda setting can imply empowerment by the facilitator of his or her students. In the case of the P4C group, students were given the power to set the course of the discussion. The facilitator mines the community for topics that are of interest to its members (Dewey, 1997b) and invites students to be active participants in dialogical inquiry (Vygotsky, 1978) and instrumental in decisions about the focus of that inquiry. This is consistent with the redistribution of power that the facilitator in the P4C group continually reinforces by inviting students to participate in group processes. The redistribution of power has significant ramifications for an antibullying intervention. By inviting students to be equal contributors to agenda setting, the facilitator strives to redress the imbalance of power that is inherent in the bully–victim relationship.

Elements of Inquiry

Low-level Questions and Responses

Table 12 captures the marked difference between the number of low-level questions in the two treatment groups. The P4C group has far fewer low-level questions and responses than the group receiving regular instruction.

Table 12. Instances of Low-level Questions Across the Treatment Groups

	P4C	Regular Instruction
Low-level questions	2	107
Low-level responses	5	223

According to Boyer (as cited in Perkins, 1993), questions that require anything beyond a low-level response typically constitute only 1% of class instruction. Brown (2003) suggests that this can be attributed to the legislative requirements that are imposed on teachers. Because of the administrative pressure to meet a number of prescribed criteria, low-level questions that can assess content mastery and move the discourse along quickly are strategically preferable. Within the parameters of the aforementioned framework, a substantially higher proportion of low-level questions in the regular-instruction group could reflect the trappings of a traditional classroom approach in which low-level questions are predominant.

This finding is important when assessing processes of group interaction that characterize a community of inquiry. Research shows that current antibullying interventions are predicated upon a model of knowledge transmission in which information about bullying is conveyed. I have argued that a dialogical paradigm holds promise because it allows students to explore bullying and all its related issues, such as fairness and respect, in a deeper, more meaningful way. The very small number of low-level questions reported for the P4C group does not automatically imply that all other questions were explored deeply and meaningfully. This is the reason why I also examined instances of high-level questions and elaborated explanations.

High-level Questions

The P4C group featured a larger number of high-level thinking questions than the regular-instruction group (Table 13). Because high-level questions are coded on the basis of the responses that they elicit, the large number of high-level questions reported in the P4C group suggests that those students were more engaged in crafting authentic, reasoned responses than the students in the group receiving regular instruction. As is characteristic in a community of inquiry, students in the P4C group had more opportunities to use language tools (inductive, deductive, and speculative reasoning) to practice high-level response construction with their peers, a result that is implicative of Vygotsky's (1978) theory of internalization. This could indicate that the students in the P4C group may be more likely to adopt a reasoned approach to the way in which they respond to and entertain the thoughts of their peers. A longer-term study could determine whether students in a P4C group would internalize the skills associated with inductive, deductive, and speculative reasoning and whether or not this would affect their beliefs about aggression.

Table 13. Instances of High-level Questions Across the Treatment Groups

	P4C	Control
High-level questions by the facilitator	120	7
High-level questions by a student	13	6

Another important component is the facilitator's willingness to share the power that is associated with a traditional classroom teacher in order to promote inductive, deductive, and speculative reasoning. As I explained in my discussion on low-level questions, teachers are often unable to devote time to the skills associated with crafting high-level responses because of the curricular requirements that are a fundamental part of the traditional classroom model. The data suggest that the facilitator in the P4C group invites students to explore reasoning as a part of the pedagogical paradigm, which is consistent with a dialogical approach that, I have argued, is necessary for an antibullying intervention. Lending itself to active participation rather than passive reception, P4C requires students to move beyond merely responding to the questions that they are asked (low-level questions), which are designed to help them attain instructional goals. Instead, the data suggest that these students answered more high-level questions, which implies that students in the P4C group supplied more authentic, reasoned, and constructed responses than the group receiving regular instruction.

Elaborated Explanation

Both groups manifested examples of elaborated explanation. However, the P4C group had more than three times as many instances of elaborated explanation (32) as the group receiving regular instruction (10). As in the case of high-level questions, the data suggest that students in the P4C group had more opportunities to construct elaborated explanations. An elaborated explanation, which requires the speaker to provide no less than two clear and cogent reasons for an opinion, position or claim, requires the speaker to posit reasonable substantiation to his or her audience.

This is particularly important for an antibullying intervention because it implies that reason and rationality can be implemented to mediate instances of injustice, such as one student tormenting another student. For bullies, aggression is used in the absence of language to achieve their goals (Eron, 1994). Substituting aggression with the skills implicit in positing an elaborated explanation by using words in a productive, constructive, and positive way could redefine the way in which a (former) bully expresses himself or herself. The judgments, persuasive arguments, and logically construed conclusions contributed and, ultimately, reached by the members of the group can serve to enlighten the bully's perspective, thus offering him or her alternative viewpoints that can be internalized to recast his or her current thinking about bullying. Thus, students use language tools as a way to mediate the socially acceptable parameters for their behavior and the behavior of others.

Exploratory Talk

Both groups had the same number (nine) of instances of exploratory talk. However, there were several occasions in the P4C group that indicated that the facilitator's status could be construed as equal to that of the other participants in the community. Gilligan's (1982) ethic of care implies that acknowledging the facilitator as an equal participant requires care on the part of the students to reciprocate the same actions that he or she has modeled, such as valuing his or her perspectives and inviting him or her to participate as an equal contributor to the talk. If the facilitator, as model and mediator, simultaneously assumes the role of equal participant, this has interesting implications for the P4C group. His or her involvement in episodes of exploratory talk as an equal participant provides a context within which he or she can model the critical, reasoned co-construction of knowledge. Using language to formulate and express concepts collectively resides within the Vygotskian (1978) framework. It also reinforces the recalibration of power among the group's participants, thus recontextualizing the issue of power, which is so central to the problem of bullying.

Following Vygotsky (1978), the facilitator, as the more experienced "peer," is teaching the other community members how to ask good questions and identifies himself as just another participant rather than supreme arbiter. This supposition presumes that the facilitator will be able to escape the role of authority figure. I would argue, though, that acknowledging the possibility of such a recharacterization (i.e., the facilitator at least temporarily becoming equal to the rest of the individuals in the community) is vital; otherwise, there is no way to support the notion that students can learn how to shift the power dynamic from someone who has modeled doing so. For example, the facilitator, who shifted his power to invite students to share in the process of nomination and agenda setting could be seen as functioning in the capacity of a more experienced peer mentor rather than a teacher-as-authority-figure. This, in a sense, permits him or her to be a part of the exploratory talk normally reserved for students. Thus, shifting power is important not only for the rich co-construction of meaning to which the facilitator-turned-participant can contribute but also for modeling the actual process of power redistribution itself.

Conclusion

The success of many existing antibullying interventions has been marginal (Fraser, 2004; Smith et al., 2004; Smith et al., 2003). This, as I have argued, appears to be attributable to the monological approach that dispossesses students of the potential to engage with and explore issues, such as respect, fairness, empathy, and caring, through community-driven, dialogical inquiry. Therefore, a pedagogical approach that features the interplay among inquiry, dialogue, and practice holds promise. Philosophy for Children is one such approach. The purpose of this study was to assess the plausibility of P4C as a potential antibullying intervention.

P4C pedagogy inherently shifts the power to all members of the community, thereby, recalibrating the imbalance that can manifest itself among schoolchildren. The facilitator can use discourse elements as a means by which to promote doing good inquiry and the dispositions that are intrinsically inherent to it. The facilitator's approach, which includes the conversational strategies that the facilitator models for his or her community and that he or she encourages its participants to appropriate, are designed to produce the democratic discourse integral to the process of reacculturation.

Thus, P4C exposes students to unique verbal and social behaviors that they are able to practice, internalize, and adapt. The data suggest that students who participate in a community of inquiry, within which dispositions, such as caring, respect, and fairness, are part of inquiry, dialogue, and doing, begin to manifest some new behaviors, such as those associated with nomination and agenda setting, and are exposed to others, such as those associated with turn-taking, back-channeling, and higher-order thinking, as a function of their participation in P4C. A key aspect for the success of all of these elements working in tandem is the role that the facilitator plays in modeling and encouraging good inquiry and empowering students to fully engage the process so that they can practice and, ultimately, internalize dispositions, such as caring and respect, which are critical to the success of any antibullying intervention.

The role of the facilitator and the way in which he or she construes and actuates that role are integral parts of P4C pedagogy. They also seem to be inextricably linked to the degree of success that a group can achieve when habituating itself to such dispositions as respect, caring, and fairness. The data show that modeling and empowerment permeated nomination, back-channeling, turn-taking, a commitment toward engaging higher-order concepts, and the time spent on agenda setting. For example, in the regular-instruction group, the teacher was the only person doing the nominating; there was no student–student nomination. On the other hand, students in the P4C group were afforded countless opportunities to negotiate nominations among themselves. Furthermore, students in the P4C group reinterpreted their roles as nominators by adopting and adapting behavior. Specifically, when the facilitator modeled nomination by prompting one student to nominate another, students adopted his behavior and felt sufficiently empowered to adapt it; as a result, they began to prompt students to nominate one another. If the literature on bullying suggests that bullying occurs when one individual wields his or her power over another, the facilitator is a critical element in modeling the recalibration of power among students. The larger implication is articulated by Vygotsky (1997), who wrote that:

All attempts at moral education, at moral sermonizing must have to be seen as quite futile. Morality has to constitute an inseparable part of education as a whole at its very roots, and he is acting morally who does not notice that he is acting morally. (p. 226)

By engaging in good inquiry, students are practicing those dispositions associated with doing good inquiry, such as entertaining multiple perspectives and being respectful of others when they speak. Following Vygotsky, students are acting morally without noticing that they are acting morally and cultivating moral behavior so that it becomes habit, which is promising for an antibullying intervention.

In an effort to formulate an antibullying intervention that reduces and, perhaps, eventually eliminates instances of aggression, it is important to consider the population of students who do not classify themselves as bullies or do not identify with a pedagogy that promotes respect, caring, fairness, and power sharing. If the goal is to shift the power dynamic within the community, this applies to everyone in the community and not just to the dynamic that exists between the facilitator and the students. Eventually, the hope is that students will begin to regulate themselves, particularly in a group that begins to chronicle a substantive shift in power among all of its participants. The reality, however, suggests that it is possible that there are simply some students who will not respond to this intervention.

Directions for Further Research

I have identified a number of natural directions for future research. First, the amount of time that students had with P4C pedagogy was limited. An analysis of the coded elements revealed some differences between the P4C group and the group receiving regular instruction. Therefore, a logical next step would be to conduct a similar study for the duration of at least one school year.

Second, I examined the impact that the consideration of complex concepts has by analyzing instances of high-level questions, elaborated explanations, and exploratory talk. A possible direction for future study could incorporate a metacognitive component, which would require students to spend the last 10 minutes of each regular classroom session and each P4C session talking about the thinking in which they engaged during that session. Then, this metacognitive component could be mined for additional data about, for example, student awareness of the ways in which they responded to one another during their session.

Third, I evaluated instances of restatement and repetition as part of back-channeling. Although the facilitator in the group receiving regular instruction used a higher percentage of repetition and the facilitator in the P4C group used a significant percentage of restatement, it is not possible to corroborate Halliday and Hasan's (1976) claims regarding the bonds that may have been cultivated between the facilitator and her students. However, a possible direction for future study would be to examine the quality of restatement and repetition between treatment groups and the impact that they have on students' attitudes and beliefs about the relationship that the facilitator has cultivated with them.

The results of this study argue for the potential that philosophical dialogue has for addressing the significant social problem of bullying and suggests that an educational intervention, such as P4C, which is centered around philosophical discussions could have the potential to affect the ways in which students approach one another and the conflicts that arise among them. The results also suggest that the role of facilitator is critical to this process. This study invites further research that will provide concerned educators with practical and empirically-supported suggestions for addressing bullying in their schools in order to help cultivate environments that promote safe, democratic, and caring communities of learning.

References

Anderson, R. C., Chinn, C., Waggoner, M., & Nguyen, K. (1998). Intellectually stimulating story discussions. In J. Osborn & F. Lehr (Eds.), *Literacy for all: Issues in teaching and learning* (pp. 170–186). New York: Guilford.

Arsenio, W. F., & Lemerise, E. A. (2001). Varieties of childhood bullying: Values, emotion processes and social competence. *Social Development, 10,* 59–73.

Banks, J. (1989). Philosophy for Children and California Achievement Test: An analytic study in a Midwestern suburb. *Analytic Teaching, 9*(2), 7–20.

Barber, B. R. (2003). *Strong democracy: Participatory politics for a new age.* Berkeley: University of California Press.

Bargh, J. A., & Schul, Y. (1980). On the cognitive benefits of teaching. *Journal of Educational Psychology, 72,* 593–604.

Batsche, G. M., & Knoff, H. M. (1994). Bullies and their victims: Understanding a pervasive problem in the schools. *School Psychology Review, 23,* 165–174.

Berelson, B. (1952). *Content analysis in communication research.* Glencoe, IL: Free Press.

Bloom, B. S., Engelhart, M. D., Furst, E. J., Hill, W. H., & Krathwohl. D. R. (1956). *Taxonomy of educational objectives, the classification of educational goals. Handbook I: The cognitive domain.* New York: McKay.

Brown, K. L. (2003). From teacher-centered curriculum: Improving learning in diverse classrooms. *Education, 124,* 49–54.

Burgh, G., Field, T., & Freakley, M. (2006). *Ethics and the community of inquiry: Education for deliberative democracy.* South Melbourne, Australia: Thomson Social Science Press.

Camhy, D., & Iberer, G. (1988). Philosophy for Children: A research project for further mental and personality development of primary and secondary school pupils. *Thinking, 7*(4), 18–26.

Cazden, C. B. (2001). *Classroom discourse: The language of teaching and learning* (2nd ed.). Portsmouth, NH: Heinemann.

Chinn, C. A., O'Donnell, A. M., & Jinks, T. S. (2000). The structure of discourse in collaborative learning. *The Journal of Experimental Education, 69*(1), 77–97.

Coupland, N. (1998). What is sociolinguistic theory? *Journal of Sociolinguistics, 2*(1), 110–117.

Coy, D. R. (2001). *Bullying.* Greensboro: University of North Carolina. (ERIC Document Reproduction Service No. ED459405)

Craig, W. M., Henderson, K., & Murphy, J. G. (2000). Prospective teachers' attitudes toward bullying and victimization. *School Psychology International, 21,* 5–21.

Crick, N. R. (1997). Engagement in gender normative versus nonnormative forms of aggression: Links to social–psychological adjustment. *Developmental Psychology, 33,* 610–617.

Crowhurst, M. (1988). *Research review: Patterns of development in writing persuasive/argumentative discourse* (Report No. 506374). Vancouver, Canada: University of British Columbia. (ERIC Document Reproduction Service No. ED299596)

Davis, M. H. (1994). *Empathy: A social psychological approach.* Dubuque, IA: Brown.

Dewey, J. (1997a). *Democracy and education: An introduction to the philosophy of education.* New York: Free Press.

Dewey, J. (1997b). *How we think.* Mineola, NY: Dover.

Duncan, S. (1972). Some signals and rules for taking speaking turns in conversation. *Journal of Personality and Social Psychology, 23,* 283–292.

—. (1974). On the structure of speaker–auditor interaction during speaking turns. *Language in Society, 2,* 161–180.

Eisenberg, N., & Fabes, R. A. (1998). Prosocial development. In W. Damon & N. Eisenberg (Eds.), *Handbook of child psychology. Vol. 3. Social, emotional and personality development* (5th ed., pp. 701–778). New York: Wiley.

Eisenberg, N., & Strayer, J. (Eds.). (1987). *Empathy and its development.* New York: Cambridge University Press.

Endresen, I. M., & Olweus, D. (2001). Self-reported empathy in Norwegian adolescents: Sex differences, age trends and relationships to bullying. In A. C. Bohart & D. J. Stipek (Eds.), *Constructive and destructive behavior: Implications for family, school & society* (pp. 147–165). Washington, DC: American Psychological Association.

Eron, L. D. (1994). Theories of aggression: From drives to cognitions. In L. R. Huesmann (Ed.), *Aggressive behavior: Current perspectives* (pp. 3–11). New York: Plenum.

Espelage, D. L., Bosworth, K., & Simon, T. R. (2001). Short-term stability and prospective correlates of bullying in middle-school students: An examination of potential demographic, psychosocial and environmental influences. *Violence and Victims, 16,* 411–426.

Fairclough, N. (2000). Discourse, social theory and social research: The discourse of welfare reform. *Journal of Sociolinguistics, 4,* 163–195.

Farrington, D. P. (1993). Understanding and preventing bullying. In M. Tonry (Ed.), *Crime and justice: A review of research* (Vol. 17, pp. 348–458). Chicago: University of Chicago Press.

Fraser, C. M. (2004). *Bully proofing your school: The effectiveness of a school-wide prevention program with middle school students.* (UMI No. AAT 3132731)

French, P., & MacLure, M. (1981). Teachers' questions, pupils' answers: An investigation of questions and answers in the infant classroom. *First Language, 2*(4), 31–45.

Gilligan, C. (1982). *In a different voice.* Cambridge, MA: Harvard University Press.

Gumperz, J. (1982). *Discourse strategies.* Cambridge, MA: Cambridge University Press.

Haidar, J., & Rodriguez, L. (1995). Power and ideology in different discursive practices. In C. Schäeffner & A. L. Wenden (Eds.), *Language and peace* (pp. 119–135). Brookfield, VT: Dartmouth.

Halliday, M. A. K., & Hasan, R. (1976). *Cohesion in English.* London: Longman.

Hoover, J. H., Oliver, R., & Thomson, K. A. (1993). Perceived victimization by school bullies: New research and future directions. *Journal of Humanistic Education and Development, 32,* 76–84.

Isernhagen, K., & Harris, S. (2003). A comparison of 9th and 10th grade boys' and girls' bullying behaviors in two states. *Journal of School Violence, 2*(2), 67–80.

John-Steiner, V., Panofsky, C. P., & Smith, L. W. (1994). *Sociocultural approaches to language and literacy: An interactionist perspective.* Cambridge, England: Cambridge University Press.

Jolliffe, D., & Farrington, D. P. (2006). Examining the relationship between low empathy and bullying. *Aggressive Behavior, 32,* 540–550.

Kennedy, D. (2004). The role of a facilitator in a community of philosophical inquiry. *Metaphilosophy, 35*(5), 744–765.

Kenny, M. C., McEachern, A. G., & Aluede, O. (2005). Female bullying: Prevention and counseling interventions. *Journal of Social Sciences, 8,* 13–19.

Lipman, M. (1982). *Kio and Gus.* Upper Montclair, NJ: Institute for the Advancement of Philosophy for Children.

—. (1988). *Philosophy goes to school.* Philadelphia, PA: Temple University Press.

—. (2003). *Thinking in education* (2nd ed.). New York: Cambridge University Press.

Lipman, M., Sharp, A. M., & Oscanyan, F. S. (1980). *Philosophy in the classroom.* Philadelphia: Temple University Press.

McCombs, B. L., & Whisler, J. S. (1997). *The learner-centered classroom and school: Strategies for increasing student motivation and achievement.* San Francisco: Jossey-Bass.

McEachern, A. G., Kenny, M., Blake, E., & Aluede, O. (2005). Bullying in the schools: International variations in school bullying. *Journal of Social Sciences, 8,* 51–58.

Mercer, N. (2002). Developing dialogues. In G. Wells & G. Claxton (Eds.), *Learning for life in the 21st century: Sociocultural perspectives on the future of education* (pp. 141–153). Oxford, England: Blackwell.

Mercer, N., Wegerif, R., Dawes, L., Sams, C., & Fernandez, M. (2007). How computers can help children think together about texts. In C. Kinzer & L. Verhoeven (Eds.), *Interactive literacy education* (pp. 245–268). New York: Taylor & Francis.

Nansel, T. R., Overpeck, M., Pilla, R. S., Ruan, W. J., Simons-Morton, B., & Scheidt, P. (2001). Bullying behaviors among U.S. youth: Prevalence and association with psychosocial adjustment. *Journal of the American Medical Association, 285,* 2094–2100.

Nystrand, M., Wu, L. L., Gamoran, A., Zeiser, S., & Long, D. A. (2003). Questions in time: Investigating the structure and dynamics of unfolding classroom discourse. *Discourse Processes, 35,* 135–198.

Olweus, D. (1991). Bully/victim problems among schoolchildren: Basic facts and effects of a school-based intervention program. In D. J. Pepler & K. H. Rubin (Eds.), *The development and treatment of childhood aggression* (pp. 411–448). Hillsdale, NJ: Erlbaum.

—. (1992). Victimization by peers: Antecedents and long-term outcomes. In K. H. Rubin & J. B. Asendorf (Eds.), *Social withdrawal, inhibition and shyness in childhood* (pp. 315–341). Hillsdale, NJ: Erlbaum.

—. (1993a). *Bullying at school: What we know and what we can do.* Oxford, England: Blackwell.

—. (1993b). Bully/victim problems among schoolchildren: Long-term consequences and an effective intervention program. In S. Hodgins (Ed.), *Mental disorder and crime* (pp. 317–349). Thousand Oaks, CA: Sage.

—. (2001). Peer harassment: A critical analysis and some important issues. In J. Juvonen & S. Graham (Eds.), *Peer harassment in school: The plight of the vulnerable and victimized* (pp. 3–20). New York: Guilford.

Oreström, B. (1983). *Turn-taking in English conversation.* Lund, Sweden: CWK Gleerup.

Perkins, D. (1993). Thinking-centered learning. *Educational Leadership, 51*(4), 84–85.

Perry, D. G., Kusel, S. J., & Perry, L. C. (1988). Victims of peer aggression. *Developmental Psychology, 24,* 807–814.

QSR International. (2008). QSR NVivo 8 [Computer software]. Melbourne, Australia: Author.

Reznitskaya, A., Anderson, R. C., Dong, T., Li, Y., & Kim, I. (2008). Learning to think well: Application of argument schema theory to literacy instruction. In C. C. Block, P. Afflerbach, & S. Parris (Eds.), *Comprehension instruction: Research-based best practices* (pp. 196–213). New York: Guilford.

Rigby, K. (1996). *Bullying in school and what to do about it.* London: Kingsley.

—. (2001). Health consequences of bullying and its prevention in schools. In J. Juvonen & S. Graham (Eds.), *Peer harassment in school: The plight of the vulnerable and victimized* (pp. 310–331). New York: Guilford.

Rigby, K., Cox, I., & Black, G. (1997). Cooperativeness and bully/victim problems among Australian schoolchildren. *Journal of Social*

Psychology, 137, 357–368.

Rigby, K., Smith, P. K., & Pepler, D. (2004). Working to prevent school bullying: Key issues. In P. K. Smith, D. Pepler, & K. Rigby (Eds.), *Bullying in schools: How successful can interventions be?* (pp. 1–12). New York: Cambridge University Press.

Roland, E., & Idsoe, T. (2001). Aggression and bullying. *Aggressive Behavior, 27,* 446–462.

Sacks, H., Schegloff, E. A., & Jefferson, G. (1974). A simplest systematics for the organisation of turn-taking for conversation. *Language, 50,* 696–735.

Smith, J. D., Schneider, B. H., Smith, P. K., & Ananiadou, K. (2004). The effectiveness of whole-school antibullying programs: A synthesis of evaluation research. *School Psychology Review, 33,* 547–560.

Smith, P. K., Ananiadou, K., & Cowie, H. (2003). Interventions to reduce school bullying. *Canadian Journal of Psychiatry, 48,* 591–599.

Smith, P. K., & Sharp, S. (1994). *School bullying: Insights and perspectives.* London: Routledge.

Smith, P. K., & Thompson, D. (1991). *Practical approaches to bullying.* London: David Fulton.

Soter, A., Wilkinson, I. A. G., Murphy, P. K., Rudge, L., & Reninger, K. B. (2007). *Analyzing the Discourse of Discussion Coding Manual.* Unpublished manuscript.

Splitter, L. J., & Sharp, A. M. (1995). *Teaching for better thinking.* Melbourne: ACER.

Sutton, J., Smith, P. K., & Swettenham, J. (1999). Social cognition and bullying: Social inadequacy or skilled manipulation? *British Journal of Developmental Psychology, 17,* 435–450.

Tannen, D. (1989). *Talking voices: Repetition, dialogue and imagery in everyday conversational discourse.* Cambridge, England: Cambridge University Press.

Thompson, D., & Sharp, S. (1998). The dynamics of victimisation and rejection in school. In D. Thompson & S. Sharp (Eds.), *Improving schools: Establishing and integrating whole school behavior policies* (pp. 11–25). London: David Fulton.

Thornbury S. (2005). *How to teach speaking.* Essex, England: Pearson.

Twemlow, S. W., Fonagy, P., & Sacco, F. C. (2004). The role of the bystander in the social architecture of bullying and violence in schools and communities. *Annals of the New York Academy of Sciences, 1036,* 215–232.

Unnever, J. D., & Cornell, D. G. (2003). The culture of bullying in middle school. *Journal of School Violence, 2*(2), 5–27.

Van der Veer, R., & Valsiner, J. (1991). *Understanding Vygotsky: A quest for synthesis.* Cambridge, MA: Blackwell.

Van Dijk, T. A. (1995). Discourse analysis as ideology analysis. In C. Schäeffner & A. L. Wenden (Eds.), *Language and peace* (pp. 17–33). Brookfield, VT: Dartmouth.

Vygotsky, L. (1926/1997). *Educational Psychology* (R. Silverman, trans.). Boca Raton, FL: St. Lucie.

Vygotsky, L. S. (1978). *Mind in society: The development of higher psychological processes.* Cambridge, MA: Harvard University Press.

Wardhaugh, R. (1992). *An introduction to sociolinguistics* (2nd ed.). Cambridge, MA: Blackwell.

Watzlawick, P., Beavin, J. H., & Jackson, D. D. (1967). *Pragmatics of human communication.* New York: Norton.

Webb, N. M., Farivar, S. H., & Mastergeorge, A. M. (2002). Productive helping in cooperative groups. *Theory into Practice, 41*(1), 13–20.

Weinhold, B. K. (2003). Uncovering the hidden causes of bullying and school violence. In J. Miller, I. R. Martin, & G. Schamess (Eds.), *School violence and children in crisis: Community and school interventions for social workers and counselors* (pp. 103–134). Denver: Love.

Wertsch, J. V. (Ed.). (1981). *The concept of activity in Soviet psychology.* Armonk, NY: Sharpe.

Whitney, I., & Smith, P. K. (1993). A survey of the nature and extent of bullying in junior/middle and secondary schools. *Educational Research, 35*(1), 3–25.

Yngve, V. H. (1970). On getting a word in edgewise. In Campbell, M. A. (Ed.), *Papers from the sixth regional meeting of the Chicago Linguistic Society* (pp. 567–577). Chicago: Chicago Linguistic Society.

Note

1. I excluded Duncan's (1974) fifth category, nonverbal gestures, because I coded written transcripts and not the videos themselves.

Appendix A: Three of Duncan's Four Categories— Repetition, Requests for Clarification, and Sentence Completion—Simultaneously Represented

Facilitator: "T, what grabbed you?"

T (female student): "That animals be educated."

Facilitator: "That animals be educated." (repetition)

T (female student): "Yes."

Facilitator: "What do you think?"

T (female student): "I think 'yes' because a lot of people enter their dogs or puppies into dog shows and they have to...the dogs need to be educated to be able to do tricks and to roll over."

Facilitator: "Okay. And that's education." (request for clarification)

T (female student): "Well, for dogs because you can't actually teach a dog or cat math or writing because we are the only people that have oppos...."

Facilitator: "Opposable thumbs?" (sentence completion)

T (female student): "Yeah. Opposable thumbs."

Facilitator: "We're the only animals with opposable thumbs."

Appendix B: Qualifies as an Episode of Exploratory Talk

S (female speaker): "I think that we should start using comics here 'cause it does help with your writing and your reading."

Facilitator: "Can you explain why you think that?"

(Episode of exploratory talk begins.)

S (female speaker): "Because you have, um, say like you don't like fiction stories, and you only like nonfiction stories. And then you start reading comics, and it's like a fiction story. So you're gonna learn what they're all about, and then you'll learn how to read a comic. You'll like comic books, and with writing, you'll learn how to actually write one and see how you're writing." (Turn 1)

Facilitator: "Um, another comment, T?" (procedural interjection, does not add to talk)

T (male speaker): "I think we should make comics, I think we should make comics in our own head of what we think of, like, some adventures that we think of, and we should put 'em in from our head to the comics." (Turn 2)

Facilitator: "Comics. Um, K?" (procedural interjection, does not add to talk)

K (female speaker): "I think we should use comics because, like J said, Miss G. has comics, and in 3rd grade, our teacher, Miss R., also had comics. She had it in this, she had it, and everyone had this, um, this book. It wasn't like, it wasn't like, it wasn't like a book, it wasn't, was like a portfolio, and it had all these, all these stories. And every day, but it wasn't, it wasn't like a comic book for, for like fun and with adventures. It actually, it actually teached us something about the lesson. Like last time, we were talking about measuring things. So it was a story about a family of mass, I mean mice, and they were trying to get through, and then they were trying to run away from this guy. So they went on top of the ramp, and they were trying to go up so they would all fit and be able to go back into their mouse hole. So they had to they had to compare all the mice, the mouses, the mice weight, and they figured out which mice should go on which balance beam and then they can get back." (Turn 3)

Facilitator: "M?" (procedural interjection, does not add to talk)

M (female speaker): "Um, also I agree with S because it does help you with writing. Like it helps you write, um, creative.

And also I know what K's talking about because it was a math comic book that um we looked at." (Turn 4)

Facilitator: "Yup, we have it here for 5th grade. We just don't use it." (substantive interjection, which ends episode of exploratory talk)

Appendix C: Disqualified as an Episode of Exploratory Talk

Facilitator: "You know how most needles the point is very, very thin so they can get into your arm and everything?"

Multiple students: "Yes."

Facilitator: "The EpiPen needles are actually much thicker and bigger because...they do not go in the arm. Anyone want to take a guess as to where they have to literally jam the needle?"

Male speaker: "Ewww!"

Facilitator: "Think of a place on your body. It could be your derrière."

(Multiple students laughing)

Facilitator: "H?"

H (female speaker): "Your shoulder."

Facilitator: "Your shoulder. Oh, that's a good, that's a good place. A?"

A (male speaker): "Your neck."

Facilitator: "Your neck. Okay, I can understand why. T?"

T (male speaker): "Your foot."

Facilitator: "Your foot, okay."

Male speaker: "Most people usually do it on their leg."

Facilitator: "On their leg. But you know what? Their leg is very big. Where on your leg?"

Male speaker: "Your thigh."

Facilitator: "The thigh area. J?"

J (male speaker): "Your neck."

Facilitator: "Your neck, K?"

K (female student): "Your stomach."

Facilitator: "Your stomach. D?"

D (female speaker): "Your back."

Facilitator: "Your back. S?"

S (male speaker): "Your derrière. Doesn't hurt there."

(Multiple students laughing)

Facilitator: "K?"

K (male speaker): "Um, your back."

Facilitator: "Your back. Okay, well, the correct area actually is your thigh, which is right here. Okay? And they have to get it in a tough place, and what they do is, you can't really, you know how they...? They always have to clean the area first and leave all the, if you're wearing long sleeve, they make you roll it up and everything."

Male speaker: *(inaudible)*

Facilitator: "Usually. Because of EpiPens, because you have to do it quick and because it's so big, you have to pass through something. So they always go through the skin or through your clothing. You know how needles, doctors are just like, you know how doctors and nurses when they're giving you a shot they go like this, okay, and do it very gently, so you barely feel anything?"

Multiple students: *(inaudible)*

Facilitator: "What happens…with an EpiPen is that person usually is, you know, if that person is having an allergic reaction that means you have to lay the person on their side, and you literally…" *(makes a jamming gesture)*

ABOUT THE AUTHORS

Beate Børresen, Ph.D., is an associate professor in the Faculty of Education and International Studies at Oslo and Akershus University College. Børresen has worked with philosophy in schools and preschools since 1997. She has led projects for the City of Oslo and the Norwegian Directorate for Education, developed courses, and written books.

Monica B. Glina, Ed.D., is a postdoctoral fellow with the Text Comprehension: Development, Instruction and Multiple Texts research group in the Department of Educational Research at the University of Oslo. Glina's research examines the relationships (a) between classroom discourse and argument literacy and (b) between classroom discourse and aggression. She also teaches a number of courses, including educational psychology and philosophy of education.

Maughn Rollins Gregory, Ph.D., J.D., is an associate professor in the Department of Educational Foundations at Montclair State University, where he is faculty advisor to the Institute for the Advancement of Philosophy for Children and Director of the Classroom Inquiry Project in Newark, New Jersey. He publishes and teaches in the areas of philosophy of education, pragmatism, Philosophy for Children, gender and education, and Socratic and contemplative pedagogy.

David Kennedy, Ed.D., is a professor in the Department of Educational Foundations at Montclair State University and a Fellow at the Institute for the Advancement of Philosophy for Children. His scholarly and research interests include philosophy for/with children, philosophy of childhood, community of inquiry theory and practice, and the reconstruction of schooling. He is the author of four books, including *Philosophical Dialogue with Children: Essays on Theory and Practice* (Mellen, 2011) and *My Name is Myshkin* (LIT Verlag, 2012), a philosophical novel for children, as well as numerous journal articles.

Nadia Kennedy, Ed.D., is an assistant professor of mathematics education at Stony Brook University. Her work is currently focused on complexity theory in education, group argumentation, and the community of inquiry as a pedagogical medium for mathematical and philosophical investigations.

Ching Ching Lin, Ed.D., is currently an instructor at the Graduate School of Education at Touro College in New York.

Christopher Parker is a doctoral student in the Department of Educational Foundations at Montclair State University, where he also teaches mythology and general humanities. Parker holds an M.F.A. in poetry from Columbia University and has run poetry workshops for the Geraldine R. Dodge Foundation Poetry Program and the New Jersey State Council on the Arts for almost 30 years.

Jon Rogers is a doctoral student in the Department of Educational Foundations at Montclair State University, and he studies how teachers in training construct and develop their conceptions of professional identity. Rogers currently teaches philosophy at William Paterson University and Bergen College.

Lavina Sequeira, Ed.D., is a lecturer affiliated with the Philosophy and Religion Department at Bergen Community College. Sequeira's research interests include cultural studies, democratic education, adolescent identity, and issues of social justice, particularly those pertaining to the identity negotiation of immigrants and the implications for education reform.

Laurance J. Splitter, Ph.D., was instrumental to the development of Philosophy for Children in Australia and is currently a professor of philosophy and education at the Hong Kong Institute of Education. In his research and teaching, he draws on the community of inquiry paradigm and his background in analytic philosophy to explore such issues as personal development and identity politics, citizenship and moral education, thinking and dialogue across ethnic and cultural boundaries, and authenticity.